Erving
Goffman

WHERE THE
ACTION IS

Three essays

Allen Lane The Penguin Press
London 1969

First published in Great Britain in 1969 by
Allen Lane The Penguin Press
Vigo Street, London w1

Printed in Great Britain by
Latimer Trend & Co. Ltd, Plymouth

Contents

On Face-Work: An Analysis of Ritual Elements in Social Interaction

This paper was written at the University of Chicago; for financial support in writing it, I am indebted to a US Public Health Grant (No. M702 6 MH 5) for a study of the characteristics of social interaction of individuals, headed by Dr William Soskin of the Department of Psychology, University of Chicago.

On Face-Work

Every person lives in a world of social encounters, involving him either in face-to-face or mediated contact with other participants. In each of these contacts, he tends to act out what is sometimes called a *line* – that is, a pattern of verbal and nonverbal acts by which he expresses his view of the situation and through this his evaluation of the participants, especially himself. Regardless of whether a person intends to take a line, he will find that he has done so in effect. The other participants will assume that he has more or less wilfully taken a stand, so that if he is to deal with their response to him he must take into consideration the impression they have possibly formed of him.

The term *face* may be defined as the positive social value a person effectively claims for himself by the line others assume he has taken during a particular contact. Face is an image of self delineated in terms of approved social attributes – albeit an image that others may share, as when a person makes a good showing for his profession or religion by making a good showing for himself.*

A person tends to experience an immediate emotional response to the face which a contact with others allows him; he cathects his face; his 'feelings' become attached to it. If the encounter sustains an image of him that he has long taken for granted, he probably will have few feelings about the matter. If events establish a face for him that is better than he might have expected, he is likely to

* For discussions of the Chinese conception of face, see the following: Hsien Chin Hu, 'The Chinese Concept of "Face", *American Anthropologist*, 1944, n.s. 46: 45–64. Martin C. Yang, *A Chinese Village* (London: Routledge & Kegan Paul, 1947), pp. 167–72. J. Macgowan, *Men and Manners of Modern China* (Unwin, 1912), pp. 301–12. Arthur H. Smith, *Chinese Characteristics* (New York, Felming H. Revell Co., 1894), pp. 16–18. For a comment on the American Indian conception of face, see Marcel Mauss, *The Gift*, tr. Ian Cunnison (Cohen & West, 1954), p. 38.

'feel good'; if his ordinary expectations are not fulfilled, one expects that he will 'feel bad' or 'feel hurt'. In general, a person's attachment to a particular face, coupled with the ease with which disconfirming information can be conveyed by himself and others, provides one reason why he finds that participation in any contact with others is a commitment. A person will also have feelings about the face sustained for the other participants, and while these feelings may differ in quantity and direction from those he has for his own face, they constitute an involvement in the face of others that is as immediate and spontaneous as the involvement he has in his own face. One's own face and the face of others are constructs of the same order; it is the rules of the group and the definition of the situation which determine how much feeling one is to have for face and how this feeling is to be distributed among the faces involved.

A person may be said to *have*, or *be in*, or *maintain* face when the line he effectively takes presents an image of him that is internally consistent, that is supported by judgements and evidence conveyed by other participants, and that is confirmed by evidence conveyed through impersonal agencies in the situation. At such times the person's face clearly is something that is not lodged in or on his body, but rather something that is diffusely located in the flow of events in the encounter and becomes manifest only when these events are read and interpreted for the appraisals expressed in them.

The line maintained by and for a person during contact with others tends to be of a legitimate institutionalized kind. During a contact of a particular type, an interactant of known or visible attributes can expect to be sustained in a particular face and can feel that it is morally proper that this should be so. Given his attributes and the conventionalized nature of the encounter, he will find a small choice of lines will be open to him and a small choice of faces will be waiting for him. Further, on the basis of a few known attributes, he is given the responsibility of possessing a vast number of others. His coparticipants are not likely to be conscious of the character of many of these attributes until he acts perceptibly in such a way as to discredit his possession of them; then everyone becomes conscious of these attributes and assumes that he wilfully gave a false impression of possessing them.

Thus while concern for face focuses the attention of the person on the current activity, he must, to maintain face in this activity, take into consideration his place in the social world beyond it. A person who can maintain face in the current situation is someone who abstained from certain actions in the past that would have been difficult to face up to later. In addition, he fears loss of face now partly because the others may take this as a sign that consideration for his feelings need not be shown in the future. There is, nevertheless, a limitation to this interdependence between the current situation and the wider social world: an encounter with people whom he will not have dealings with again leaves him free to take a high line that the future will discredit, or free to suffer humiliations that would make future dealings with them an embarrassing thing to have to face.

A person may be said to *be in wrong face* when information is brought forth in some way about his social worth which cannot be integrated, even with effort, into the line that is being sustained for him. A person may be said to *be out of face* when he participates in a contact with others without having ready a line of the kind participants in such situations are expected to take. The intent of many pranks is to lead a person into showing a wrong face or no face, but there will also be serious occasions, of course, when he will find himself expressively out of touch with the situation.

When a person senses that he is in face, he typically responds with feelings of confidence and assurance. Firm in the line he is taking, he feels that he can hold his head up and openly present himself to others. He feels some security and some relief – as he also can when the others feel he is in wrong face but successfully hide these feelings from him.

When a person is in wrong face or out of face, expressive events are being contributed to the encounter which cannot be readily woven into the expressive fabric of the occasion. Should he sense that he is in wrong face or out of face, he is likely to feel ashamed and inferior because of what has happened to the activity on his account and because of what may happen to his reputation as a participant. Further, he may feel bad because he had relied upon the encounter to support an image of self to which he has become emotionally attached and which he now finds threatened. Felt lack of judgemental support from the encounter may take him

aback, confuse him, and momentarily incapacitate him as an interactant. His manner and bearing may falter, collapse, and crumble.
He may become embarrassed and chagrined; he may become
shamefaced. The feeling, whether warranted or not, that he is
perceived in a flustered state by others, and that he is presenting
no usable line, may add further injuries to his feelings, just as his
change from being in wrong face or out of face to being shamefaced can add further disorder to the expressive organization of
the situation. Following common usage, I shall employ the term
poise to refer to the capacity to suppress and conceal any tendency
to become shamefaced during encounters with others.

In our Anglo-American society, as in some others, the phrase
'to lose face' seems to mean to be in wrong face, to be out of face,
or to be shamefaced. The phrase 'to save one's face' appears to
refer to the process by which the person sustains an impression
for others that he has not lost face. Following Chinese usage, one
can say that 'to give face' is to arrange for another to take a better
line than he might otherwise have been able to take,* the other
thereby gets face given him, this being one way in which he can
gain face.

As an aspect of the social code of any social circle, one may expect to find an understanding as to how far a person should go
to save his face. Once he takes on a self-image expressed through
face he will be expected to live up to it. In different ways in different
societies he will be required to show self-respect, abjuring certain
actions because they are above or beneath him, while forcing
himself to perform others even though they cost him dearly. By
entering a situation in which he is given a face to maintain, a person takes on the responsibility of standing guard over the flow of
events as they pass before him. He must ensure that a particular
expressive order is sustained – an order that regulates the flow of
events, large or small, so that anything that appears to be expressed by them will be consistent with his face. When a person
manifests these compunctions primarily from duty to himself, one
speaks in our society of pride; when he does so because of duty
to wider social units, and receives support from these units in
doing so, one speaks of honour. When these compunctions have

* See, for example, Smith, *op. cit.*, p. 13.

to do with postural things, with expressive events derived from the way in which the person handles his body, his emotions, and the things with which he has physical contact, one speaks of dignity, this being an aspect of expressive control that is always praised and never studied. In any case, while his social face can be his most personal possession and the centre of his security and pleasure, it is only on loan to him from society; it will be withdrawn unless he conducts himself in a way that is worthy of it. Approved attributes and their relation to face make of every man his own jailer; this is a fundamental social constraint even though each man may like his cell.

Just as the member of any group is expected to have self-respect, so also he is expected to sustain a standard of considerateness; he is expected to go to certain lengths to save the feelings and the face of others present, and he is expected to do this willingly and spontaneously because of emotional identification with the others and with their feelings.* In consequence, he is disinclined to witness the defacement of others.† The person who can witness another's humiliation and unfeelingly retain a cool countenance himself is said in our society to be 'heartless', just as he who can unfeelingly participate in his own defacement is thought to be 'shameless'.

The combined effect of the rule of self-respect and the rule of considerateness is that the person tends to conduct himself during an encounter so as to maintain both his own face and the face of

* Of course, the more power and prestige the others have, the more a person is likely to show consideration for their feelings, as H. E. Dale suggests in *The Higher Civil Service of Great Britain* (Oxford, O.U.P., 1941), p. 126*n*. 'The doctrine of "feelings" was expounded to me many years ago by a very eminent civil servant with a pretty taste in cynicism. He explained that the importance of feelings varies in close correspondence with the importance of the person who feels. If the public interest requires that a junior clerk should be removed from his post, no regard need be paid to his feelings; if it is a case of an Assistant Secretary, they must be carefully considered, within reason; if it is a Permanent Secretary, his feelings are a principal element in the situation, and only imperative public interest can override their requirements.'

† Salesmen, especially street 'stemmers', know that if they take a line that will be discredited unless the reluctant customer buys, the customer may be trapped by considerateness and buy in order to save the face of the salesman and prevent what would ordinarily result in a scene.

the other participants. This means that the line taken by each participant is usually allowed to prevail, and each participant is allowed to carry off the role he appears to have chosen for himself. A state where everyone temporarily accepts everyone else's line is established.* This kind of mutual acceptance seems to be a basic structural feature of interaction, especially the interaction of face-to-face talk. It is typically a 'working' acceptance, not a 'real' one, since it tends to be based not on agreement of candidly expressed heart-felt evaluations, but upon a willingness to give temporary lip service to judgements with which the participants do not really agree.

The mutual acceptance of lines has an important conservative effect upon encounters. Once the person initially presents a line, he and the others tend to build their later responses upon it, and in a sense become stuck with it. Should the person radically alter his line, or should it become discredited, then confusion results, for the participants will have prepared and committed themselves for actions that are now unsuitable.

Ordinarily, maintenance of face is a condition of interaction, not its objective. Usual objectives, such as gaining face for oneself, giving free expression to one's true beliefs, introducing depreciating information about the others, or solving problems and performing tasks, are typically pursued in such a way as to be consistent with the maintenance of face. To study face-saving is to study the traffic rules of social interaction; one learns about the

* Surface agreement in the assessment of social worth does not, of course, imply equality; the evaluation consensually sustained of one participant may be quite different from the one consensually sustained of another. Such agreement is also compatible with expression of differences of opinion between two participants, provided each of the disputants shows 'respect' for the other, guiding the expression of disagreement so that it will convey an evaluation of the other that the other will be willing to convey about himself. Extreme cases are provided by wars, duels, and bar-room fights, when these are of a gentlemanly kind, for they can be conducted under consensual auspices, with each protagonist guiding his action according to the rules of the game, thereby making it possible for his action to be interpreted as an expression of a fair player openly in combat with a fair opponent. In fact, the rules and etiquette of any game can be analysed as a means by which the image of a fair player can be expressed, just as the image of a fair player can be analysed as a means by which the rules and etiquette of a game are sustained.

code the person adheres to in his movement across the paths and designs of others, but not where he is going, or why he wants to get there. One does not even learn why he is ready to follow the code, for a large number of different motives can equally lead him to do so. He may want to save his own face because of his emotional attachment to the image of self which it expresses, because of his pride or honour, because of the power his presumed status allows him to exert over the other participants, and so on. He may want to save the others' face because of his emotional attachment to an image of them, or because he feels that his coparticipants have a moral right to this protection, or because he wants to avoid the hostility that may be directed towards him if they lose their face. He may feel that an assumption has been made that he is the sort of person who shows compassion and sympathy towards others, so that to retain his own face, he may feel obliged to be considerate of the line taken by the other participants.

By *face-work* I mean to designate the actions taken by a person to make whatever he is doing consistent with face. Face-work serves to counteract 'incidents' – that is, events whose effective symbolic implications threaten face. Thus poise is one important type of face-work, for through poise the person controls his embarrassment and hence the embarrassment that he and others might have over his embarrassment. Whether or not the full consequences of face-saving actions are known to the person who employs them, they often become habitual and standardized practices; they are like traditional plays in a game or traditional steps in a dance. Each person, subculture, and society seems to have its own characteristic repertoire of face-saving practices. It is to this repertoire that people partly refer when they ask what a person or culture is 'really' like. And yet the particular set of practices stressed by particular persons or groups seems to be drawn from a single logically coherent framework of possible practices. It is as if face, by its very nature, can be saved only in a certain number of ways, and as if each social grouping must make its selections from this single matrix of possibilities.

The members of every social circle may be expected to have some knowledge of face-work and some experience in its use. In our society, this kind of capacity is sometimes called tact, *savoir-faire*, diplomacy, or social skill. Variation in social skill pertains more to the efficacy of face-work than to the frequency of its application, for almost all acts involving others are modified, prescriptively or proscriptively, by considerations of face.

If a person is to employ his repertoire of face-saving practices, obviously he must first become aware of the interpretations that others may have placed upon his acts and the interpretations that he ought perhaps to place upon theirs. In other words, he must exercise perceptiveness.* But even if he is properly alive to symbolically conveyed judgements and is socially skilled, he must yet be willing to exercise his perceptiveness and his skill; he must, in short, be prideful and considerate. Admittedly, of course, the possession of perceptiveness and social skill so often leads to their application that in our society terms such as politeness or tact fail to distinguish between the inclination to exercise such capacities and the capacities themselves.

I have already said that the person will have two points of view – a defensive orientation towards saving his own face and a protective orientation towards saving the others' face. Some practices will be primarily defensive and others primarily protective, although in general one may expect these two perspectives to be taken at the same time. In trying to save the face of others, the person must choose a tack that will not lead to loss of his own; in trying to save his own face, he must consider the loss of face that his action may entail for others.

In many societies there is a tendency to distinguish three levels of responsibility that a person may have for a threat to face that his actions have created. First, he may appear to have acted innocently; his offence seems to be unintended and unwitting, and those who perceive his act can feel that he would have attempted to avoid it had he foreseen its offensive consequences. In our society one calls such threats to face *faux pas*, *gaffes*, boners, or bricks.

* Presumably social skill and perceptiveness will be high in groups whose members frequently act as representatives of wider social units such as lineages or nations, for the player here is gambling with a face to which the feelings of many persons are attached. Similarly, one might expect social skill to be well developed among those of high station and those with whom they have dealings, for the more face an interactant has, the greater the number of events that may be inconsistent with it, and hence the greater the need for social skill to forestall or counteract these inconsistencies.

Secondly, the offending person may appear to have acted maliciously and spitefully, with the intention of causing open insult. Thirdly, there are incidental offences; these arise as an unplanned but sometimes anticipated by-product of action – action the offender performs in spite of its offensive consequences, although not out of spite. From the point of view of a particular participant, these three types of threat can be introduced by the participant himself against his own face, by himself against the face of the others, by the others against their own face, or by the others against himself. Thus the person may find himself in many different relations to a threat to face. If he is to handle himself and others well in all contingencies, he will have to have a repertoire of face-saving practices for each of these possible relations to threat.

THE BASIC KINDS OF FACE-WORK

The avoidance process. The surest way for a person to prevent threats to his face is to avoid contacts in which these threats are likely to occur. In all societies one can observe this in the avoidance relationship* and in the tendency for certain delicate transactions to be conducted by go-betweens.† Similarly, in many societies, members know the value of voluntarily making a gracious withdrawal before an anticipated threat to face has had a chance to occur.‡

* In our own society an illustration of avoidance is found in the middle- and upper-class Negro who avoids certain face-to-face contacts with whites in order to protect the self-evaluation projected by his clothes and manner. See, for example, Charles Johnson, *Patterns of Negro Segregation* (New York: Harper, 1943), Ch. 13. The function of avoidance in maintaining the kinship system in small preliterate societies might be taken as a particular illustration of the same general theme.

† An illustration is given by K. S. Latourette, *The Chinese: Their History and Culture* (London: Collier-Macmillan, 1964): 'A neighbor or a group of neighbors may tender their good offices in adjusting a quarrel in which each antagonist would be sacrificing his face by taking the first step in approaching the other. The wise intermediary can effect the reconciliation while preserving the dignity of both' (vol. 2: p. 211).

‡ In an unpublished paper Harold Garfinkel has suggested that when the person finds that he has lost face in a conversational encounter, he may feel a desire to disappear or 'drop through the floor,' and that this may involve a wish not only to conceal loss of face but also to return magically to a point in time when it would have been possible to save face by avoiding the encounter.

B

Once the person does chance an encounter, other kinds of avoidance practices come into play. As defensive measures, he keeps off topics and away from activities that would lead to the expression of information that is inconsistent with the line he is maintaining. At opportune moments he will change the topic of conversation or the direction of activity. He will often present initially a front of diffidence and composure, suppressing any show of feeling until he has found out what kind of line the others will be ready to support for him. Any claims regarding self may be made with belittling modesty, with strong qualifications, or with a note of unseriousness; by hedging in these ways he will have prepared a self for himself that will not be discredited by exposure, personal failure, or the unanticipated acts of others. And if he does not hedge his claims about self, he will at least attempt to be realistic about them, knowing that otherwise events may discredit him and make him lose face.

Certain protective manoeuvres are as common as these defensive ones. The person shows respect and politeness, making sure to extend to others any ceremonial treatment that might be their due. He employs discretion; he leaves unstated facts that might implicitly or explicitly contradict and embarrass the positive claims made by others.* He employs circumlocutions and deceptions, phrasing his replies with careful ambiguity so that the others' face is preserved even if their welfare is not.† He employs courtesies, making slight modifications of his demands on

* When the person knows the others well, he will know what issues ought not to be raised and what situations the others ought not to be placed in, and he will be free to introduce matters at will in all other areas. When the others are strangers to him, he will often reverse the formula, restricting himself to specific areas he knows are safe. On these occasions, as Simmel suggests, '. . . discretion consists by no means only in the respect for the secret of the other, for his specific will to conceal this or that from us, but in staying away from the knowledge of all that the other does not expressly reveal to us.' See *The Sociology of Georg Simmel* (Kurt H. Wolff, tr. and ed.) (Glencoe, Ill.: The Free Press, 1950), pp. 320–21.

† The Western traveller used to complain that the Chinese could never be trusted to say what they meant but always said what they felt their Western listener wanted to hear. The Chinese used to complain that the Westerner was brusque, boorish, and unmannered. In terms of Chinese standards, presumably, the conduct of a Westerner is so gauche that he creates an emergency, forcing the Asian to forgo any kind of direct reply in order to rush in with a

or appraisals of the others so that they will be able to define the situation as one in which their self-respect is not threatened. In making a belittling demand upon the others, or in imputing uncomplimentary attributes to them, he may employ a joking manner, allowing them to take the line that they are good sports, able to relax from their ordinary standards of pride and honour. And before engaging in a potentially offensive act, he may provide explanations as to why the others ought not to be affronted by it. For example, if he knows that it will be necessary to withdraw from the encounter before it has terminated, he may tell the others in advance that it is necessary for him to leave, so that they will have faces that are prepared for it. But neutralizing the potentially offensive act need not be done verbally; he may wait for a propitious moment or natural break – for example, in conversation, a momentary lull when no one speaker can be affronted – and then leave, in this way using the context instead of his words as a guarantee of inoffensiveness.

When a person fails to prevent an incident, he can still attempt to maintain the fiction that no threat to face has occurred. The most blatant example of this is found where the person acts as if an event that contains a threatening expression has not occurred at all. He may apply this studied nonobservance to his own acts – as when he does not by any outward sign admit that his stomach is rumbling – or to the acts of others, as when he does not 'see' that another has stumbled.* Social life in mental hospitals owes much to this process; patients employ it in regard to their own peculiarities, and visitors employ it, often with tenuous desperation, in regard to patients. In general, tactful blindness of this kind is applied only to events that, if perceived at all, could be perceived and interpreted only as threats to face.

A more important, less spectacular kind of tactful overlooking is practised when a person openly acknowledges an incident

---

remark that might rescue the Westerner from the compromising position in which he has placed himself. (See Smith, op. cit., Ch. 8, 'The Talent for Indirection.') This is an instance of the important group of misunderstandings which arise during interaction between persons who come from groups with different ritual standards.

* A pretty example of this is found in parade-ground etiquette which may oblige those in a parade to treat anyone who faints as if he were not present at all.

as an event that has occurred, but not as an event that contains a threatening expression. If he is not the one who is responsible for the incident, then his blindness will have to be supported by his forbearance; if he is the doer of the threatening deed, then his blindness will have to be supported by his willingness to seek a way of dealing with the matter, which leaves him dangerously dependent upon the co-operative forbearance of the others.

Another kind of avoidance occurs when a person loses control of his expressions during an encounter. At such times he may try not so much to overlook the incident as to hide or conceal his activity in some way, thus making it possible for the others to avoid some of the difficulties created by a participant who has not maintained face. Correspondingly, when a person is caught out of face because he had not expected to be thrust into inter-action, or because strong feelings have disrupted his expressive mask, the others may protectively turn away from him or his activity for a moment, to give him time to assemble himself.

The corrective process. When the participants in an undertaking or encounter fail to prevent the occurrence of an event that is expressively incompatible with the judgements of social worth that are being maintained, and when the event is of the kind that is difficult to overlook, then the participants are likely to give it accredited status as an incident – to ratify it as a threat that deserves direct official attention – and to proceed to try to correct for its effects. At this point one or more participants find themselves in an established state of ritual disequilibrium or disgrace, and an attempt must be made to re-establish a satisfactory ritual state for them. I use the term *ritual* because I am dealing with acts through whose symbolic component the actor shows how worthy he is of respect or how worthy he feels others are of it. The imagery of equilibrium is apt here because the length and intensity of the corrective effort is nicely adapted to the persistence and intensity of the threat.* One's face, then, is a sacred thing, and the expressive order required to sustain it is therefore a ritual one.

* This kind of imagery is one that social anthropologists seem to find naturally fitting. Note, for example, the implications of the following statement by Margaret Mead in her 'Kinship in the Admiralty Islands', *Anthropological Papers of the American Museum of Natural History*, 34: 183–358: 'If a husband

The sequence of acts set in motion by an acknowledged threat to face, and terminating in the re-establishment of ritual equilibrium, I shall call an *interchange*.* Defining a message or move as everything conveyed by an actor during a turn at taking action, one can say that an interchange will involve two or more moves and two or more participants. Obvious examples in our society may be found in the sequence of 'Excuse me' and 'Certainly', and in the exchange of presents or visits. The interchange seems to be a basic concrete unit of social activity and provides one natural empirical way to study interaction of all kinds. Face-saving practices can be usefully classified according to their position in the natural sequence of moves that comprise this unit. Aside from the event which introduces the need for a corrective interchange, four classic moves seem to be involved.

There is, first, the challenge, by which participants take on the responsibility of calling attention to the misconduct; by implication they suggest that the threatened claims are to stand firm and that the threatening event itself will have to be brought back into line.

The second move consists of the offering, whereby a participant, typically the offender, is given a chance to correct for the offence and re-establish the expressive order. Some classic ways of making this move are available. On the one hand, an attempt can be made to show that what admittedly appeared to be a threatening expression is really a meaningless event, or an unintentional act, or a joke not meant to be taken seriously, or an unavoidable, 'understandable' product of extenuating circumstances. On the other hand, the meaning of the event may be granted and effort concentrated on the creator of it. Information may be provided to

---

beats his wife, custom demands that she leave him and go to her brother real or officiating, and remain a length of time commensurate with the degree of her offended dignity' (p. 274).

* The notion of interchange is drawn in part from Eliot D. Chapple, 'Measuring Human Relations', *Genetic Psychol. Monographs* (1940) 22: 3–147, especially pp. 26–30, and from A. B. Horsfall and C. A. Arensberg, 'Teamwork and Productivity in a Shoe Factory', *Human Organization* (1949) 8: 13–25, especially p. 19. For further material on the interchange as a unit see E. Goffman, 'Communication Conduct in an Island Community', unpublished Ph.D. dissertation, Department of Sociology, University of Chicago, 1953, especially Chs. 12 and 13, pp. 165–95.

show that the creator was under the influence of something and not himself, or that he was under the command of somebody else and not acting for himself. When a person claims that an act was meant in jest, he may go on and claim that the self that seemed to lie behind the act was also projected as a joke. When a person suddenly finds that he has demonstrably failed in capacities that the others assumed him to have and to claim for himself – such as the capacity to spell, to perform minor tasks, to talk without malapropisms, and so on – he may quickly add, in a serious or unserious way, that he claims these incapacities as part of his self. The meaning of the threatening incident thus stands, but it can now be incorporated smoothly into the flow of expressive events.

As a supplement to or substitute for the strategy of redefining the offensive act or himself, the offender can follow two other procedures: he can provide compensations to the injured – when it is not his own face that he has threatened; or he can provide punishment, penance, and expiation for himself. These are important moves or phases in the ritual interchange. Even though the offender may fail to prove his innocence, he can suggest through these means that he is now a renewed person, a person who has paid for his sin against the expressive order and is once more to be trusted in the judgemental scene. Further, he can show that he does not treat the feelings of the others lightly, and that if their feelings have been injured by him, however innocently, he is prepared to pay a price for his action. Thus he assures the others that they can accept his explanations without this acceptance constituting a sign of weakness and a lack of pride on their part. Also, by his treatment of himself, by his self-castigation, he shows that he is clearly aware of the kind of crime he would have committed had the incident been what it first appeared to be, and that he knows the kind of punishment that ought to be accorded to one who would commit such a crime. The suspected person thus shows that he is thoroughly capable of taking the role of the others towards his own activity, that he can still be used as a responsible participant in the ritual process, and that the rules of conduct which he appears to have broken are still sacred, real, and unweakened. An offensive act may arouse anxiety about the ritual code; the offender allays this anxiety by showing that both the code and he as an upholder of it are still in working order.

After the challenge and the offering have been made, the third move can occur: the persons to whom the offering is made can accept it as a satisfactory means of re-establishing the expressive order and the faces supported by this order. Only then can the offender cease the major part of his ritual offering.

In the terminal move of the interchange, the forgiven person conveys a sign of gratitude to those who have given him the indulgence of forgiveness.

The phases of the corrective process – challenge, offering, acceptance, and thanks – provide a model for inter-personal ritual behaviour, but a model that may be departed from in significant ways. For example, the offended parties may give the offender a chance to initiate the offering on his own before a challenge is made and before they ratify the offence as an incident. This is a common courtesy, extended on the assumption that the recipient will introduce a self-challenge. Further, when the offended persons accept the corrective offering, the offender may suspect that this has been grudgingly done from tact, and so he may volunteer additional corrective offerings, not allowing the matter to rest until he has received a second or third acceptance of his repeated apology. Or the offended persons may tactfully take over the role of the offender and volunteer excuses for him that will, perforce, be acceptable to the offended persons.

An important departure from the standard corrective cycle occurs when a challenged offender patently refuses to heed the warning and continues with his offending behaviour, instead of setting the activity to rights. This move shifts the play back to the challengers. If they countenance the refusal to meet their demands, then it will be plain that their challenge was a bluff and that the bluff has been called. This is an untenable position; a face for themselves cannot be derived from it, and they are left to bluster. To avoid this fate, some classic moves are open to them. For instance, they can resort to tactless, violent retaliation, destroying either themselves or the person who had refused to heed their warning. Or they can withdraw from the undertaking in a visible huff – righteously indignant, outraged, but confident of ultimate vindication. Both tacks provide a way of denying the offender his status as an interactant, and hence denying the reality of the offensive judgement he has made. Both strategies are ways of salvaging face, but for all concerned the costs are usually high. It is partly to forestall such scenes that an offender is usually quick to offer apologies; he does not want the affronted persons to trap themselves into the obligation to resort to desperate measures.

It is plain that emotions play a part in these cycles of response, as when anguish is expressed because of what one has done to another's face, or anger because of what has been done to one's own. I want to stress that these emotions function as moves, and fit so precisely into the logic of the ritual game that it would seem difficult to understand them without it.* In fact, spontaneously expressed feelings are likely to fit into the formal pattern of the ritual interchange more elegantly than consciously designed ones.

MAKING POINTS –
THE AGGRESSIVE USE OF FACE-WORK

Every face-saving practice which is allowed to neutralize a particular threat opens up the possibility that the threat will be wilfully introduced for what can be safely gained by it. If a person knows that his modesty will be answered by others' praise of him, he can fish for compliments. If his own appraisal of self will be checked against incidental events, then he can arrange for favourable incidental events to appear. If others are prepared to overlook an affront to them and act forbearantly, or to accept apologies, then he can rely on this as a basis for safely offending them. He can attempt by sudden withdrawal to force the others into a ritually unsatisfactory state, leaving them to flounder in an interchange that cannot readily be completed. Finally, at some expense to himself, he can arrange for the others to hurt his feelings,

---

* Even when a child demands something and is refused, he is likely to cry and sulk not as an irrational expression of frustration but as a ritual move, conveying that he already has a face to lose and that its loss is not to be permitted lightly. Sympathetic parents may even allow for such display, seeing in these crude strategies the beginnings of a social self.

thus forcing them to feel guilt, remorse, and sustained ritual disequilibrium.*

When a person treats face-work not as something he need be prepared to perform, but rather as something that others can be counted on to perform or to accept, then an encounter or an undertaking becomes less a scene of mutual considerateness than an arena in which a contest or a match is held. The purpose of the game is to preserve everyone's line from an inexcusable contradiction, while scoring as many points as possible against one's adversaries and making as many gains as possible for oneself. An audience to the struggle is almost a necessity. The general method is for the person to introduce favourable facts about himself and unfavourable facts about the others in such a way that the only reply the others will be able to think up will be one that terminates the interchange in a grumble, a meagre excuse, a face-saving I-can-take-a-joke laugh, or an empty stereotyped comeback of the 'Oh yeah?' or 'That's what you think' variety. The losers in such cases will have to cut their losses, tacitly grant the loss of a point, and attempt to do better in the next interchange. Points made by allusion to social class status are sometimes called snubs; those made by allusions to moral respectability are sometimes called digs; in either case one deals with a capacity at what is sometimes called 'bitchiness'.

In aggressive interchanges the winner not only succeeds in introducing information favourable to himself and unfavourable to the others, but also demonstrates that as interactant he can handle himself better than his adversaries. Evidence of this capacity is often more important than all the other information the person conveys in the interchange, so that the introduction of a 'crack' in verbal interaction tends to imply that the initiator is better at footwork than those who must suffer his remarks. However, if they succeed in making a successful parry of the thrust and then a successful riposte, the instigator of the play must not only face the disparagement with which the others have answered

* The strategy of manoeuvring another into a position where he cannot right the harm he has done is very commonly employed but nowhere with such devotion to the ritual model of conduct as in revengeful suicide. See, for example, M. D. W. Jeffreys, 'Samsonic Suicide, or Suicide of Revenge Among Africans', *African Studies* (1952) 11: 118–22.

him but also accept the fact that his assumption of superiority in footwork has proven false. He is made to look foolish; he loses face. Hence it is always a gamble to 'make a remark'. The tables can be turned and the aggressor can lose more than he could have gained had his move won the point. Successful ripostes or comebacks in our society are sometimes called squelches or toppers; theoretically it would be possible for a squelch to be squelched, a topper to be topped, and a riposte to be parried with a counterriposte, but except in staged interchanges this third level of successful action seems rare.*

THE CHOICE OF APPROPRIATE FACE-WORK

When an incident occurs, the person whose face is threatened may attempt to reinstate the ritual order by means of one kind of strategy, while the other participants may desire or expect a practice of a different type to be employed. When, for example, a minor mishap occurs, momentarily revealing a person in wrong face or out of face, the others are often more willing and able to act blind to the discrepancy than is the threatened person himself. Often they would prefer him to exercise poise,† while he feels that he cannot afford to overlook what has happened to his

* In board and card games the player regularly takes into consideration the possible responses of his adversaries to a play that he is about to make, and even considers the possibility that his adversaries will know that he is taking such precautions. Conversational play is by comparison surprisingly impulsive; people regularly make remarks about others present without carefully designing their remarks to prevent a successful comeback. Similarly, while feinting and sandbagging are theoretical possibilities during talk, they seem to be little exploited.

† Folklore imputes a great deal of poise to the upper classes. If there is truth in this belief it may lie in the fact that the upper-class person tends to find himself in encounters in which he outranks the other participants in ways additional to class. The ranking participant is often somewhat independent of the good opinion of the others and finds it practical to be arrogant, sticking to a face regardless of whether the encounter supports it. On the other hand, those who are in the power of a fellow-participant tend to be very much concerned with the valuation he makes of them or witnesses being made of them, and so find it difficult to maintain a slightly wrong face without becoming embarrassed and apologetic. It may be added that people who lack awareness of the symbolism in minor events may keep cool in difficult situations, showing poise that they do not really possess.

face and so becomes apologetic and shamefaced, if he is the creator of the incident, or destructively assertive, if the others are responsible for it.* Yet on the other hand, a person may manifest poise when the others feel that he ought to have broken down into embarrassed apology – that he is taking undue advantage of their helpfulness by his attempts to brazen it out. Sometimes a person may himself be undecided as to which practice to employ, leaving the others in the embarrassing position of not knowing which tack they are going to have to follow. Thus when a person makes a slight *gaffe*, he and the others may become embarrassed not because of inability to handle such difficulties, but because for a moment no one knows whether the offender is going to act blind to the incident, or give it joking recognition, or employ some other face-saving practice.

CO-OPERATION IN FACE-WORK

When a face has been threatened, face-work must be done, but whether this is initiated and primarily carried through by the person whose face is threatened, or by the offender, or by a mere witness,† is often of secondary importance. Lack of effort on the part of one person induces compensative effort from others; a contribution by one person relieves the others of the task. In fact, there are many minor incidents in which the offender and the offended simultaneously attempt to initiate an apology.‡ Resolution of the situation to everyone's apparent satisfaction is the

* Thus, in our society, when a person feels that others expect him to measure up to approved standards of cleanliness, tidiness, fairness, hospitality, generosity, affluence, and so on, or when he sees himself as someone who ought to maintain such standards, he may burden an encounter with extended apologies for his failings, while all along the other participants do not care about the standard, or do not believe the person is really lacking in it, or are convinced that he is lacking in it and see the apology itself as a vain effort at self-elevation.

† Thus one function of seconds in actual duals, as well as in figurative ones, is to provide an excuse for not fighting that both contestants can afford to accept.

‡ See, for instance, Jackson Toby, 'Some Variables in Role Conflict Analysis', *Social Forces* (1952) 30: 323–37: 'With adults there is less likelihood for essentially trivial issues to produce conflict. The automatic apology of two strangers who accidentally collide on a busy street illustrates the

first requirement; correct apportionment of blame is typically a secondary consideration. Hence terms such as tact and *savoir-faire* fail to distinguish whether it is the person's own face that his diplomacy saves or the face of the others. Similarly, terms such as *gaffe* and *faux pas* fail to specify whether it is the actor's own face he has threatened or the face of other participants. And it is understandable that if one person finds he is powerless to save his own face, the others seem especially bound to protect him. For example, in polite society, a handshake that perhaps should not have been extended becomes one that cannot be declined. Thus one accounts for the *noblesse oblige* through which those of high status are expected to curb their power of embarrassing their lessers,*

---

integrative function of etiquette. In effect, each of the parties to the collision says, "I don't know whether I am responsible for this situation, but *if* I am, you have a right to be angry with me, a right that I pray you will not exercise." By defining the situation as one in which both parties must abase themselves, society enables each to keep his self-respect. Each may feel in his heart of hearts, "Why can't that stupid ass watch where he's going?" But overtly *each plays the role of the guilty party* whether he feels he has been miscast or not.' (p. 325.)

* Regardless of the person's relative social position, in one sense he has power over the other participants and they must rely upon his considerateness. When the others act towards him in some way, they presume upon a social relationship to him, since one of the things expressed by interaction is the relationship of the interactants. Thus they compromise themselves, for they place him in a position to discredit the claims they express as to his attitude towards them. Hence in response to claimed social relationships every person, of high estate or low, will be expected to exercise *noblesse oblige* and refrain from exploiting the compromised position of the others.

Since social relationships are defined partly in terms of voluntary mutual aid, refusal of a request for assistance becomes a delicate matter, potentially destructive of the asker's face. Chester Holcombe, *The Real Chinaman* (New York: Dodd, Mead, 1895), provides a Chinese instance: 'Much of the falsehood to which the Chinese as a nation are said to be addicted is a result of the demands of etiquette. A plain, frank "no" is the height of discourtesy. Refusal or denial of any sort must be softened and toned down into an expression of regretted inability. Unwillingness to grant a favor is never shown. In place of it there is seen a chastened feeling of sorrow that unavoidable but quite imaginary circumstances render it wholly impossible. Centuries of practice in this form of evasion have made the Chinese matchlessly fertile in the invention and development of excuses. It is rare, indeed, that one is caught at a loss for a bit of artfully embroidered fiction with which to hide an unwelcome truth.' (pp. 274–5.)

as well as the fact that the handicapped often accept courtesies that they can manage better without.

Since each participant in an undertaking is concerned, albeit for differing reasons, with saving his own face and the face of the others, then tacit co-operation will naturally arise so that the participants together can attain their shared but differently motivated objectives.

One common type of tacit co-operation in face-saving is the tact exerted in regard to face-work itself. The person not only defends his own face and protects the face of the others, but also acts so as to make it possible and even easy for the others to employ face-work for themselves and him. He helps them to help themselves and him. Social etiquette, for example, warns men against asking for New Year's Eve dates too early in the season, lest the girl find it difficult to provide a gentle excuse for refusing. This second-order tact can be further illustrated by the widespread practice of negative-attribute etiquette. The person who has an unapparent negatively valued attribute often finds it expedient to begin an encounter with an unobtrusive admission of his failing, especially with persons who are uninformed about him. The others are thus warned in advance against making disparaging remarks about his kind of person and are saved from the contradiction of acting in a friendly fashion to a person towards whom they are unwittingly being hostile. This strategy also prevents the others from automatically making assumptions about him which place him in a false position and saves him from painful forbearance or embarrassing remonstrances.

Tact in regard to face-work often relies for its operation on a tacit agreement to do business through the language of hint – the language of innuendo, ambiguities, well-placed pauses, carefully worded jokes, and so on.* The rule regarding this unofficial kind of communication is that the sender ought not to act as if he had officially conveyed the message he has hinted at, while the recipients have the right and the obligation to act as if they have not officially received the message contained in the hint. Hinted

* Useful comments on some of the structural roles played by unofficial communication can be found in a discussion of irony and banter in Tom Burns, 'Friends, Enemies, and the Polite Fiction', *American Sociological Revue* (1953), 18: 654–62.

communication, then, is deniable communication; it need not be faced up to. It provides a means by which the person can be warned that his current line or the current situation is leading to loss of face, without this warning itself becoming an incident.

Another form of tacit co-operation, and one that seems to be much used in many societies, is reciprocal self-denial. Often the person does not have a clear idea of what would be a just or acceptable apportionment of judgements during the occasion, and so he voluntarily deprives or depreciates himself while indulging and complimenting the others, in both cases carrying the judgements safely past what is likely to be just. The favourable judgements about himself he allows to come from the others; the unfavourable judgements of himself are his own contributions. This 'after you, Alphonse' technique works, of course, because in depriving himself he can reliably anticipate that the others will compliment or indulge him. Whatever allocation of favours is eventually established, all participants are first given a chance to show that they are not bound or constrained by their own desires and expectations, that they have a properly modest view of themselves, and that they can be counted upon to support the ritual code. Negative bargaining, through which each participant tries to make the terms of trade more favourable to the other side, is another instance; as a form of exchange perhaps it is more widespread than the economist's kind.

A person's performance of face-work, extended by his tacit agreement to help others perform theirs, represents his willingness to abide by the ground rules of social interaction. Here is the hallmark of his socialization as an interactant. If he and the others were not socialized in this way, interaction in most societies and most situations would be a much more hazardous thing for feelings and faces. The person would find it impractical to be oriented to symbolically conveyed appraisals of social worth, or to be possessed of feelings – that is, it would be impractical for him to be a ritually delicate object. And as I shall suggest, if the person were not a ritually delicate object, occasions of talk could not be organized in the way they usually are. It is no wonder that trouble is caused by a person who cannot be relied upon to play the face-saving game.

THE RITUAL ROLES OF THE SELF

So far I have implicitly been using a double definition of self: the self as an image pieced together from the expressive implications of the full flow of events in an undertaking; and the self as a kind of player in a ritual game who copes honourably or dishonourably, diplomatically or undiplomatically, with the judgemental contingencies of the situation. A double mandate is involved. As sacred objects, men are subject to slights and profanation; hence as players of the ritual game they have had to lead themselves into duels, and wait for a round of shots to go wide of the mark before embracing their opponents. Here is an echo of the distinction between the value of a hand drawn at cards and the capacity of the person who plays it. This distinction must be kept in mind, even though it appears that once a person has gotten a reputation for good or bad plays this reputation may become a part of the face he must later play at maintaining.

Once the two roles of the self have been separated, one can look to the ritual code implicit in face-work to learn how the two roles are related. When a person is responsible for introducing a threat to another's face, he apparently has a right, within limits, to wriggle out of the difficulty by means of self-abasement. When performed voluntarily these indignities do not seem to profane his own image. It is as if he had the right of insulation and could castigate himself *qua* actor without injuring himself *qua* object of ultimate worth. By token of the same insulation he can belittle himself and modestly underplay his positive qualities, with the understanding that no one will take his statements as a fair representation of his sacred self. On the other hand, if he is forced against his will to treat himself in these ways, his face, his pride, and his honour will be seriously threatened. Thus, in terms of the ritual code, the person seems to have a special licence to accept mistreatment at his own hands that he does not have the right to accept from others. Perhaps this is a safe arrangement because he is not likely to carry this licence too far, whereas the others, were they given this privilege, might be more likely to abuse it.

Further, within limits the person has a right to forgive other participants for affronts to his sacred image. He can forbearantly overlook minor slurs upon his face, and in regard to somewhat greater injuries he is the one person who is in a position to accept apologies on behalf of his sacred self. This is a relatively safe prerogative for the person to have in regard to himself, for it is one that is exercised in the interests of the others or of the undertaking. Interestingly enough, when the person commits a *gaffe* against himself, it is not he who has the licence to forgive the event; only the others have that prerogative, and it is a safe prerogative for them to have because they can exercise it only in his interests or in the interests of the undertaking. One finds, then, a system of checks and balances by which each participant tends to be given the right to handle only those matters which he will have little motivation for mishandling. In short, the rights and obligations of an interactant are designed to prevent him from abusing his role as an object of sacred value.

SPOKEN INTERACTION

Most of what has been said so far applies to encounters of both an immediate and mediated kind, although in the latter the interaction is likely to be more attenuated, with each participant's line being gleaned from such things as written statements and work records. During direct personal contacts, however, unique informational conditions prevail and the significance of face becomes especially clear. The human tendency to use signs and symbols means that evidence of social worth and of mutual evaluations will be conveyed by very minor things, and these things will be witnessed, as will the fact that they have been witnessed. An unguarded glance, a momentary change in tone of voice, an ecological position taken or not taken, can drench a talk with judgemental significance. Therefore, just as there is no occasion of talk in which improper impressions could not intentionally or unintentionally arise, so there is no occasion of talk so trivial as not to require each participant to show serious concern with the way in which he handles himself and the others present. Ritual factors which are present in mediated contacts are here present in an extreme form.

In any society, whenever the physical possibility of spoken interaction arises, it seems that a system of practices, conventions, and procedural rules comes into play which functions as a means of guiding and organizing the flow of messages. An understanding will prevail as to when and where it will be permissible to initiate talk, among whom, and by means of what topics of conversation. A set of significant gestures is employed to initiate a spate of communication and as a means for the persons concerned to accredit each other as legitimate participants.* When this process of reciprocal ratification occurs, the persons so ratified are in what might be called a *state of talk* – that is, they have declared themselves officially open to one another for purposes of spoken communication and guarantee together to maintain a flow of words. A set of significant gestures is also employed by which one or more new participants can officially join the talk, by which one or more accredited participants can officially withdraw, and by which the state of talk can be terminated.

A single focus of thought and visual attention, and a single flow of talk, tends to be maintained and to be legitimated as officially representative of the encounter. The concerted and official visual attention of the participants tends to be transferred smoothly by means of formal or informal clearance cues, by which the current speaker signals that he is about to relinquish the floor and the prospective speaker signals a desire to be given the floor. An understanding will prevail as to how long and how frequently each participant is to hold the floor. The recipients convey to the speaker, by appropriate gestures, that they are according him their attention. Participants restrict their involvement in matters external to the encounter and observe a limit to involvement in any one message of the encounter, in this way ensuring that they will be able

* The meaning of this status can be appreciated by looking at the kinds of unlegitimated or unratified participation that can occur in spoken interaction. A person may overhear others unbeknownst to them; he can overhear them when they know this to be the case and when they choose either to act as if he were not overhearing them or to signal to him informally that they know he is overhearing them. In all of these cases, the outsider is officially held at bay as someone who is not formally participating in the occasion. Ritual codes, of course, require a ratified participant to be treated quite differently from an unratified one. Thus, for example, only a certain amount of insult from a ratified participant can be ignored without this avoidance practice causing loss of face to the insulted persons; after a point they must challenge the offender and demand redress. However, in many societies apparently, many kinds of verbal abuse from unratified participants can be ignored, without this failure to challenge constituting a loss of face.

C

to follow along whatever direction the topic of conversation takes them. Interruptions and lulls are regulated so as not to disrupt the flow of messages. Messages that are not part of the officially accredited flow are modulated so as not to interfere seriously with the accredited messages. Nearby persons who are not participants visibly desist in some way from exploiting their communication position and also modify their own communication, if any, so as not to provide difficult interference. A particular ethos or emotional atmosphere is allowed to prevail. A polite accord is typically maintained, and participants who may be in real disagreement with one another give temporary lip service to views that bring them into agreement on matters of fact and principle. Rules are followed for smoothing out the transition, if any, from one topic of conversation to another.*

These rules of talk pertain not to spoken interaction considered as an ongoing process, but to *an* occasion of talk or episode of interaction as a naturally bounded unit. This unit consists of the total activity that occurs during the time that a given set of participants have accredited one another for talk and maintain a single moving focus of attention.†

The conventions regarding the structure of occasions of talk represent an effective solution to the problem of organizing a flow of spoken messages. In attempting to discover how it is that these conventions are maintained in force as guides to action, one finds evidence to suggest a functional relationship between the structure of the self and the structure of spoken interaction.

The socialized interactant comes to handle spoken interaction as he would any other kind, as something that must be pursued with ritual care. By automatically appealing to face, he knows how to conduct himself in regard to talk. By repeatedly and automatically asking himself the question, 'If I do or do not act in this way, will I or others lose face?' he decides at each moment, consciously

---

*For a further treatment of the structure of spoken interaction see Goffman, 'Communication Conduct in an Island Community', op. cit.

† I mean to include formal talks where rules of procedure are explicitly prescribed and officially enforced, and where only certain categories of participants may be allowed to hold the floor – as well as chats and sociable talks where rules are not explicit and the role of speaker passes back and forth among the participants.

or unconsciously, how to behave. For example, entrance into an occasion of spoken interaction may be taken as a symbol of intimacy or legitimate purpose, and so the person must, to save his face, desist from entering into talk with a given set of others unless his circumstances justify what is expressed about him by his entrance. Once approached for talk, he must accede to the others in order to save their face. Once engaged in conversation, he must demand only the amount of attention that is an appropriate expression of his relative social worth. Undue lulls come to be potential signs of having nothing in common, or of being insufficiently self-possessed to create something to say, and hence must be avoided. Similarly, interruptions and inattentiveness may convey disrespect and must be avoided unless the implied disrespect is an accepted part of the relationship. A surface of agreement must be maintained by means of discretion and white lies, so that the assumption of mutual approval will not be discredited. Withdrawal must be handled so that it will not convey an improper evaluation.* The person must restrain his emotional involvement so as not to present an image of someone with no self-control or dignity who does not rise above his feelings.

The relation between the self and spoken interaction is further displayed when one examines the ritual interchange. In a conversational encounter, interaction tends to proceed in spurts, an interchange at a time, and the flow of information and business is parcelled out into these relatively closed ritual units.† The lull between interchanges tends to be greater than the lull between turns at talking in an interchange, and there tends to be a less

---

* Among people who have had some experience in interacting with one another, conversational encounters are often terminated in such a way as to give the appearance that all participants have independently hit upon the same moment to withdraw. The disbandment is general, and no one may be conscious of the exchange of cues that has been required to make such a happy simultaneity of action possible. Each participant is thus saved from the compromising position of showing readiness to spend further time with someone who is not as ready to spend time with him.

† The empirical discreteness of the interchange unit is sometimes obscured when the same person who provides the terminating turn at talking in one interchange initiates the first turn at talking in the next. However, the analytical utility of the interchange as a unit remains.

meaningful relationship between two sequential interchanges than between two sequential speeches in an interchange.

This structural aspect of talk arises from the fact that when a person volunteers a statement or message, however trivial or commonplace, he commits himself and those he addresses, and in a sense places everyone present in jeopardy. By saying something, the speaker opens himself up to the possibility that the intended recipients will affront him by not listening or will think him forward, foolish, or offensive in what he has said. And should he meet with such a reception, he will find himself committed to the necessity of taking face-saving action against them. Furthermore, by saying something the speaker opens his intended recipients up to the possibility that the message will be self-approving, presumptuous, demanding, insulting, and generally an affront to them or to their conception of him, so that they will find themselves obliged to take action against him in defence of the ritual code. And should the speaker praise the recipients, they will be obliged to make suitable denials, showing that they do not hold too favourable an opinion of themselves and are not so eager to secure indulgencies as to endanger their reliability and flexibility as interactants.

Thus when one person volunteers a message, thereby contributing what might easily be a threat to the ritual equilibrium, someone else present is obliged to show that the message has been received and that its content is acceptable to all concerned or can be acceptably countered. This acknowledging reply, of course, may contain a tactful rejection of the original communication, along with a request for modification. In such cases, several exchanges of messages may be required before the interchange is terminated on the basis of modified lines. The interchange comes to a close when it is possible to allow it to do so – that is, when everyone present has signified that he has been ritually appeased to a degree satisfactory to him.* A momentary lull between inter-

* The occurrence of the interchange unit is an empirical fact. In addition to the ritual explanation for it, others may be suggested. For example, when the person makes a statement and receives a reply at once, this provides him with a way of learning that his statement has been received and correctly received. Such 'metacommunication' would be necessary on functional grounds even were it unnecessary on ritual ones.

changes is possible, for it comes at a time when it will not be taken as a sign of something untoward.

In general, then, a person determines how he ought to conduct himself during an occasion of talk by testing the potentially symbolic meaning of his acts against the self-images that are being sustained. In doing this, however, he incidentally subjects his behaviour to the expressive order that prevails and contributes to the orderly flow of messages. His aim is to save face; his effect is to save the situation. From the point of view of saving face, then, it is a good thing that spoken interaction has the conventional organization given it; from the point of view of sustaining an orderly flow of spoken messages, it is a good thing that the self has the ritual structure given it.

I do not mean, however, to claim that another kind of person related to another kind of message organization would not do as well. More important, I do not claim that the present system is without weakness or drawbacks; these must be expected, for everywhere in social life a mechanism or functional relation which solves one set of problems necessarily creates a set of potential difficulties and abuses all its own. For example, a characteristic problem in the ritual organization of personal contacts is that while a person can save his face by quarrelling or by indignantly withdrawing from the encounter, he does this at the cost of the interaction. Furthermore, the person's attachment to face gives others something to aim at; they can not only make an effort to wound him unofficially, but may even make an official attempt utterly to destroy his face. Also, fear over possible loss of his face often prevents the person from initiating contacts in which important information can be transmitted and important relationships re-established; he may be led to seek the safety of solitude rather than the danger of social encounters. He may do this even though others feel that he is motivated by 'false pride' – a pride which suggests that the ritual code is getting the better of those whose conduct is regulated by it. Further, the 'after you, Alphonse' complex can make the termination of an interchange difficult. So, too, where each participant feels that he must sacrifice a little more than has been sacrificed for him, a kind of vicious indulgence cycle may occur – much like the hostility cycle that can lead to open quarrels – with each person receiving things he does not want and giving in return things he would rather keep. Again, when people are on formal terms, much energy may be spent in ensuring that events do not occur which might effectively carry an improper expression. And on the other hand, when a set of persons are on familiar terms and feel that they need not stand on ceremony with one another, then inattentiveness and interruptions are likely to become rife, and talk may degenerate into a happy babble of disorganized sound.

The ritual code itself requires a delicate balance, and can be easily upset by anyone who upholds it too eagerly or not eagerly enough, in terms of the standards and expectations of his group. Too little perceptiveness, too little *savoir-faire*, too little pride and considerateness, and the person ceases to be someone who can be trusted to take a hint about himself or give a hint that will save others embarrassment. Such a person comes to be a real threat to society; there is nothing much that can be done with him, and often he gets his way. Too much perceptiveness or too much pride, and the person becomes someone who is thin-skinned, who must be treated with kid gloves, requiring more care on the part of others than he may be worth to them. Too much *savoir-faire* or too much considerateness, and he becomes someone who is too socialized, who leaves the others with the feeling that they do not know how they really stand with him, nor what they should do to make an effective long-term adjustment to him.

In spite of these inherent 'pathologies' in the organization of talk, the functional fitness between the socialized person and spoken interaction is a viable and practical one. The person's orientation to face, especially his own, is the point of leverage that the ritual order has in regard to him; yet a promise to take ritual care of his face is built into the very structure of talk.

FACE AND SOCIAL RELATIONSHIPS

When a person begins a mediated or immediate encounter, he already stands in some kind of social relationship to the others concerned, and expects to stand in a given relationship to them after the particular encounter ends. This, of course, is one of the ways in which social contacts are geared into the wider society. Much of the activity occurring during an encounter can be understood as an effort on everyone's part to get through the occasion and all the unanticipated and unintentional events that can cast participants in an undesirable light, without disrupting the relationships of the participants. And if relationships are in the process of change, the object will be to bring the encounter to a satisfactory close without altering the expected course of development. This perspective nicely accounts, for example, for the little ceremonies of greeting and farewell which occur when people begin a conversational encounter or depart from one. Greetings provide a way of showing that a relationship is still what it was at the termination of the previous coparticipation, and, typically, that this relationship involves sufficient suppression of hostility for the participants temporarily to drop their guards and talk. Farewells sum up the effect of the encounter upon the relationship and show what the participants may expect of one another when they next meet. The enthusiasm of greetings compensates for the weakening of the relationship caused by the absence just terminated, while the enthusiasm of farewells compensates the relationship for the harm that is about to be done to it by separation.*

It seems to be a characteristic obligation of many social relationships that each of the members guarantees to support a given face for the other members in given situations. To prevent disruption of these relationships, it is therefore necessary for each member to avoid destroying the other's face. At the same time, it is often the person's social relationship with others that leads him to participate in certain encounters with them, where, incidentally, he will be dependent upon them for supporting his

---

* Greetings, of course, serve to clarify and fix the roles that the participants will take during the occasion of talk and to commit participants to these roles, while farewells provide a way of unambiguously terminating the encounter. Greetings and farewells may also be used to state, and apologize for, extenuating circumstances – in the case of greetings for circumstances that have kept the participants from interacting until now, and in the case of farewells for circumstances that prevent the participants from continuing their display of solidarity. These apologies allow the impression to be maintained that the participants are more warmly related socially than may be the case. This positive stress, in turn, assures that they will act more ready to enter into contacts than they perhaps really feel inclined to do, thus guaranteeing that diffuse channels for potential communication will be kept open in the society.

face. Furthermore, in many relationships, the members come to share a face, so that in the presence of third parties an improper act on the part of one member becomes a source of acute embarrassment to the other members. A social relationship, then, can be seen as a way in which the person is more than ordinarily forced to trust his self-image and face to the tact and good conduct of others.

THE NATURE OF THE RITUAL ORDER

The ritual order seems to be organized basically on accommodative lines, so that the imagery used in thinking about other types of social order is not quite suitable for it. For the other types of social order a kind of schoolboy model seems to be employed: if a person wishes to sustain a particular image of himself and trust his feelings to it, he must work hard for the credits that will buy this self-enhancement for him; should he try to obtain ends by improper means, by cheating or theft, he will be punished, disqualified from the race, or at least made to start all over again from the beginning. This is the imagery of a hard, dull game. In fact, society and the individual join in one that is easier on both of them, yet one that has dangers of its own.

Whatever his position in society, the person insulates himself by blindness, half-truths, illusions, and rationalizations. He makes an 'adjustment' by convincing himself, with the tactful support of his intimate circle, that he is what he wants to be and that he would not do to gain his ends what the others have done to gain theirs. And as for society, if the person is willing to be subject to informal social control – if he is willing to find out from hints and glances and tactful cues what his place is, and keep it – then there will be no objection to his furnishing this place at his own discretion, with all the comfort, elegance, and nobility that his wit can muster for him. To protect this shelter he does not have to work hard, or join a group, or compete with anybody; he need only be careful about the expressed judgements he places himself in a position to witness. Some situations and acts and persons will have to be avoided; others, less threatening, must not be pressed too far. Social life is an uncluttered, orderly thing because the person voluntarily stays away from the places and topics and times where he is not wanted and where he might be disparaged for going. He co-operates to save his face, finding that there is much to be gained from venturing nothing.

Facts are of the schoolboy's world – they can be altered by diligent effort but they cannot be avoided. But what the person protects and defends and invests his feelings in is an idea about himself, and ideas are vulnerable not to facts and things but to communications. Communications belong to a less punitive scheme than do facts, for communications can be by-passed, withdrawn from, disbelieved, conveniently misunderstood, and tactfully conveyed. And even should the person misbehave and break the truce he has made with society, punishment need not be the consequence. If the offence is one that the offended persons can let go by without losing too much face, then they are likely to act forbearantly, telling themselves that they will get even with the offender in another way at another time, even though such an occasion may never arise and might not be exploited if it did. If the offence is great, the offended persons may withdraw from the encounter, or from future similar ones, allowing their withdrawal to be reinforced by the awe they may feel towards someone who breaks the ritual code. Or they may have the offender withdrawn, so that no further communication can occur. But since the offender can salvage a good deal of face from such operations, withdrawal is often not so much an informal punishment for an offence as it is merely a means of terminating it. Perhaps the main principle of the ritual order is not justice but face, and what any offender receives is not what he deserves but what will sustain for the moment the line to which he has committed himself, and through this the line to which he has committed the interaction.

Throughout this paper it has been implied that underneath their differences in culture, people everywhere are the same. If persons have a universal human nature, they themselves are not to be looked to for an explanation of it. One must look rather to the fact that societies everywhere, if they are to be societies, must mobilize their members as self-regulating participants in social encounters. One way of mobilizing the individual for this purpose is through ritual; he is taught to be perceptive, to have feelings attached to self and a self expressed through face, to have pride, honour, and dignity, to have considerateness, to have tact and a certain amount of poise. These are some of the elements of behaviour which must be built into the person if practical use is to be made of him as an interactant, and it is these elements that are referred to in part when one speaks of universal human nature.

Universal human nature is not a very human thing. By acquiring it, the person becomes a kind of construct, built up not from inner psychic propensities but from moral rules that are impressed upon him from without. These rules, when followed, determine the evaluation he will make of himself and of his fellow-participants in the encounter, the distribution of his feelings, and the kinds of practices he will employ to maintain a specified and obligatory kind of ritual equilibrium. The general capacity to be bound by moral rules may well belong to the individual, but the particular set of rules which transforms him into a human being derives from requirements established in the ritual organization of social encounters. And if a particular person or group or society seems to have a unique character all its own, it is because its standard set of human-nature elements is pitched and combined in a particular way. Instead of much pride, there may be little. Instead of abiding by the rules, there may be much effort to break them safely. But if an encounter or undertaking is to be sustained as a viable system of interaction organized on ritual principles, then these variations must be held within certain bounds and nicely counterbalanced by corresponding modifications in some of the other rules and understandings. Similarly, the human nature of a particular set of persons may be specially designed for the special kind of undertakings in which they participate, but still each of these persons must have within him something of the balance of characteristics required of a usable participant in any ritually organized system of social activity.

Role Distance

I am grateful to the Center for the Integration of
Social Science Theory, of the University of California, Berkeley,
and the Society for the Study of Human Ecology, New York,
for support during the preparation of this paper. I have
profited from criticisms by Aaron Cicourel, John Clausen,
Fred Davis, Melvin Kohn, Sheldon Messinger, Theodore Sarbin,
David Schneider, and Gregory Stone.

Role Distance

In sociology there are few concepts more commonly used than 'role', few that are accorded more importance, and few that waver so much when looked at closely. In this paper I want to consider a broadened version of role and one of the concepts required to do this systematically.

ROLE CONCEPTS

The classic formulation of role concepts comes from the social-anthropological tradition* and has led to the development of a conceptual framework sometimes called 'role theory'. A *status* is a position in some system or pattern of positions and is related to the other positions in the unit through reciprocal ties, through rights and duties binding on the incumbents. *Role* consists of the activity the incumbent would engage in were he to act solely in terms of the normative demands upon someone in his position. Role in this normative sense is to be distinguished from *role performance* or role enactment, which is the actual conduct of a particular individual while on duty in his position. (Accordingly, it is a position that can be entered, filled, and left, not a role, for a role can only be performed; but no student seems to hold to these consistencies, nor will I.) In describing a role there is, of course, a problem of how much detail to give, the amount sometimes being tacitly determined unsystematically by the degree of familiarity the reader is assumed to have with the role in question.

The individual's role enactment occurs largely through a cycle of face-to-face situations with *role others*, that is, relevant audiences. These various kinds of role others for an individual in role,

* Principally Ralph Linton, *The Study of Man* (New York: Appleton-Century, 1936), especially Ch. 8, 'Status and Rôle'.

when taken together, have recently been termed a *role-set*.* The role-set for a doctor, for example, contains colleagues, nurses, patients, and hospital administrators. The norms relating the individual to performers of one of the roles in his role-set will have a special and non-conflictful relation to one another – more so than the norms relating the individual to different kinds of role others. The over-all role associated with a position falls into *role sectors*† or subroles, each having to do with a particular kind of role other. Doctor-nurse is a role sector of the doctor role; doctor-patient, another. Social changes in a role can be traced by the loss or gain to the role-set of types of role other. However, even within the special sector of a role relating the performer to one type of role other, the activities involved may themselves fall into different, somewhat independent, parcels or bundles, and through time these may also be reduced or added to, a bundle at a time. In any case, we ought not to be embarrassed by the fact that what is handled from one kind of position in one organization may be apportioned to two or three kinds of positions in another organization. We need only claim to know how a role is likely to be broken up should it come to be divided – the points of cleavage – and what roles are likely to be combined at times of organizational retrenchment.

The elementary unit of role analysis, as Linton was at pains to point out,‡ is not the individual but the individual enacting his bundle of obligatory activity. The system or pattern borrows only a part of the individual, and what he does or is at other times and places is not the first concern. The role others for whom he performs similarly represent only slices of these others. Presumably his contribution and their contribution, differentiated and interdependent, fit together into a single assemblage of activity,

* R. K. Merton, 'The Role-Set: Problems in Sociological Theory', *British Journal of Sociology*, 8 (1957), pp. 106–20. Presumably, a term will be needed to refer to the complement of individuals within *one* element in the role set, so that we can discuss the fact that some role others, such as wife, contain only one performer, while other role others, such as patient, contain many.

† Neal Gross, Ward Mason and Alexander McEachern, *Explorations in Role Analysis* (Wiley, 1958), especially p. 62. This book provides a very useful treatment of role. See also the helpful article by F. L. Bates, 'Position, Role, and Status: A Reformulation of Concepts', *Social Forces*, 34 (1956), pp. 313–21.

‡ Linton, *op. cit.*, p. 113.

this *system* or pattern being the real concern of role analysis. The role perspective has definite implications of a social-psychological kind. In entering the position, the incumbent finds that he must take on the whole array of action encompassed by the corresponding role, so role implies a social determinism and a doctrine about socialization. We do not take on items of conduct one at a time but rather a whole harness-load of them and may anticipatorily learn to be a horse even while being pulled like a wagon.* Role, then, is the basic unit of socialization. It is through roles that tasks in society are allocated and arrangements made to enforce their performance.

Recruitment for positions is restrictively regulated in some way, assuming that the incumbents will possess certain minimal qualifications, official and unofficial, technically relevant and irrelevant.† Incumbency tends to be symbolized through status cues of dress and manner, permitting those who engage in a situation to know with whom they are dealing. In some cases there will also be a role term of reference and address. Each position tends to be accorded some invidious social value, bringing a corresponding amount of prestige or contamination to the individual who fills it.

For this paper, it is important to note that in performing a role the individual must see to it that the impressions of him that are conveyed in the situation are compatible with role-appropriate personal qualities effectively imputed to him: a judge is supposed to be deliberate and sober; a pilot, in a cockpit, to be cool; a book-keeper to be accurate and neat in doing his work. These personal qualities, effectively imputed and effectively claimed, combine with a position's title, when there is one, to provide a basis of *self-image* for the incumbent and a basis for the image that his role others will have of him. A self, then, virtually awaits the individual entering a position; he need only conform to the pressures on him and he will find a *me* ready-made for him. In the language of Kenneth Burke, doing is being.

Sociologists have added several concepts to round out the Lintonian perspective; these can be introduced here, along with some effort at clarification.

* See Orville Brim, unpublished paper, 'Socialization as Role Learning'.
† E. C. Hughes, 'Dilemmas and Contradictions of Status', *American Journal of Sociology*, 50 (1945), pp. 353–9.

It can be useful to distinguish between the *regular performance* of a role and a *regular performer* of a role. If, for example, a funeral parlour is to stay in business, then the role of the director, of the immediately bereaved, and of the deceased must be performed regularly; but, of these regularly performed roles, only the director will be a regular performer. The immediately bereaved may play the same role on a few other occasions, but certainly the role of the deceased is played but once by any one individual. We can now see that to speak in common-sense terms of an 'irregular' performer is to refer to someone performing only a few times what is usually performed by a regular performer.

The *function* of a role is the part it plays in the maintenance or destruction of the system or pattern as a whole, the terms *eufunction* and *dysfunction* sometimes being employed to distinguish the supportive from the destructive effects.* Where the functional effect of a role is openly known and avowed, the term *manifest* function is sometimes employed; where these effects are not regularly foreseen and, especially, where this foresight might alter effects, the term *latent* is sometimes used.†

A concept that is often employed in the discussion of roles is that of *commitment*. I propose to restrict this term to questions of impersonally enforced structural arrangements. An individual becomes committed to something when, because of the fixed and interdependent character of many institutional arrangements, his doing or being this something irrevocably conditions other important possibilities in his life, forcing him to take courses of action, causing other persons to build up their activity on the basis of his continuing in his current undertakings, and rendering him vulnerable to unanticipated consequences of these undertakings.‡ He

* M. J. Levy, Jr, *The Structure of Society* (Princeton: Princeton University Press, 1952), pp. 76–9. It sometimes seems to be the hope of so-called functional analysis to transform all role analysis into role-function analysis.

† R. K. Merton, *Social Theory and Social Structure* (London: Collier-Macmillan, 1957), Ch. 1, 'Manifest and Latent Functions', pp. 19–84, especially definitions, p. 51.

‡ This last point is based on the thorough statement by Philip Selznick, *TVA and the Grass Roots* (Berkeley: University of California Press, 1953), pp. 255–9. A general consideration of the term 'commitment' may be found in Howard S. Becker, 'Notes on the Concept of Commitment', *American Journal of Sociology*, 66 (1960), pp. 32–40.

thus becomes locked into a position and coerced into living up to the promises and sacrifices built into it. Typically, a person will become deeply committed only to a role he regularly performs, and it is left to gallants, one-shot gamblers, and the foolhardy to become committed to a role they do not perform regularly.

The self-image available for anyone entering a particular position is one of which he may become affectively and cognitively enamoured, desiring and expecting to see himself in terms of the enactment of the role and the self-identification emerging from this enactment. I will speak here of the individual becoming *attached* to his position and its role, adding only that in the case of larger social units – groups, not positions – attachment is more likely to have a selfless component.* An appreciation can grow up concerning how attached an individual ought properly to be to a particular role, giving rise to the possibility that, compared to this moral norm, a performer may be over-attached to his role or alienated from it. For example, it is said that a new capitalist of the seventeenth century in Europe who entered and left an area of trade according to the temporary profit in it was felt by members of crafts and guilds to be sinfully unattached to what he dealt in.† Currently, it is felt to be sound mental hygiene for an individual to be attached to the role he performs, especially if he is a committed and regular performer of it. In all this there may be a middle-class bias, with our understanding of attachment coming from the learned professions, where attachment traditionally is great, to the neglect of the many roles that persons play with detachment, shame, or resentment.

In describing individuals' attachment to a role, it is sometimes said that they have committed their self-feelings to it, but in this paper I shall try to restrict the concept of commitment to the

---

* Strictly speaking, while it is possible for an individual to become attached to a position (as when a queen becomes convinced of the public value of monarchical government), to be attached to a position usually means to be attached to one's own incumbency of it.

† See, for example, Werner Sombart, *The Jews and Modern Capitalism* (London: Collier-Macmillan, 1962), Ch. 7, 'The Growth of a Capitalistic Point of View in Economic Life'.

D

forced-consequence sense previously suggested.* We will then be able to see that while attachment and commitment are often found together, as virtue doth cover necessity, there may also be discrepancies. Adoption agencies, for example, deal with two kinds of couples, the too fertile and the insufficiently fertile, the first being committed to the parent role without being attached to it, and the second being attached to the role without yet being committed to it.

Although traditional role analysis starts by focusing on the pattern or system arising from the differentiation and integration of roles, a second concern has emerged, related to, but analytically quite different from, the first, with the individual as the central unit. It is a basic assumption of role analysis that each individual will be involved in more than one system or pattern and, therefore, perform more than one role. Each individual will, therefore, have several selves, providing us with the interesting problem of how these selves are related. The model of man according to the initial role perspective is that of a kind of holding company for a set of not relevantly connected roles: it is the concern of the second perspective to find out how the individual runs this holding company.

While manifestly participating in one system of roles, the individual will have some capacity to hold in abeyance his involvement in other patterns, thus sustaining one or more dormant roles that are enacted roles on other occasions. This capacity supports a life cycle, a calendar cycle, and a daily cycle of role enactments; such scheduling implies some jurisdictional agreements as to where and what the individual is to be when. This *role-segregation* may be facilitated by *audience-segregation*, so that those who figure in one of the individual's major role-sets do not figure in another, thereby allowing the individual to possess contradictory qualities. Nevertheless, a person such as a surgeon, who keeps his surgical tools off his kitchen table and his wife off his other

* K. T. Erikson, in an interesting paper, 'Patient Role and Social Uncertainty – A Dilemma of the Mentally Ill', *Psychiatry*, 20 (1957), pp. 263–74, suggests a differing pairing of terms: 'commitment' to refer to the process by which an individual comes to take a role to heart, and 'validation' to refer to the process by which the community comes to accord a given role to the individual, ratifying his right to perform it.

table, may someday find himself with the role dilemma of treating another both as a kinsman and as a body. The embarrassment and vacillation characteristic of *role conflict* presumably result. The identification of this kind of trouble is not a limitation of role analysis but one of its main values, for we are led to consider mechanisms for avoiding such conflict or dealing with unavoidable conflict.*

Given the role perspective, it is of course possible to have a clinical, historical, or biographical interest, and to be concerned with all the roles performed by a particular concrete individual. Usually, however, role analysis is pitched in terms of the roles of some particular category of person, such as doctor or female. Often, in addition, concern is narrowed to some sphere of life, such as a formal organization, a social establishment, an occupational group, or a task activity. It may be added that while these distinctions in focus are easy enough to stipulate, it is apparently much less easy to keep within one focus once it has been selected.†

LIMITATIONS OF THE ROLE FRAMEWORK

Although the classic conceptions of position and role can deal adequately with many difficulties, there remain some issues that are less easy to resolve.

For example, if we look more closely at the notion of rights and duties we see that these were not well-chosen terms. Linton seems to have had in mind the normative world and the two general ways in which this world could impinge upon the individual: as *obligation*, in terms of an action of his own that he or others can legitimately demand he perform, and as *expectation*,‡ in terms of an action of others that he or they can legitimately insist upon. But the terms 'rights' and 'duties' carry other meanings. Sometimes these words refer to normative involvements – whether

* For example, see S. E. Perry and L. C. Wynne, 'Role Conflict, Role Redefinition, and Social Change in a Clinical Research Organization', *Social Forces*, 38 (1959), pp. 62–5.

† A very useful treatment of these issues can be found in Gross, *op. cit.*, pp. 56–7, under the heading 'situational specifications'.

‡ This term has the disadvantage of referring to both statistical and normative understandings; Gross, *op. cit.*, p. 59, suggests the term 'anticipations' be used for the former. See also A. W. Gouldner, *Wildcat Strike* (London: Routledge & Kegan Paul, 1955), p. 22.

obligation or expectation – that are desired or undesired in themselves, apart from moral considerations.* The term 'rights' is
especially ambiguous. Sometimes it means an obligation that can
be fulfilled by any one of a class of acts, choice within the class
being open to the actor, as when an executive finds he is at
liberty to wear any one of his seven business suits to work just
as long as he wears a business suit. Sometimes it means an obligation or expectation of one's own that one is allowed to forgo,
out of consideration for the other's distaste for it.

These verbal difficulties can easily be corrected. A more important issue is that while social scientists may formally espouse
Linton's normative approach, many of these students, and Linton
himself, do not adhere to it in practice. What students have in
mind when they refer to position and role is something much
broader and more adaptable than Linton's definitions provide.

An individual's position, defining position as it tends to be
used, is a matter of life chances – the likelihood of his undergoing
certain fateful experiences, certain trials, tribulations, and
triumphs. His position in some sphere of life is his 'situation'
there, in the sense employed by existentialists: the image that he
and others come to have of him; the pleasures and anxieties he is
likely to experience; the contingencies he meets in face-to-face
interaction with others; the relationships he is likely to form; his
probable alignment and stand on public issues, leading various
kinds of persons in various connexions to oppose him or support
him. I include also the obligations and expectations that very often
come to guide his action relative to specified others,† admitting
as one usual but not inevitable aspect of the scene what Linton
defined as the whole picture.‡ From this starting point we can

* See E. Goffman, 'The Nature of Deference and Demeanor', *American
Anthropologist*, 58 (1956), pp. 473–4.

† There is an asymmetry in the impingement of these two normative
domains. The individual's role, being his response to his position, will presumably be more directly involved in his obligations than in his expectations –
in what he ought to do, as opposed to what others ought to do in regard to
him. It is, therefore, natural to speak of the normative components of a
position but the obligatory components of role.

‡ I draw this revision of the term 'position' from Herbert Blumer, in 'Race
Prejudice as a Sense of Group Position', *Pacific Sociological Review*, 1 (1958),
pp. 3–7.

turn to consider either a role system or the manner in which the individual manages his multiple roles; we can also address ourselves without embarrassment to ways in which these two main aims of role analysis impinge on one another.

Role may now be defined, in this corrected version, as the *typical* response of individuals in a particular position. Typical role must, of course, be distinguished from the actual role performance of a concrete individual in a given position. Between typical response and actual response we can usually expect some difference, if only because the position of an individual, in the terms now used, will depend somewhat on the varying fact of how he perceives and defines his situation. Where there is a normative framework for a given role, we can expect that the complex forces at play upon individuals in the relevant position will ensure that typical role will depart to some degree from the normative model, despite the tendency in social life to transform what is usually done to what ought to be done. In general, then, a distinction must be made among typical role, the normative aspects of role, and a particular individual's actual role performance.

Another issue must now be considered. Earlier it was suggested that role analysis tends to concern itself with categories of persons and not with individuals as such. This formulation permits a troublesome ambiguity. In many cases, the category selected for study is one that is well established as a category in daily life with a role term and stereotyped image all its own: doctor, priest, housewife. In other cases, the category is one that is created by the student, who sees that a given set of persons can profitably be treated together, even if persons in everyday life have not done so. Typically, when a student uses a traditional category, the first issue is not the category's character as a 'collective representation', but whether – just as with a category fabricated solely for study – it brackets off a set of persons whose common life situation is worth looking at sociologically. I shall use the term *analytical category* to refer to a set of persons classed together for purposes of study, whether or not these persons have heretofore been brought together and categorized by the public at large.

To set up an analytical category, one must establish a defining or name attribute, possession of which leads to inclusion in the category. Once this is done, however, we must be careful to see that an analytical category (or the corresponding defining attribute) only provides us with a means of *discerning* or *disclosing* the social fate common to the members of the category. Categories and attributes *may* determine an allocation of social fate, as well as merely disclose it (although hardly determining what is available for allocation), but this stronger possibility must not be read into the discussion unless specifically mentioned. Traditional role analysis is often ambiguous and confusing on this point. For example, all persons called 'Doctor' in a given hospital may enjoy and suffer a common social fate. Legal claims to the title, however, tell us who will fall within the category, and hence who will receive this fate, but will not tell us why or how this particular fate has come to be allocated to members of this category, nor the part played by the title in this determination. We say, loosely, that legal entitlement to the term of address 'Doctor' determines how the entitled person will be treated, when, in fact, we usually merely mean that if we know how a person is addressed, we will know which of the available modes of treatment will be accorded him.

The notion that position is part of a pattern or system must now be reappraised. Some formal organizations, especially ones wholly contained in the physically bounded region of a walled-in social establishment, provide a concrete system of activity that can be used as a contextual point of reference. Even here the system-like properties of the organization cannot be taken for granted; but when we take a wider unit, such as a community or a society, there is no obvious concrete system of activity to point to as the pattern or system in which the position has its place. I suggest that a more atomistic frame of reference must be used – and is in fact used in actual studies. When we study role we study the situation of someone of a particular analytical category, and we usually limit our interest to the situation of this kind of person in a place and time: the home during non-working hours; the factory during working hours; the community during one's lifetime; the school during the academic term. But any identification of these contexts as social systems is surely hazardous, requiring for justification an extensive preliminary study seldom undertaken.

SITUATED ACTIVITY SYSTEMS

An object of this paper is to adapt role concepts for us in close studies of moment-to-moment behaviour. At the same time, I do not want to gloss over the fact – already stressed – that the 'system of reference' in role analysis is often vague and shifting. I therefore limit myself to activity that occurs entirely within the walls of single social establishments. This is already a grave limitation. The role of doctor can hardly be considered fully by noting what he does in a particular hospital that employs him; a full treatment must cover his round of work visits in the community and, what is more, the special treatment he is given when not ostensibly involved in medical matters at all – a treatment he facilitates by having a special licence plate, a special door plate, a special term of address, and a special title on his official documents.

But even limiting interest to a particular establishment is not enough. We can look at the individual's regular participation in such an establishment as a regular sequence of daily activities: our doctor makes rounds, writes out clinical notes, places calls to his office, has staff conferences, spends time in surgery, has coffee and lunch breaks, and so forth. Some of these activities will bring him into face-to-face interaction with others for the performance of a single joint activity, a somewhat closed, self-compensating, self-terminating circuit of interdependent actions – what might be called a *situated activity system*. The performance of a surgical operation is an example. Illustrations from other spheres of life would be: the playing-through of a game; the execution of one run of a small-group experiment; the giving and getting of a haircut. Such systems of activity are to be distinguished from a task performed wholly by a single person, whether alone or in the presence of others, and from a joint endeavour that is 'multi-situated', in that it is executed by subgroups of persons operating from different rooms. I would like to add that in English it is convenient to allow the context to decide the class-member issue, that is, whether one is referring to a class of like activities and a pattern of similarities, or referring to any occasion, trial, or run during which one complete cycle of phases occurs and provides a single illustration of the class and pattern.

Given any individual's sequence of regular activities in a social establishment, *one* regular activity involving a situated system can be singled out for study, since this provides the student with a context in which he can get as close as he is able to raw conduct. We deal, then, with 'small group' phenomena in a natural setting.

When the runs of a situated system are repeated with any frequency fairly well-developed *situated roles* seem to emerge: action comes to be divided into manageable bundles, each a set of acts that can be compatibly performed by a single participant. In addition to this role formation, there is a tendency for role differentiation to occur, so that the package of activity that the members of one class of participants perform is different from, though dependent on, the set performed by members of another category. A situated role, then, is a bundle of activities visibly performed before a set of others and visibly meshed into the activity these others perform. These kinds of roles, it may be added, differ from roles in general, not only because they are realized and encompassed in a face-to-face social situation, but also because the pattern of which they are a part can be confidently identified as a concrete self-compensating system.

The part that an individual plays in a situated circuit of activity inevitably expresses something about him, something out of which he and the others fashion an image of him. Often, this will be more than what is conveyed by mere accidents and incidents, and different from what is conveyed by membership in the establishment as such and by location in its ranks and offices. A situated self, then awaits the individual.

As an initial example of a situated system, I would like to draw on some brief observations of merry-go-rounds. There are senses in which any patronized ride on a merry-go-round provides an instance of a natural and objective social unit, an activity circuit, providing we follow the ride through its full cycle of activity involving a cohort of persons, each one getting a ticket and using it up together on the same ride. As is often the case with situated activity systems, mechanical operations and administrative purpose provide the basis of the unit. Yet persons are placed on this floor and something organic emerges. There is a mutual orientation of the participants and – within limits, it is true – a meshing together of their activity. As with any face-to-face interaction, there is much chance for communication and its feedback through a wide variety of signs, for the damping and surging of response, and for the emergence of homeostatic-like controls. As soon as the ride gets under way, there is a circulation of feeling among the participants and an 'involvement contour' may emerge, with collective shifts in the intensity, quality, and objects of involvement. Every ride, then, can be fruitfully viewed as an instance or run of a somewhat closed self-realized system. And this is so even though we know that this episode of reality is tied in with the day's activity at the merry-go-round, the state of the amusement park as a whole, the park season, and the community from which the riders come, just as we know that, for the man who runs the merry-go-round, a single ride may appear as a hardly distinguishable part of a day's work.

Some of the concepts introduced earlier regarding positions and roles can be applied, *mutatis mutandis*, to situated activity circuits. Certainly in the case of the merry-go-round there is role differentiation: those who ride; those who watch; and those who run the machine. Further, a role in such a system does imply an image of self, even a well-rounded one. For the merry-go-round rider, for example, the self awaiting is one that entails a child's portion of bravery and muscular control, a child's portion of manliness, and often a child's title. So, too, we know that children can become attached to such a role, since some will scream when finally taken off their horses. Further, some concepts, such as function, can be applied to a situated circuit of activity better perhaps than anywhere else, since here at least we deal with a clear-cut, well-bounded, concrete system.

The application of other role concepts to situated activity systems must be more carefully considered. To what, for example, can a child commit himself in becoming a rider? In coming to the amusement park, the child may be forgoing another kind of amusement that day. In paying his dime, he is committing some measure of purchasing power, but even for him perhaps no great amount. And once the machine starts, he may have some commitment to finishing the ride, as a person piloting a plane has a commitment to stay with his task until a landing is made. But, in the main, a rider's commitment is small. He can, for example, easily arrange to take on the role or divest himself of it.

The role of merry-go-round operator might constitute a greater commitment, since this role is not only performed regularly but also is likely to be enacted by a regular performer. In following his present line of work, the operator may well have automatically excluded himself from the recruitment channels leading to other kinds of jobs. The money he can make on the job, further, may be committed to the upkeep of his domestic establishment, and his budget may have been planned on the basis of his continuing to operate the concession. Relative to the individuals who ride his steeds, then, he is committed to his position and locked into it.

But this is a loose way of talking, derived from traditional role analysis. If the operator is employed by the amusement park, then he is committed to performing some job in connexion with the organization. Within the organization's formal setting, however, he may, in fact, change his situated role, managing the candy and popcorn concession one day and the merry-go-round the next – and on some days even both. Although these changes entail a radical shift in the tasks he performs and in the intimate system of situated activity in which these tasks fit, he may find little change in his situation in life. Even where he owns the concession and has invested all his money in the merry-go-round, he need not be committed to the role of operator but merely to hiring someone to perform the role whose hire he can afford to pay.

The point about looking at situated activity systems, however, is not that some traditional role concepts can be applied in this situational setting, but that the complexities of concrete conduct can be examined instead of by-passed. Where the social content of a situated system faithfully expresses in miniature the structure of the broader social organization in which it is located, then little change in the traditional role analysis is necessary; situated roles would merely be our means of sampling, say, occupational or institutional roles. But where a discrepancy is found, we would be in a position to show proper respect for it.

THE PROBLEM OF EXPRESSION

With this preliminary review and revision of role concepts, and the introduction of the notion of situated activity systems, we can begin to look at the special concern of this paper, the issue of

expression. I must backtrack a little at first, however, before pro-
ceeding with expression on merry-go-rounds and other situated
systems.

I have already reviewed the assumption that when an individual
makes an appearance in a given position, he will be the person
that the position allows and obliges him to be and will continue
to be this person during role enactment. The performer will
attempt to make the expressions that occur consistent with the
identity imputed to him; he will feel compelled to control and
police the expressions that occur. Performance will, therefore,
be able to express identity. But we need only state that doing is
being to become aware of apparent exceptions, which, furthermore, arise at different points, each throwing light on a different
source of instability in the presumed expressiveness of role.

One issue is that roles may not only be *played* but also *played at*,
as when children, stage actors, and other kinds of cut-ups mimic
a role for the avowed purpose of make-believe; here, surely,
doing is not being. But this is easy to deal with. A movie star
who plays at being a doctor is not in the role of doctor but in the
role of actor; and this latter role, we are told, he is likely to take
quite seriously. The work of his role is to portray a doctor, but
the work is only incidental; his actual role is no more make-
believe than that of a real doctor – merely better paid. Part of the
confusion here, perhaps, has been that actors do not have a right
to keep amateurs from playing at being actors in amateur theatricals, a fact that helps give the whole trade a bad name.

A professional actor differs from a child in the degree of perseverance and perfection the professional must manifest in the role
he simulates. Professional and child are similar, however, in
making no continued effort to convince any audience that performer and performed character are the same, and they are
similarly embarrassed when this over-belief occurs. Both are to
be contrasted with actors employed in one version or another
of the cloak-and-dagger business. These desperate performers are
caught exactly between illusion and reality, and must lead one
audience to accept the role portrait as real, even while assuring
another audience that the actor in no way is convincing himself.

Further, under certain rare and colourful circumstances, a man
who first appears, say, to be a surgeon, accepting others' acceptance

of him in this role, may in fact be a knowing impostor, knowing of radical grounds that others do not know they have for not accepting him. And in addition to this classic kind of misrepresentation, there is the situation in which an individual may, against his will, be temporarily misidentified by others who have accepted the wrong cues regarding him. It is a sad fact that a Negro intern or resident in a predominantly white hospital is likely to acquire experience in telling patients and visitors that he cannot see to minor requests because he is not an attendant.

Whether an individual plays a role or plays at it, we can expect that the mechanics of putting it on will typically expose him as being out of character at certain regular junctures. Thus, while a person may studiously stay *in role* while in the staging area of its performance, he may nonetheless *break role* or go out of role when he thinks that no one or no one important can see him. Even a performer of one of our most splendid roles, such as a surgeon, may allow himself to 'go out of play' – to stare vacantly, pick his nose, or comb his hair, all in a manner unbecoming a surgeon – just before he enters the operating room or just after he leaves it. But again, it is just these expressive incongruities that role analysis allows us to perceive and account for.

Furthermore, students these days are increasingly examining 'role dissensus', in connexion with the plurality of cultural and group affiliations which differentially impinge upon persons present in a role to one another.* Thus, some surgeons are more alive than others to the opinion of patients, others to the opinion of their colleagues, and still others to the view that the hospital management has of them. Each of these audiences is likely to have a somewhat different view of ideal standards of performance; what is one man's ideal for role performance may to another seem almost an infraction.

I want to add a point that is insufficiently appreciated. Before a set of task-like activities can become an identity-providing role, these activities must be clothed in a moral performance of some kind. Mere efficient enactment is not enough to provide the identity; activities must be built up socially and made something

* For example, Gross, *op. cit.*, and A. W. Gouldner, 'Cosmopolitans and Locals: Toward an Analysis of Latent Social Roles – I', *Administrative Science Quarterly*, 2 (1957), pp. 281–306.

of. Although this role formation or social capitalization of jobs seems the usual practice in urban life, it is by no means universal. There are, for example, ancient inbred island communities of Britain where kinship and fellow-islander status is so fundamental that a native who is employed in a local shop to sell to members of the community is unlikely to build this work activity into a stance to be taken to customers. Such clerks take the point of view of the other not only in manner, as in the case of urban sellers, but also in spirit, the other in this case being treated not as a customer but as a kinsman, as a neighbour, or as a friend. Often, no variation can be observed in tone or manner as the clerk weaves personal gossipy conversation in amongst the words of advice he offers as to which of the local shops (not just his own) sells which product at the most advantageous price. Here, the richness of communal life entails an impoverishment of the self-defining aspects of occupational roles: required tasks are done, but they are scarcely allowed to form the base for the development of a special loyalty and a special orientation to the world.* Here doing is not being. The person who is the salesman has a self, but it is not the self of a salesman. Only the manager of the store will display identification with his role, and even he appreciates that he must not throw himself too much into his calling.

The next issue concerning expression requires a more extended consideration.

Whatever an individual does and however he appears, he knowingly and unknowingly makes information available concerning the attributes that might be imputed to him and hence the categories in which he might be placed. The status symbolism in his 'personal front' provides information about his group and aggregate affiliations; his treatment at the hands of others conveys a conception of him; the physical milieu itself conveys implications

---

* Interestingly enough, in such communities there is often an appreciation that traditional bases for defining the self must be put aside and those of urban repute encouraged. In the Shetland Islands, where almost every man can do a surprising range of mechanical, electrical and construction work, one may observe tacit agreements among islanders to support one of their number as a 'specialist' in a skill, allowing him payment for jobs they might have done themselves. Once these specialists are established by reputation, if not by the volume and constancy of their trade, the islanders point to them with pride as evidence of the modernity of the community.

concerning the identity of those who are in it. Face-to-face situations, it may be added, are ones in which a great variety of sign vehicles become available, whether desired or not, and are, therefore, situations in which much information about oneself can easily become available. Face-to-face situations are, in fact, ideal projective fields that the participant cannot help but structure in a characterizing way, so that conclusions can be drawn about him, correct or incorrect, whether he wants it or not.

It should be appreciated that the information the situation provides about an individual who is in it need not be a direct reflection or extension of the local scene itself. By working on a charity case in a slum dwelling, a physician does not become identified with the status of his client; social dirt does not rub off on him. (The socio-economic attributes of those who make up his office practice, however, present another problem.) Similarly, the tourist does not lose caste in appearing in an unsophisticated peasant milieu; the very presence of natives establishes him as a traveller.

The individual stands in a double relationship to attributes that are, or might be, imputed to him. Some attributes he will feel are rightfully his, others he will not; some he will be pleased and able to accept as part of his self-definition, others he will not.* There is some relationship between these two variables – between what is right and what is pleasing – in that the individual often feels that pleasing imputations regarding himself are in addition rightful, and unpleasing imputations are, incidentally, undeserved and illegitimate. But this happy relationship between the two variables does not always hold.

Ordinarily, the information that arises in a social situation concerning one of the participants consistently confirms for him and others a particular conception of himself which is, in addition, one that he is prepared to accept, more or less, as both right and desirable. Here, in fact, we have two basic assumptions of the role perspective – that one accepts as an identification of oneself what one is doing at the time, and that once cues have been conveyed about one's positions, the rest of the information becoming available in the situation confirms these initial cues.

* Psychiatrically, this is sometimes referred to as a difference between ego-syntonic and ego-alien.

But expressive consistency and acceptability are not always in fact maintained. Information incompatible with the individual's image of himself does get conveyed. In some cases, this inopportune information may give the individual more credit than he feels he could properly accept; in more cases, apparently, the troublesome information undercuts the individual's self-image. Some of this self-threatening information may be valid, referring to facts which the individual wishes would not be raised concerning him. Some of the information may be invalid, implying an unwarranted image of himself that he ought not to have to accept.

In any case, it should be clear that the individual cannot completely control the flow of events in a social situation and hence cannot completely control the information about himself that becomes available in the situation. Even the best-run interactions throw up events that are expressively somewhat inconsistent with effective claims regarding self. Men trip, forget names, wear slightly inappropriate clothes, attempt to buy a too-small amount of some commodity, fail to score well in a game, arrive a few minutes late for an appointment, become a trifle overheated in argument, fail to finish a task quite on time. In all these cases, a momentary discrepancy arises between what the individual anticipated being and what events imply he is.

Whether a social situation goes smoothly or whether expressions occur that are in discord with a participant's sense of who and what he is, we might expect – according to the usual deterministic implications of role analysis – that he will fatalistically accept the information that becomes available concerning him. Yet when we get close to the moment-to-moment conduct of the individual we find that he does not remain passive in the face of the potential meanings that are generated regarding him, but, so far as he can, actively participates in sustaining a definition of the situation that is stable and consistent with his image of himself.

Perhaps the simplest example of this 'control of implications' response is the 'explanation'. Here, the individual volunteers information which is designed to alter radically the information that has been, or otherwise will be, generated in the situation. Another is that of the 'apology', through which the individual begs not to be judged in the way that appears likely, implying that his own standards are offended by his act and that therefore some part of him, at least, cannot be characterized by the unseemly action.* A display of righteous indignation has the same effect, but it is the other who is cast in a bad light instead of a split-off portion of oneself. Similarly, by introducing an unserious style, the individual can project the claim that nothing happening at the moment to him or through him should be taken as a direct reflection of him, but rather of the person-in-situation that he is mimicking. Thus, there is in our society a special tone of voice and facial posture through which 'baby talk' is conveyed at strategic moments, for example when a second helping is requested by an individual who does not want to appear to be intemperate.

Explanations, apologies, and joking are all ways in which the individual makes a plea for disqualifying some of the expressive features of the situation as sources of definitions of himself. Since these manoeuvres are often accepted by the others present, we must see that the individual's responsibility for the self-expressive implications of the events around him has definite limits.

ROLE DISTANCE

The occurrence of explanations and apologies as limitations on the expressiveness of role leads us to look again at what goes on in concrete face-to-face activity. I return to our situated example, the merry-go-round.

A merry-go-round horse is a thing of some size, some height, and some movement; and while the track is never wet, it can be very noisy. American middle-class two-year-olds often find the prospect too much for them. They fight their parents at the last moment to avoid being strapped into a context in which it had been hoped they would prove to be little men. Sometimes they become frantic halfway through the ride, and the machine must be stopped so that they can be removed.

Here we have one of the classic possibilities of life. Participation in any circuit of face-to-face activity requires the participant

* Explanations and apologies are, of course, often combined into the 'excuse' through which both restructuring information and self-abasement are introduced at the same time. See the treatment in Jackson Toby, 'Some Variables in Role Conflict Analysis', *Social Forces*, 30 (1952), pp. 323–37.

to keep command of himself, both as a person capable of executing physical movements and as one capable of receiving and transmitting communications. A flustered failure to maintain either kind of role poise makes the system as a whole suffer. Every participant, therefore, has the function of maintaining his own poise, and one or more participants are likely to have the specialized function of modulating activity so as to safeguard the poise of the others. In many situated systems, of course, all contingencies are managed without such threats arising. However, there is no such system in which these troubles might not occur, and some systems, such as those in a surgery ward, presumably provide an especially good opportunity to study these contingencies.

Just as a rider may be disqualified during the ride because he proves to be unable to handle riding, so a rider will be removed from his saddle at the very beginning of the ride because he does not have a ticket or because, in the absence of his parents, he makes management fear for his safety. There is an obvious distinction, then, between qualifications required for permission to attempt a role and attributes required for performing suitably once the role has been acquired.

At three and four, the task of riding a wooden horse is still a challenge, but apparently a manageable one, inflating the rider to his full extent with demonstrations of capacity. Parents need no longer ride alongside to protect their youngsters. The rider throws himself into the role in a serious way, playing it with verve and an admitted engagement of all his faculties. Passing his parents at each turn, the rider carefully lets go one of his hands and grimly waves a smile or a kiss – this, incidentally, being an example of an act that is a typical part of the role but hardly an obligatory feature of it. Here, then, doing is being, and what was designated as a 'playing at' is stamped with serious realization.

Just as 'flustering' is a classic possibility in all situated systems, so also is the earnest way these youngsters of three or four ride their horses. Three matters seem to be involved: an admitted or expressed attachment to the role; a demonstration of qualifications and capacities for performing it; an active *engagement* or spontaneous involvement in the role activity at hand, that is, a visible investment of attention and muscular effort. Where these

E

three features are present, I will use the term *embracement*. To embrace a role is to disappear completely into the virtual self available in the situation, to be fully seen in terms of the image, and to confirm expressively one's acceptance of it. To embrace a role is to be embraced by it. Particularly good illustrations of full embracement can be seen in persons in certain occupations: team managers during baseball games; traffic policemen at intersections during rush hours; landing-signal officers who wave-in planes landing on the decks of aircraft carriers; in fact, anyone occupying a directing role where the performer must guide others by means of gestural signs.*

An individual may affect the embracing of a role in order to conceal a lack of attachment to it, just as he may affect a visible disdain for a role, thrice refusing the kingly crown, in order to defend himself against the psychological dangers of his actual attachment to it. Certainly an individual may be attached to a role and fail to be able to embrace it, as when a child proves to have no ticket or to be unable to hang on.

Returning to the merry-go-round, we see that at five years of age the situation is transformed, especially for boys. To be a merry-go-round horse rider is now apparently not enough, and this fact must be demonstrated out of dutiful regard for one's own character. Parents are not likely to be allowed to ride along, and the strap for preventing falls is often disdained. One rider may keep time to the music by clapping his feet or a hand against the horse, an early sign of utter control. Another may make a wary stab at standing on the saddle or changing horses without touching the platform. Still another may hold on to the post with one hand and lean back as far as possible while looking up to the sky in a challenge to dizziness. Irreverence begins, and the horse may be held on to by his wooden ear or his tail. The child says by his actions: 'Whatever I am, I'm not just someone who can barely manage to stay on a wooden horse.' Note that what the rider is apologizing for is not some minor untoward event that has cropped up during the interaction, but the whole role. The image of him that is generated for him by the routine entailed in his mere participation – his virtual self in the context – is an

* Here, as elsewhere, I am indebted to Gregory Stone.

image from which he apparently withdraws by *actively* manipulating the situation. Whether this skittish behaviour is intentional or unintentional, sincere or affected, correctly appreciated by others present or not, it does constitute a wedge between the individual and his role, between doing and being. This 'effectively' expressed pointed separateness between the individual and his putative roll I shall call *role distance*. A shorthand is involved here: the individual is actually denying not the role but the virtual self that is implied in the role for all accepting performers.

In any case, the term 'role distance' is not meant to refer to all behaviour that does not directly contribute to the task core of a given role but only to those behaviours that are seen by someone present as relevant to assessing the actor's attachment to his particular role and relevant in such a way as to suggest that the actor possibly has some measure of disaffection from, and resistance against, the role. Thus, for example, a four-year-old halfway through a triumphant performance as a merry-go-round rider may sometimes go out of play, dropping from his face and manner any confirmation of his virtual self, yet may indulge in this break in role without apparent intent, the lapse reflecting more on his capacity to sustain any role than on his feelings about the present one. Nor can it be called role distance if the child rebels and totally rejects the role, stomping off in a huff, for the special facts about self that can be conveyed by holding a role off a little are precisely the ones that cannot be conveyed by throwing the role over.

At seven and eight, the child not only dissociates himself self-consciously from the kind of horseman a merry-go-round allows him to be but also finds that many of the devices that younger people use for this are now beneath him. He rides no-hands, gleefully chooses a tiger or a frog for a steed, clasps hands with a mounted friend across the aisle. He tests limits, and his antics may bring negative sanction from the adult in charge of the machine. And he is still young enough to show distance by handling the task with bored, nonchalant competence, a candy bar languidly held in one hand.

At eleven and twelve, maleness for boys has become a real responsibility, and no easy means of role distance seems to be available on merry-go-rounds. It is necessary to stay away or to exert creative acts of distancy, as when a boy jokingly treats his wooden horse as if it were a racing one: he jogs himself up and down, leans far over the neck of the horse, drives his heels mercilessly into its flanks, and uses the reins for a lash to get more speed, brutally reining in the horse when the ride is over. He is just old enough to achieve role distance by defining the whole undertaking as a lark, a situation for mockery.

Adults who choose to ride a merry-go-round display adult techniques of role distance. One adult rider makes a joke of tightening the safety belt around him; another crosses his arms, giving popcorn with his left hand to the person on his right and a coke with his right hand to the person on his left. A young lady riding sidesaddle tinkles out, 'It's cold', and calls to her watching boy friend's boy friend, 'Come on, don't be chicken.' A dating couple riding adjacent horses holds hands to bring sentiment, not daring, to the situation. Two double-dating couples employ their own techniques: the male in front sits backwards and takes a picture of the other male rider taking a picture of him. And, of course, some adults, riding close by their threatened two-and-a-half-year-old, wear a face that carefully demonstrates that they do not perceive the ride as an event in itself, their only present interest being their child.

And finally there is the adult who runs the machine and takes the tickets. Here, often, can be found a fine flowering of role distance. Not only does he show that the ride itself is not – as a ride – an event to him, but he also gets off and on and around the moving platform with a grace and ease that can only be displayed by safely taking what for children and even adults would be chances.

Some general points can be made about merry-go-round role distance. First, while the management of a merry-go-round horse in our culture soon ceases to be a challenging 'developmental task', the task of expressing that it is not continues for a long time to be a challenge and remains a felt necessity. A full twist must be made in the iron law of etiquette: the act through which one can afford to try to fit into the situation is an act that can be styled to show that one is somewhat out of place. One enters the situation to the degree that one can demonstrate that one does not belong.

A second general point about role distance is that immediate audiences figure very directly in the display of role distance. Merry-go-round horsemen are very ingenuous and may frankly wait for each time they pass their waiting friends before playing through their gestures of role distance. Moreover, if persons above the age of twelve or so are to trust themselves to making a lark of it, they almost need to have a friend along on the next horse, since persons who are 'together' seem to be able to hold off the socially defining force of the environment much more than a person alone.

A final point: two different means of establishing role distance seem to be found. In one case the individual tries to isolate himself as much as possible from the contamination of the situation, as when an adult riding along to guard his child makes an effort to be completely stiff, affectless, and preoccupied. In the other case the individual co-operatively projects a childish self, meeting the situation more than halfway, but then withdraws from this cast-off self by a little gesture signifying that the joking has gone far enough. In either case the individual can slip the skin the situation would clothe him in.

A summary of concepts is now in order. I have tried to distinguish among three easily confused ideas: *commitment, attachment,* and *embracement.** It is to be noted that these sociological terms are of a different order from that of *engagement,* a psychobiological process that a cat or a dog can display more beautifully than man. Finally, the term *role distance* was introduced to refer to actions which effectively convey some disdainful detachment of the performer from a role he is performing.

ROLE DISTANCE AND SERIOUS ACTIVITY

The role of merry-go-round rider can be regularly performed at any amusement park but hardly by a regular performer. After a few years each of us 'outgrows' the role and can only perform it as an occasional thing and as an occasion for the display of much

* A somewhat different and more differentiated analysis may be found in G. P. Stone, 'Clothing and Social Relations: A Study of Appearance in the Context of Community Life' (unpublished Ph.D. dissertation, Department of Sociology, University of Chicago, 1959).

role distance. As an example, then, merry-go-round riding is not a very serious one; furthermore, it is somewhat misleading, since it implies that role distance is displayed in connexion with roles no adult can take seriously.

Actually, we deal with a more general phenomenon, with roles that categories of individuals find it unwise to embrace. Even a short step away from merry-go-rounds shows this. Take, for example, six lower-middle-class high-school girls, not of the horsey set, taking a vacation in a national park and deciding to 'do' horseback riding on one of their mornings. As long as they come to the riding stable in self-supporting numbers, they can nicely illustrate distance from a role that persons of another social class and region might take seriously all their lives. The six I observed came in clothing patently not designed as a consolidation of the horsewoman role: pedal pushers, cotton leotards, ballet-type flats, frilly blouses. One girl, having been allotted the tallest horse, made a mock scene of declining to get on because of the height, demanding to be allowed to go home. When she did get on, she called her horse 'Daddy-O', diverting her conversation from her friends to her horse. During the ride, one girl pretended to post while the horse walked, partly in mockery of a person not in their party who was posting. Another girl leaned over the neck of her horse and shouted racing cries, again while the horse was locked in a walking file of other horses. She also slipped her right foot out of the stirrup and brought it over the saddle, making a joke of her affectation of riding sidesaddle and expressing that both positions were much alike to her – both equally unfamiliar and uncongenial; at the same time she tested the limits of the wrangler's permissiveness. Passing under low branches, the girls made a point of making a point of this by pulling off branches, waving them like flags, then feeding them to their horses. Evidences of the excretory capacities of the steeds were greeted with merriment and loud respect. During the latter part of the two-hour ride, two of the girls became visibly bored, dropped the reins over the saddlehorn, let their hands fall limply to their sides, and gave up all pretence at being in role.

Again we can detect some general facts about role distance. We can see that a role that some persons take seriously most of their lives may be one that others will never take seriously at any age.

We see that participation with a group of one's similars can lend strength to the show of role distance and to one's willingness to express it. In the presence of age-peers elegantly attired for riding and skilled at it, the girls I observed might falter in displaying role distance, feeling hostile, resentful, and unconfident. Presumably, if one of these girls were alone with thoroughgoing horsewomen she would be even less prone to flourish this kind of distance. We can suspect, then, that role distance will have defensive functions. By manifesting role distance, the girls give themselves some elbow room in which to manoeuvre. 'We are not to be judged by this incompetence,' they say. Should they make a bad showing, they are in a position to dodge the reflection it could cast on them. Whatever their showing, they avoid having to be humbled before those who are socially placed to make a much better showing. By exposing themselves in a guise to which they have no serious claim, they leave themselves in full control of shortcomings they take seriously.

While horse trails and children's playgrounds provide fine places for studying repertoires of role distance, we need not look to situations that are so close to being unserious, situations where it is difficult to distinguish role playing from playing at. We know, for example, that tasks that might be embraced by a housewife or maid may be tackled by the man of the house with carefully expressed clumsiness and with self-mockery. Perhaps it should be noted that similar out-of-character situations can easily be created experimentally by asking subjects to perform tasks that are inappropriate to persons of their kind.

The published literature on some of our occupational byways provides serious material on role distance. Psychoanalysts, for example, who have told us so much about the contingencies of a particular trade (even when not telling us all we might want to know about their patients), provide interesting data on role distance in connexion with 'resistance' on the part of the patient. Resistance here takes the form of the patient refusing to provide relevant associations or refusing to allow the therapist to function solely as a 'therapist'. From the therapist's view of the patient's motivation, then, resistance expresses some rejection of the constraints of one's role as patient:

Up to this point I found myself, as the doctor, comfortably installed in my explicit instrumental role; the role assignment given me by the patient appeared to be concerned with her 'problem'. The system of roles was complementary and apparently well integrated. The next moment, however, the patient initiated a new role assignment. She asked me if I had seen a recent performance of 'Don Juan in Hell' from *Man and Superman*. The question seemed a simple enough request for information regarding my playgoing habits. But since I did not know what role I was being invited to take, and because I suspected that behind whatever explicit role this might turn out to be there lurked a more important implicit one, I did not answer the question. The patient paused for a moment, and then, perceiving that I would not answer the question, she continued. . . .

In continuing after the pause, the patient delivered a highly perceptive account of Shaw's intention in the Don Juan interlude, of the actors' interpretations, and of her reactions. The account was so long that I finally interrupted to ask if she knew why she wanted to tell all this. At the point of interruption I had become aware that my new role was an expressive one – to play the appreciative audience to her role as a gifted art and drama critic.*

The therapist then goes on to explain that had he merely fallen in with the patient's manoeuvres to keep herself at a distance from the role of patient he would have had to pass up 'the opportunity to get more information regarding the hidden, implicit role buried in this transaction and thus to learn more about her motivation for shifting out of her initial instrumental role in which she had started the interview.'† The therapist could have added that to ask the patient why she felt it necessary to run on so is a classic therapist's ploy to put the patient in her place, back in role.

Situated roles that place an individual in an occupational setting he feels is beneath him are bound to give rise to much role distance. A good example is provided by Isaac Rosenfeld in a reminiscence about a summer job as a barker at Coney Island. The writer begins his description by telling of his return after many years, seeing someone else handling his old job:

He was sneering, just as I used to do in the old days, and no doubt

---

* J. P. Spiegel, 'The Social Roles of Doctor and Patient in Psychoanalysis and Psychotherapy', *Psychiatry*, 17 (1954), pp. 372–3.
† *Ibid.*, p. 373.

for the same reason: because the summer was hot, and the work hard, sweaty and irritating, stretching over long hours for poor pay. It was absolutely indispensable, now as it was then, to separate oneself from the job – one had to have a little ledge to stand on all to himself; otherwise perish. I used to pitch this ledge very high. The higher I stood, the greater my contempt, and the more precious the moments of freedom I won for myself by this trick of balancing above the crowd. I remembered how I used to mix T. S. Eliot with my spiel (in those days there was hardly anyone in Freshman English who did not know a good deal of *The Waste Land* by heart): 'Step right up ladies and gentlemen mingling memory with desire for the greatest thrill show on earth only a dime the tenth part of a dollar will bring you to Carthage then I come burning burning burning O Lord thou pluckest me out ten cents!'*

Some of the most appealing data on role distance come from situations where a subordinate must take orders or suggestions and must go along with the situation as defined by superordinates. At such times, we often find that although the subordinate is careful not to threaten those who are, in a sense, in charge of the situation, he may be just as careful to inject some expression to show, for any who care to see, that he is not capitulating completely to the work arrangement in which he finds himself.† Sullenness, muttering, irony, joking, and sarcasm may all allow one to show that something of oneself lies outside the constraints of the moment and outside the role within whose jurisdiction the moment occurs.

Given these various examples of role distance, I want to go on to argue that this conduct is something that falls between role obligations on one hand and actual role performance on the other. This gap has always caused trouble for sociologists. Often, they try to ignore it. Faced with it, they sometimes despair and turn

---

* Isaac Rosenfeld, 'Coney Island Revisited', in *Modern Writing*, eds. William Phillips and Philip Rahv (New York: Avon Publications, 1953), p. 219.

† Some excellent illustrations of this may be found in Tom Burns, 'Friends, Enemies and the Polite Fiction', *American Sociological Review*, 18 (1953), pp. 654–62, a paper to which I am very much indebted. A good illustration from army life is provided in William Styron's story, *The Long March* (Harmondsworth: Penguin Books, 1964), in connexion with a captain's minor remonstrances against orders issued by his colonel.

from their own direction of analysis; they look to the biography of the performer and try to find in his history some particularistic explanation of events, or they rely on psychology, alluding to the fact that in addition to playing the formal themes of his role, the individual always behaves personally and spontaneously, phrasing the standard obligations in a way that has a special psychological fit for him.

The concept of role distance provides a *sociological* means of dealing with one type of divergence between obligation and actual performance. First, we know that often distance is not introduced on an individual basis but can be predicted on the grounds of the performers' gross age-sex characteristics. Role distance is a part (but, of course, only one part) of *typical* role, and this routinized sociological feature should not escape us merely because role distance is not part of the normative framework of role. Secondly, that which one is careful to point out one is not, or not merely, necessarily has a directing and intimate influence on one's conduct, especially since the means for expressing this disaffection must be carved out of the standard materials available in the situation.

We arrive, then, at a broadened sociological way of looking at the trappings of a social role. A set of visible qualifications and known certifications, along with a social setting well designed as a showplace, provides the individual with something more than an opportunity to play his role self to the hilt, for this scene is just what he needs to create a clear impression of what he chooses not to lay claim to. The more extensive the trappings of a role, the more opportunity to display role distance. Personal front and social setting provide precisely the field an individual needs to cut a figure in – a figure that romps, sulks, glides, or is indifferent. Later in this paper, some additional social determinants of role distance will be considered.

SURGERY AS AN ACTIVITY SYSTEM

I have suggested some cases where the scene of activity generates for the individual a self which he is apparently loath to accept openly for himself, since his conduct suggests that some disaffiliation exists between himself and his role. But a peek into some odd corners of social life provides no basis, perhaps, for generalizing about social life. As a test, then, of the notion of role distance (and role), let us take a scene in which activity generates a self for the individual that appears to be a most likely one for self-attachment. Let us take, for example, the activity system sustained during a surgical operation. The components consist of verbal and physical acts and the changing state of the organism undergoing the operation. Here, if anywhere in our society, we should find performers flushed with a feeling of the weight and dignity of their action. A Hollywood ideal is involved: the white-coated chief surgeon strides into the operating theatre after the patient has been anaesthetized and opened by assistants. A place is automatically made for him. He grunts a few abbreviated preliminaries, then deftly, almost silently, gets to work, serious, grim, competently living up to the image he and his team have of him, yet in a context where momentary failure to exhibit competence might permanently jeopardize the relation he is allowed to have to his role. Once the critical phase of the operation is quite over, he steps back and, with a special compound of tiredness, strength, and disdain, rips off his gloves; he thus contaminates himself and abdicates his role, but at a time when his own labours put the others in a position to 'close up'. While he may be a father, a husband, or a baseball fan at home, he is here one and only one thing, a surgeon, and being a surgeon provides a fully rounded impression of the man. If the role perspective works, then, surely it works here, for in our society the surgeon, if anyone, is allowed and obliged to put himself into his work and get a self out of it.*

As a contrast, then, to the insubstantial life of horses-for-ride, I want to report briefly on some observations of activity in surgery wards.†

* Much the same conceit has already been employed by Temple Burling in *Essays on Human Aspects of Administration*, Bulletin 25 (August 1953) of the New York States School of Industrial and Labor Relations, Cornell University, pp. 9–10. The fullest published accounts of conduct in the operating room that I know of are to be found in T. Burling, E. Lentz and R. Wilson, *The Give and Take in Hospitals* (New York: Putnam, 1956), Ch. 17, pp. 260–83, and R. Wilson, 'Teamwork in the Operating Room', *Human Organization*, 12 (1954), pp. 9–14.

† My own material on interaction during surgery, from which all staff practices and verbal responses cited in this paper are drawn, derives from

If we start with the situation of the lesser medical personnel, the intern and the junior resident, the test will not be fair, for here, apparently, is a situation much like the ones previously mentioned. The tasks these juniors are given to do – such as passing haemostats, holding retractors, cutting small tied-off veins, swabbing the operating area before the operation, and perhaps suturing or closing at the end – are not large enough to support much of a surgical role. Furthermore, the junior person may find that he performs even these lowly tasks inadequately, and that the scrub nurse as well as the chief surgeon tells him so. And when the drama is over and the star performer has dropped his gloves and gown and walked out, the nurses may underline the intern's marginal position by lightly demanding his help in moving the body from the fixed table to the movable one, while automatically granting him a taste of the atmosphere they maintain when real doctors are absent. As for the intern himself, surgery is very likely *not* to be his chosen speciality; the three-month internship is a course requirement and he will shortly see the last of it. The intern may confirm all this ambivalence to his work on occasions away from the surgery floor, when he scathingly describes surgery as a plumber's craft exercised by mechanics who are told what to look for by internists.

The surgical junior, especially the intern, has, then, a humbling position during surgery. Whether as a protection against this condition or not, the medical juniors I observed, like over-age merry-go-round riders, analysands, and carnival pitchmen, were not prepared to embrace their role fully; elaborate displays of role distance occurred.* A careful, bemused look on the face is

_____

brief observations in the medical building of a mental hospital and the operating rooms of a suburban community hospital. Not deriving from the most formal hospitals, these data load the facts a little in my favour.

I am grateful to Dr Otis R. Farley, and his staff in the Medical and Surgical Branch of St Elizabeth's Hospital, Washington, DC, and to John F. Wight, Administrative Director, and Lenore Jones, Head Surgical Nurse, of Herrick Memorial Hospital, Berkeley, California, for full research freedom and great courtesy.

* Some of the interns I observed had plans to take a psychiatric residency and, apparently because of this, were doing their stint of surgical internship in the medical building of a mental hospital; they therefore had wider institutional support for their lack of interest in physical techniques.

sometimes found, implying, 'This is not the real me.' Sometimes
the individual will allow himself to go 'away', dropping off into a
brown study that removes him from the continuity of events, increases the likelihood that his next contributory act will not quite
fit into the flow of action, and effectively gives the appearance of
occupational disaffection; brought back into play, he may be careful to evince little sign of chagrin. He may rest himself by leaning
on the patient or by putting a foot on an inverted bucket but in a
manner too contrived to allow the others to feel it is a matter of
mere resting. Interestingly enough, he sometimes takes on the
function of the jester, endangering his reputation with antics that
temporarily place him in a doubtful and special position, yet
through this providing the others present with a reminder of less
exalted worlds:

CHIEF SURGEON JONES (*in this case a senior resident*): A small
Richardson please.
SCRUB NURSE: Don't have one.
DR JONES: O.K., then give me an Army and Navy.
SCRUB NURSE: It looks like we don't have one.
DR JONES (*lightly joking*): No Army or Navy man here.
INTERN (*dryly*): No one in the armed forces, but Dr Jones here is in
the Boy Scouts.

SCRUB NURSE: Will there be more than three [sutures] more? We're
running out of sutures.
CHIEF SURGEON: I don't know.
INTERN: We can finish up with Scotch tape.

INTERN (*looking for towel clamps around body*): Where in the
world . . . ?
SCRUB NURSE: Underneath the towel.
(*Intern turns to the nurse and in slow measure makes a full cold bow to
her.*)

SCRUB NURSE (*to Intern*): Watch it, you're close to my table! [*A
Mayo stand containing instruments whose asepsis she must guard and
guarantee.*]
(*Intern performs a mock gasp and clownishly draws back.*)

As I have suggested, just as we cannot use a child over four riding a merry-go-round as an exhibition of how to embrace an activity role, so also we cannot use the junior medical people on a surgical team. But surely the chief surgeon, at least, will demonstrate the embracing of a role. What we find, of course, is that even this central figure expresses considerable role distance.

Some examples may be cited. One can be found in medical etiquette. This body of custom requires that the surgeon, on leaving the operation, turn and thank his assistant, his anaesthetist, and ordinarily his nurses as well. Where a team has worked together for a long time and where the members are of the same age-grade, the surgeon may guy this act, issuing the thanks in what he expects will be taken as an ironical and farcical tone of voice: 'Miss Westly, you've done a simply wonderful job here.' Similarly, there is a formal rule that in preparing a requested injection the nurse show the shelved vial to the surgeon before its sealed top is cracked off so that he can check its named contents and thereby take the responsibility on himself. If the surgeons are very busy at the time, this checking may be requested but not given. At other times, however, the checking may be guyed.

CIRCULATING NURSE: Dr James, would you check this?

DR JAMES (*in a loud ministerial voice, reading the label*): Three cubic centimetres of heparin at ten-milligramme strength, put up by Invenex and held by Nurse Jackson at a forty-five-degree angle. That is right, Nurse Jackson.

Instead of employing technical terms at all times, he may tease the nurses by using homey appellations: 'Give me the small knife, we'll get in just below the belly button'; and he may call the electric cauterizer by the apt name of 'sizzler', ordering the assistant surgeon to 'sizzle here, and here.' Similarly, when a nurse allows her non-sterile undergown to be exposed a little, a surgeon may say in a pontifical and formal tone, 'Nurse Bevan, can I call your attention to the anterior portion of your gown. It is exposing you. I trust you will correct this condition', thereby instituting social control, reference to the nurse's non-nursing attributes, and satire of the profession all with one stroke. So, too, a nurse, returning to the operating room with a question, 'Dr Williams?' may be answered by a phrase of self-satirization: 'In person', or 'This is

Dr Williams'. And a well-qualified surgeon, in taking the situated role of assistant surgeon for the duration of a particular operation, may tell the nurses, when they have been informed by the chief surgeon that two electric cauterizers will be employed, 'I'm going to get one too, just like the big doctors, that's what I like to hear'. A chief surgeon, then, may certainly express role distance. Why he does so, and with what effect, are clearly additional questions, and ought to be considered.

THE FUNCTIONS OF ROLE DISTANCE FOR SURGERY

I have suggested that in surgery, in a room that pridefully keeps out germs and gives equal medical treatment to bodies of different socio-economic status, there is no pretence at expressional asepsis. Role distance is routinely expressed.

But why should the individual be disinclined to embrace his role self? The situation of the junior medical man suggests that defensive activity is at work. We cannot say, however, that role distance protects the individual's ego, self-esteem, personality, or integrity from the implications of the situation without introducing constructs which have no place in a strictly sustained role perspective. We must find a way, then, of getting the ego back into society.

We can begin to do this by noting that when the individual withdraws from a situated self he does not withdraw into some psychological world that he creates himself but rather acts in the name of some other socially created identity. The liberty he takes in regard to a situated self is taken because of other, equally social, constraints. A first example of this is provided us when we try to obtain a systematic view of the functions performed by role distance in surgery, for immediately we see a paradoxical fact: one of the concerns that prevent the individual from fully accepting his situated self is his commitment to the situated activity system itself. We see this when we shift our point of view from the individual to the situated system and look at the functions that role distance serves for it. We find that certain manoeuvres which act to integrate the system require for their execution individuals who do not fully embrace their situated selves. System-irrelevant roles can thus themselves be exploited for the system as a whole. In other words, one of the claims upon himself that the individual must balance against all others is the claim created by the over-all 'needs'* of the situated activity system itself, apart from his particular role in it.

An illustration of these contingencies is provided by the chief surgeon. Like those in many other occupational positions, the chief surgeon finds that he has the obligation to direct and manage a particular activity system, in this case a surgical operation. He is obliged to see that the operation is effectively carried through, regardless of what this may sometimes express about himself.

Now for the surgical team to function usefully, each member, as already suggested, must sustain his capacity as a communicator, an individual capable of giving and receiving verbal communications and their substitutes. And, as in other activity systems, each member must be able to execute physical actions requiring some coolness and self-command. Anything that threatens either this verbal or physical poise threatens the participant's capacity to contribute, and hence the activity system itself. Each individual member of the surgical team must be in command of himself, and where he is not able to handle himself, others, especially the chief surgeon, must help him do it.

In order to ensure that the members of his team keep their heads during the operation, the chief surgeon finds himself under pressure to modulate his own demands and his own expectations of what is due him. If he exercises his situated rights openly to criticize incompetent conduct, the surgeon may only further weaken the defaulter's self-command and further endanger the particular operation. In short, the chief surgeon is likely to find himself with the situated role function of anxiety management† and may find that he must draw on his own dignity, on what is owed his station, in order to fulfil this function. A kind of bargaining

---

* In the sense used by Philip Selznick in 'Foundations of the Theory of Organization', *American Sociological Review*, 13 (1948), pp. 29–30.

† This role function is one which the M.D. anaesthetist often performs, or tries to perform, sometimes apparently quite intentionally, as a filler for a position that might otherwise not have enough weight for the person who fills it.

or bribery* occurs, whereby the surgeon receives a guarantee of equability from his team in return for being 'a nice guy' – someone who does not press his rightful claims too far. Of course, the surgeon may save his dignity and lose the operation, but he is under pressure not to do so.

Given the conflict between correcting a subordinate and helping him maintain his poise, it is understandable that surgeons will employ joking means of negative sanction, so that it is difficult to determine whether the joke is a cover for the sanction, or the sanction a cover for the joke. In either case, some distance from usual surgical decorum is required:

(*Intern holds retractor at wrong end of incision and goes 'away', being uninterested in the operation.*)
CHIEF SURGEON (*in mock English accent*): You don't have to hold that up there, old chap, perhaps down here. Going to sleep, old boy?

CHIEF SURGEON (*on being accidentally stabbed in the finger by the assistant surgeon, who is using the electric scalpel*): If I get syphalis [*sic*] I'll know where I got it from, and I'll have witnesses.

If some of these jokes seem weak and unnecessary, we must appreciate that to let a small error of conduct go by without comment has its own dangers, apart from what this laxness might mean for staff training. In the presence of a mistake, staff members can ready themselves for the occurrence of a corrective sanction, and unless something pertinent is said, this readiness may act as an anxiety-producing distraction. The immediate expression of a joking sanction, however laboured, grounds this source of tension.

Just as a negative sanction may be toned down to prevent the offender from acting still more disruptively, so also direct commands may be softened into requests even though the surgeon's general occupational status and particular situated role empower him to command. Where he has a right to issue a peremptory order for an instrument, he may instead employ courtesies: 'Let's have another Richardson', 'Could I have a larger retractor'. In-

* The notion of 'role bargain' is usefully developed in W. J. Goode, 'A Theory of Role Strain', *American Sociological Review*, 25 (1960), pp. 483–96.

F

stead of flaring up when no suitable ready-made instrument is available, he may choose to express a boyish mechanical ingenuity, constructing on the spot a make-do instrument.*

I am suggesting that he who would effectively direct an operation at times may have to employ a touch so light as to embarrass the dark dignities of his position. In fact, we can expect that the more that is demanded from a subordinate in the way of delicacy, skill, and pure concentration, the more informal and friendly the superordinate is likely to become. If one person is to participate in a task as if he were an extension of another participant, opening himself up to the rapid and delicate feedback control that an individual ordinarily obtains only of and for himself, then, apparently, he must be favourably disposed to the person in command, for such co-operativeness is much easier to win than to exact.†

* In some face-to-face activity systems a participant may be so close to losing poise that a responsible other may have to modify his whole manner, not merely his commands and negative sanctions, if the unreliable participant is to be kept on his feet, and this modification is likely to be at the expense of formal behaviour patterns associated with the superordinate's role. To prevent the full weight of his role from frightening or freezing subordinates, the superordinate may therefore employ informalities. The official who asks an interviewee to join him in a cigarette provides the classic example, known as 'putting a subordinate at his ease'. The strategy employed by a child analyst provides another illustration:

'It is so desirable for the psychoanalyst to remain on the less active side with the child patient that for her to knit is often a good device. The knitting should be on something for the patient so that he will not feel that the busy-work takes away from him. The knitting serves to occupy the therapist who may have an inclination to play with the child or the need to press the child into some significant productions. It also serves to modify the seductiveness of the analytical experience of the small patient, who has the exciting opportunity to have a mother figure all alone five hours a week intently engrossed with him and his ideas and encouraging him to express more.' (Helen Arthur, 'A Comparison of the Techniques Employed in Psychotherapy and Psychoanalysis of Children', *American Journal of Orthopsychiatry*, 22 [1952], pp. 493–4.)

I am told by Charlotte Green Schwartz that some male analysts knit or hook rugs during treatment of adult patients, in part, apparently, to divert enough attention to keep themselves from interrupting too frequently.

† This is nicely illustrated in multi-situated activity systems on board ship, where, it has been claimed, the one time when the captain unbends and uses easy language not ordinarily associated with his role is when an engine

I would like to note here that the chief surgeon may feel obliged to introduce distractions as well as to dispel them. When the spontaneous engagement of the participants in the task activity itself seems likely to tax them too much, the chief surgeon may distract them, for example, by joking. This is just the reverse of the process previously described. Thus, at a point of high tension, when a large renal tumour had been completely exposed and was ready to be pierced by a draining-needle, a chief surgeon lightly warned before he pierced: 'Now don't get too close'. Another instance of this easing process is found in the fact that the others often seem to look to the chief surgeon to mark the end of a critical phase of action and the beginning of a less critical phase, one that can be used for a general letdown in the sustained concentration of attention and effort. In order to set the tone for these functionally useful relaxations, at the end of a phase of action, the surgeon may stretch himself in a gawky, exaggerated, and clownish way and utter a supportive informality such as 'okey-dokey' or 'th'ar sh' be'. Before the critical phase is begun, and after it has been terminated, he may engage others present in talk about last night's party, the recent ball game, or good places to fish.* And when the patient is being closed up and the critical

---

steersman must be counted on to respond exquisitely to steering directions from the helm.

By the same logic, however, we should be prepared for the fact that at times the task-management obligations of the individual may force him to draw back to the formal position accorded him and exact the full swift measure of his authority, for there are times when a flustered subordinate will be steadied better by a sharp negative sanction than by sympathy.

* Under strictest possible procedure, no talking would be tolerated except when technically necessary, since germs can apparently be spread through masks in this way. My own experience was in relatively informal hospitals where irrelevant talk and byplays did occur. Burling and Wilson report a similar experience. Presumably the medical traditions of different regions differ in this regard, as suggested by Eugene de Savitsch, *In Search of Complications* (New York: Simon & Schuster, 1940), pp. 374–5:

'In a clinic or operating room almost anywhere in the world all would be silence, soft lights, and sustained tension. In France everybody chatters away as merrily as in a café. While a brain tumor, for instance, is removed, the surgeon, his assistants, and the audience – if any – argue over the merits of the present cabinet, disclose the shortcomings of their wives, and exchange advice about stocks and bonds.'

work is quite over, the chief surgeon may initiate and tolerate joking with nurses, bantering with them about their lack of proficiency or about the operation not being nearly over. If no male nurse is present to lift the patient from the operating table to the trolley, the chief surgeon, if he is still in the operating room, may gallantly brush aside the efforts of one of the nurses and insist on lifting the heaviest part of the patient, the middle, himself, acting now in the capacity of a protective male, not a medical person.

Just as the chief surgeon may mark the point where attentiveness may be usefully relaxed, so he, and sometimes others on the team, will put brackets around the central task activity with the result that the level of concern required for it will not be demanded of the team before matters actually get under way and after they have ended. This is nicely shown not merely in the ritual of tearing off one's gloves and immediately leaving the operating room, by which the chief surgeon tells the team that teacher is no longer checking up on them and they can relax, but also in the way in which the body is handled. During the operation, the body of the patient is the rightful focus of a great deal of respectful sustained consideration, technically based, especially in connexion with the maintenance of asepsis, blood levels, and respiration. It is as if the body were a sacred object, regardless of the socioeconomic character of its possessor, but in this case the consideration given is rational as well as ritual. As might be expected, then, before and after the operation proper there can be observed minor acts of desacralization, whereby the patient is reduced to more nearly profane status. At the beginning of the task the surgeon may beat a tattoo on the leg of the anaesthetized patient, and at the end he may irreverently pat the patient on the bottom, commenting that he is now better than new. The surgeon is not alone in this activity. While scrubbing the anaesthetized patient, the nurse may lift up a foot by the toe and speak to it: 'You're not sterile, are you?' In moving the now groggy patient from the operating table to the trolley for the trip to the recovery room, the anaesthetist, taking charge of this relatively unskilled physical action, may obtain concerted effort from the other persons helping him by saying: 'Ready, aim, fire.' Similarly, in moving an anaesthetized patient on his left side for a thoracotomy, the anaesthetist may say: 'O.K., kids, are we ready to play flip flop? Ready? O.K.'

In addition to maintaining the capacities and poise of other members of the team, the chief surgeon has, of course, an obligation to maintain his own. Morever, he must be concerned not only with sustaining his own mobilization of personal resources, but also with the anxious attention that other members of the team might give to this. If they feel he is about to lose his temper, or that he has lost his skill, they themselves can become extremely uneasy and inefficient. Thus, when the surgeon runs into trouble that could cause his team-mates a distracting and suppressed concern over how he might react to his trouble, we find him engaging in quite standard strategies of tension management, sometimes concealing his own real concerns to do so. He alludes openly to the incident in such a way as to rob it of its capacity to distract the team.* When he drops an instrument, he may respond unseriously to his own action by a word such as 'oopsadaisy'. If he must give an order to one of his assistants which might leave the others not knowing if he were angry or not, he may deliver it in a false English accent, in adolescent slang, or in some other insulating way. Unable to find the right spot for a lumbar puncture, he may, after three tries, shake his head a little, as if to suggest that he, as a person sensitive to ideal standards, is still sensitive to them and yet in quiet control of himself, in short, that the implied discrediting of him has not made him lose poise.

Since the chief surgeon's own self-control is crucial in the operation, and since a question concerning it could have such a disquieting effect upon the other members of the team, he may feel obliged to demonstrate that he is in possession of himself, not merely at times of crisis and trouble, but even at times when he would otherwise be silent and so be providing no information one way or the other about his state of mind. Thus, when puzzled about what to do, he may ruminate half out loud, ingenuously allowing others present a close glimpse of his thoughts. During quite delicate tasks, he may softly sing incongruous undignified tunes such as 'He flies through the air with the greatest of ease'. In clamping haemostats, he may let them go from his fingers, flipping them back upon the patient's body in a neat row with the verve and control that parking attendants manifest while parking

* For a general analysis of this view of tension, see E. Goffman, 'Fun in Games', *Encounters* (Indianapolis: Bobbs-Merrill, 1961).

cars, or merry-go-round managers display in collecting tickets while moving around on the turning platform.

What we have here is a kind of 'externalization' of such feelings and thoughts as are likely to give security and confidence to the other members of the team. This externalization, as well as the constant cutting back of any distractive concern that might have arisen for the team in the course of action, also provides a constant stimulus to team members' attentiveness and task engagement, in both ways helping to hold them to the task as usable participants. Some surgeons, in fact, maintain something of a running line of patter during the operation, suggesting that whenever there is team-work, someone is likely to have the role function of 'talking it up.'

We see that the chief surgeon is something of a host to persons at his party, as well as the director of his operating team. He is under pressure (however he responds to this pressure) to make sure that those at his table feel good about what is happening so that what-ever their capacities they can better exploit them. And to do this morale-maintaining job, at least in America, the surgeon makes use of and draws upon activities not expected of one in his dignified position. When he himself does not perform the clown function, he may encourage someone else, such as the intern or circulating nurse, to take on the job.

In discussing the special responsibilities of the chief surgeon and his frequent need to draw on informality in order to meet these responsibilities, it was implied that the superordinate present may have some special reasons for exhibiting role distance. A further comment should be added concerning the relation between role distance and social ranking.

It seems characteristic of the formalities of a role that adherence to them must be allowed and confirmed by the others involved in the situation; this is one of the basic things we mean by the notion that something is formal and official. Adherence to formalities seems to guarantee the *status quo* of authority and social distance; under the guidance of this style, one can be assured that the others will not be able to move in on one. Reversing the role point of view, we can see that adherence to the formalities one owes to others can be a relatively protective matter, guaranteeing that one's conduct will have to be accepted by the others, and, often, that it will not be difficult to dissociate one's purely covert personal attachments from one's role projection. Finally, it should be added that in general we assume that it is to the advantage of the subordinate to decrease distance from the superordinate and to the advantage of the latter to sustain or increase it.

From these considerations it should be apparent that the exercise of role distance will take on quite different meanings, depending on the relative rank of the individual who exercises it. Should a subordinate exercise role distance, this is likely to be seen as a sign of his refusal to keep his place (thereby moving towards greater intimacy with the superordinate, which the latter is likely to disapprove), or as rejection of authority,* or as evidence of low morale. On the other hand, the manifestation of role distance on the part of the superordinate is likely to express a willingness to relax the *status quo*, and this the subordinate is likely to approve because of its potential profitability for him. In the main, therefore, the expression of role distance is likely to be the prerogative of the superordinate in an interaction. In fact, since informality on the part of the inferior is so suspect, a tacit division of labour may arise, whereby the inferior contributes respect for the *status quo* on behalf of both parties, while the superior contributes a glaze of sociability that all can enjoy. Charm and colourful little informalities are thus usually the prerogatives of those in higher office, leading us mistakenly to assume that an individual's social graces helped bring him to his high position, instead of what is perhaps more likely, that the graces become possible for anyone who attains the office.† Hence, it is the surgeon, not the surgical nurse, who injects irony into medical etiquette. All of this, it may be added, fits other things we know about relations between unequals. It is the ship's captain who has a right to enter the territory

---

* For example, I know of a nurse who was transferred from an experimental surgery team, in part because she enacted simulated yawns, meant to be humorous, during the ticklish part of a delicate surgical technique, thereby showing role distance above her station.

† An empirical illustration of this is presented in an excellent paper by Rose Coser in which she demonstrates the special joking prerogatives of senior psychiatrists during ward meetings; see her 'Laughter Among Colleagues', *Psychiatry*, 23 (1960), pp. 81–95. For further illustrations of role distance on the part of superordinates, see Ralph Turner, 'The Navy Disbursing Officer as a Bureaucrat', *American Sociological Review*, 12 (1947), pp. 342–8.

of the ordinary seamen, the 'fo'c'sle', not they to enter his. An officer has a right to penetrate the private life of a soldier serving under him, whereas the private does not have a similar right. In this connexion, one student has been led to speak of the social distance between two individuals as being of different extent depending from whose place one starts.*

But, of course, subordinates can exercise much role distance, and not merely through grumbling. By sacrificing the seriousness of their claim to being treated as full-fledged persons, they can exercise liberties not given to social adults.

We can now see that with the chief surgeon on one side and the intern on the other there appears to be a standard distribution of role-distance rights and role-distance tendencies. The intern may sacrifice his character as a full and serious person, becoming, thereby, a half-child in the system, in return for which he is allowed to offend medical role requirements with impunity. The person with dominating status can also offend with impunity because his position gives others present a special reason for accepting the offence.

I would like to add that although the person who manifests much role distance may, in fact, be alienated from the role, still, the opposite can well be true: in some cases only those who feel secure in their attachment may be able to chance the expression of distance. And, in fact, in spite of interns, it appears that conformity to the prescriptive aspects of role often occurs most thoroughly at the neophyte level, when the individual must prove his competence, sincerity, and awareness of his place, leaving the showing of distance from a role to a time when he is firmly 'validated' in that role.

Another peculiarity should be mentioned. To express role-irrelevant idiosyncracies of behaviour is to expose oneself to the situation, making more of oneself available in it than is required by one's role. The executive's family picture on his desk, telling us that he is not to be considered entirely apart from his loved ones, also tells us, in a way, that they are in this occupation with him, and that they might understand his having to work late or open up his house to politically wise sociability.

* Donald MacRae, 'Class Relationships and Ideology', *The Sociological Review*, n.s., 6 (1958), pp. 263–4.

The differing bases of role distance displayed by the chief surgeon and by the intern imply a division of labour or role differentiation. The nursing personnel exhibit a similar kind of differentiation among themselves: the division of labour and responsibility between the scrub nurse and the circulating nurse is associated with a difference in manifestation of role distance. The scrub nurse, in addition to her continued task obligation during the operation, may feel obliged to maintain the role function of standard-maintainer, policing the aseptic character of the order that is maintained, as well as keeping a Management's eye on the skills of the physicians. Any withdrawal of herself into the role of female might, therefore, jeopardize the situated system. The circulating nurse, on the other hand, has no such responsibilities, and, apparently, these sexual considerations can be displaced onto her. Further, not needing to be 'in' the operation as must the scrub nurse, she can withdraw into herself, or into a conversation with the anaesthetist or the nurses in the adjacent operating room, without jeopardizing matters. To place her in a female capacity does not reduce manpower. It is not surprising, therefore, that the circulating nurse, in addition to the intern, is allowed to be flighty – to act without character.

The division of role-function labour that I have described has a characteristic subtlety that should be mentioned again in conclusion. A person with a specialized task not only performs a service needed by the system but also provides a way of being, a selfhood, with which others in the system can identify, thus allowing them to sustain an image of themselves that would disrupt matters if sustained other than vicariously. The 'good guy' informality of the chief surgeon can give his subordinates a feeling that they are not the sort to tolerate strict subordination, that in fact the surgeon must see this and has adjusted himself correspondingly, yet this is, of course, a vicarious rebelliousness carried out principally by the very agency against which one would ordinarily rebel. In the same way, the circulating nurse can establish the principle of female sexuality in which the surgical nurse can see her own reflection, even while the surgeon is calling her by a masculine last-name term of address and receiving a man-sized work contribution from her.

Some final points may now be mentioned concerning the

function of role distance, now not merely in surgery but in situated systems in general.

First, by not demanding the full rights of his position, the individual finds that he is not completely committed to a particular standard of achievement; should an unanticipated discrediting of his capacity occur, he will not have committed himself and the others to a hopelessly compromised position. Second, it appears that social situations as such retain some weight and reality in their own right by drawing on role distance – on the margin of reservation the individual has placed between himself and his situated role.

An interesting confirmation of the functional significance of role distance in situated activity systems is to be had by examining situations where roles are played *at*.

There seems to be little difficulty in getting stage actors to portray a character who is inflated with pomposity or bursting with emotion, and directors often have to restrain members of the cast from acting too broadly. The actor is apparently pleased to express before a large audience a lack of reservation which he would probably blush to express off the stage. However, this willingness to embrace a staged role is understandable. Since the actor's performed character is not his real one, he feels no need to safeguard himself by hedging his taken stand. Since the staged drama is not a real one, over-involvement will simply constitute the following of a script, not a threat to one's capacity to follow it. An acted lack of poise has none of the dysfunctions of real flustering.

More significant, there is the fact that in prisons and mental hospitals, where some inmates may constantly sustain a heroic edifice of withdrawal, unco-operativeness, insolence, and combativeness, the same inmates may be quite ready to engage in theatricals in which they enact excellent portraits of civil, sane, and compliant characters. But this very remarkable turnabout is understandable too. Since the staged circumstances of the portrayed character are not the inmate's real ones, he has no need (in the character's name) to exhibit distance from them, unless, of course, the script calls for it.

A SIMULTANEOUS MULTIPLICITY OF SELVES

It is common in sociology to study the individual in terms of the conception he and others have of him, and to argue that these conceptions are made available to him through the role that he plays. In this paper, the focus of role is narrowed down to a situated activity system. And it is argued that the individual must be seen as someone who organizes his expressive situational behaviour *in relation* to situated activity roles, but that in doing this he uses whatever means are at hand to introduce a margin of freedom and manoeuvrability, of pointed dis-identification, between himself and the self virtually available for him in the situation.

Instead, then, of starting with the notion of a definition of the situation we must start with the idea that a particular definition is *in charge of the situation*, and that as long as this control is not overtly threatened or blatantly rejected, much counter-activity will be possible. The individual acts to say: 'I do not dispute the direction in which things are going and I will go along with them, but at the same time I want you to know that you haven't fully contained me in the state of affairs.' Thus, the person who mutters, jokes, or responds with sarcasm to what is happening in the situation is nevertheless going along with the prevailing definition of the situation – with whatever bad spirit. The current system of activity tells us what situated roles will be in charge of the situation, but these roles at the same time provide a framework in which role distance can be expressed. Again, it should be noted that face-to-face interaction provides an admirable context for executing a double stance – the individual's task actions unrebelliously adhere to the official definition of the situation, while gestural activity that can be sustained simultaneously and yet non-interferingly shows that he has not agreed to having all of himself defined by what is officially in progress.

In whatever name the individual exerts role distance, it is plain, by definition, that the injected identification will be more or less in opposition to the one available in the situated role. But we must now see that role distance is merely an extreme instance of expressions not a part of the self virtually available in a role, and that many other, less opposing, expressions can also occur. As long as the dominion of the situated role is not challenged, other role identities, ones different from but not necessarily opposed to the officially available self, can be sustained too. Role distance directs attention to the fact that situated roles allow for non-relevant expressions but does not tell us much about the range of these expressions.

Our problem can now be rephrased. Given a situated role and the self that virtually awaits the performer and given, too, a range of self-expression not intrinsically required by this role, what can we say about the affiliative cross-pressures that seem to arise wherever there is a situated activity system? What is there about the context in which these systems are situated that leads systematically to the appearance of certain alternate identifications?

In the previous section it was suggested that the exigencies of maintaining an activity system themselves develop needs that can be fulfilled through the exercise of role distance. The chief surgeon's commitment and attachment to the activity system may override his immediate concern about maintaining an officially correct stance. If we revert to the case of the surgical junior, a similar kind of fact emerges. It was suggested that one source of the young doctor's restiveness in the situation is that he is, after all, a graduated medical man, and the assistant's situated role may not be of sufficient weight in his eyes to be consistent with his conception of himself as a doctor. Here, we see a conflict or discrepancy between the self generated in a situated circuit of vital hospital activity and the self associated with a formal status and identity: medical man. No doubt we have here an exaggeration of the kind of discrepancy that can exist between a broad social title and a particular activity system sustained while on duty. Surely in every case, however, there will be *some* discrepancy between the self emerging from a situated activity role and the self associated with the role title in the name of which the activity is carried on. Role distance attests to this discrepancy. One basic limit, then, to embracement of a situated role is the claims of the institutional role in terms of which the participant officially participates. Surgery requires acts unbecoming a surgeon, just as mothering requires acts that are unmaternal. Only where a situated role was not seen as part of a wider institutional complex would the issue not arise.

The next issue to consider is that while an activity system situated in a social establishment may provide a fairly coherent, self-consistent bundle of tasks for a given participant, he will, at the same time, be *officially* involved in other, multi-situated matters that have a relevant claim on his time – a claim that he may be able to honour only by diverting some of the concern that is owed the situated activity. For example, in the many cases where the surgery ward is carrying on some kind of training programme, the surgeon directing the operation will periodically halt or slow up the flow of action to instruct the residents and interns in what is happening and about the character of the pathology, its frequency, likely course, and forms of treatment. This benefits surgery in general but neither the particular instance of its application nor the particular patient. Similarly, new techniques may be tested, and ones not used for a long time re-employed, not so much to keep surgery up to the mark but rather the particular surgeon, again to the possible disadvantage of the particular patient. So, too, the surgeon may momentarily check engagement in the task to answer the loudspeaker's request about his plans for next day, or to ask the circulating nurse to phone his office to rearrange some appointments, or he may briefly discuss with the nursing supervisor the effect of the current operation on the ward's schedule for the day. In all these ways in which the individual may properly act as a hospital staff man, he may find that he must express some small distance from the specific operation at hand.

In addition to these task-like claims of a multi-situated kind, there are other claims we must consider that are more purely social in character. In any work establishment, the individual becomes involved in social relationships and group formation. As units of interpersonal solidarity, these may or may not coincide with the boundaries of the various administrative units, such as the establishment itself, divisions within the establishment, and teams formally designated as responsible for specific activity systems. A required administrative action that inhibits the formation of these solidarizing social bonds or threatens bonds already formed may then have to be softened in the interests of solidarity. This softening is often accomplished by means of expressed withdrawal from situated role.

A classic instance of this softening of formal behaviour is found in situated activity systems where 'personal' interests have begun to develop. A nice illustration may be taken from a short story by William Sansom, where he describes the protracted and partially successful effort of a man to court a girl he has found serving as a clerk in the garden equipment section of a large store:

> Slowly we grew to know one another. I kept a most reserved distance. I bought my seeds and went quickly away – scarcely noticing her, scarcely giving her the usual words of polite encounter. . . . I kept my distance – until the day when I judged sincerity to be established and consulted her upon the roller. From then on our acquaintance grew. But not apace. It may sound as if all this were coldly and carefully calculated – but nothing of the sort. My simple hopes were the companions of unbearable terror, of failures of strength and sudden exits, of tentative pleasantries that smothered me as I stammered them – it was then like balancing on some impelling precipice – and I was dogged by an overwhelming distaste for the falsehoods I had to tell. I had, for instance, to invent a garden. But gradually we grew to know each other.
>
> And there were aspects of great charm in our development. When, for instance, I noticed how in her very words she began to change towards me. At first she had spoken to me only in the aloof, impersonal vernacular of gardens. When I enquired how to use an insecticide – I was told that I must 'broadcast among the plants'. About a carton of lime – this must be dusted along the rows of peas to 'hasten pod-filling'. But as time went on and ease overcame her, it was 'just scatter it everywhere' – and 'pod-filling' became 'the peas come quicker'.*

Since Mr Sansom's heroine marries another suitor met and cultivated in the same way, she presumably also performed her occupational duties informally for the luckier man, and what Mr Sansom is telling us is that situated role behaviour may be modified not by something that is intrinsically 'human' or 'personal' but by conduct suitable for male-female courting relationships, conduct so well formalized in our society that it can be initiated and sustained between persons who start out as strangers. In the same way, when a surgeon feels his assistant has made a strategic blunder, and finds himself bursting forth in negative sanction of the assistant, he may suddenly inject a first name or nickname

* William Sansom, *A Touch of the Sun* (New York: Reynal, 1958), pp. 54–5.

term of address to bolster up the personal relationship in the face of action that might jeopardize it. He does so much as a spouse uses the term 'dear' in careful measured tones, to make sure the entire marital relationship is not threatened by the sanctioning occurring within it. Again, what we see here is not the mere reduction of formality but rather an identification with one type of structure at the expense of another.

Just as the individual must manage his social relationships to his fellow participants, apart from the role demands of the situated system, so also he gives some concern to his relationships to persons not present – and this in the face of any assumptions we have about role segregation. A surgeon may not operate on his wife, as the traditional arguments about role segregation suggest, and once an operation has begun he can easily decline to be called to an urgent telephone call from her or anyone else, but the surgeons I observed wore wedding rings underneath their rubber gloves, discussed their wives' health during the operation, and joked with the nurses about being fully married men. Like the executives I mentioned earlier, some kept in their clinic offices a picture of wife and children to attest to the fact that even here, in the citadel of the profession, they had not put their family entirely away from them. Patients presumably might then be led to keep in mind that the person they dealt with was something more than a doctor.

Beginning with our surgical example, we find, more important still, that there are sources of self-identification such as age and sex categorization which penetrate the surgical activity system in a diffuse way, qualifying and modifying conduct where this can be done without threatening the task that controls the situation. Thus, while a surgical nurse may be accorded a last-name term of address, perhaps as a compliment to, and reinforcement of, her purely technical capacities, her last name is as frequently prefaced by a sexual placement: 'Miss'. Further, female nurses are traditionally excused from 'prepping' the male genitalia, and from having to lift the patient from the trolley to the operating table and back again. And it is always touching to see, when a patient is on the table and his insides are being sliced, pried, and tied, that, if the point of incision allows, his private parts will be carefully kept covered by actions that have decency and modesty in their style, whether out of respect for him, for the mixture of sexes that are likely to be present, or for society at large.

Age-sex identifications during task performances typically express concerns that are felt in addition to the task, not in opposition to it. Sometimes, however, there is an 'overdetermined' flavour to these expressions, suggesting that role distance is involved and requiring the individual to withdraw a little from the occupational game in order to be momentarily active in the older one:

SCRUB NURSE (*to intern*): Take one [haemostat] in each hand, he'll need 'em.
INTERN: Yes, Mama.
SCRUB NURSE (*half apologetically*): I'm really interested in you learning.
INTERN (*with mock intrigue*): Well, how about teaching me?
SCRUB NURSE: I gave you a book, what else can I do?
INTERN: Oh there's lots else you can do.
SCRUB NURSE (*to Chief Surgeon*): Do you want me here or on the other side?
INTERN (*next to whom she had been standing*): Stay here close to me.

I would like to add that it would be wrong indeed to overestimate the sexuality of these sexual references. They resemble a tickle much more than a caress. Sex here seems to be made a convenience of, seized upon not for itself but to demonstrate a little independence regarding one's situated role. If serious at all, these joking remarks allow the surgeon to stake a claim to roles he might want to be available to him at another time and in another setting.

Although it is obvious that principles of identity and social organization such as age and sex are always receiving their small due, the reason why we have not constructed an approach that gives appropriate place to them is not as apparent. Perhaps our concern about prejudice and discrimination – the introduction of bases of identity that we feel ought not to have been introduced – has led us to see all this play of identification around the central task theme as a kind of illegitimate and unfortunate deviation from the norm – a particularistic invasion of sacred universalistic ground. In fact, of course, to embrace a situated role fully and exclusively is more the exception than the rule.

I have argued that the individual does not embrace the situated role that he finds available to him while holding all his other selves in abeyance. I have argued that a situated activity system provides an arena for conduct and that in this arena the individual constantly twists, turns, and squirms, even while allowing himself to be carried along by the controlling definition of the situation. The image that emerges of the individual is that of a juggler and synthesizer, an accommodator and appeaser, who fulfils one function while he is apparently engaged in another; he stands guard at the door of the tent but lets all his friends and relatives crawl in under the flap. This seems to be the case even in one of our most sacred occupational shows – surgery.

I have also argued that these various identificatory demands are not created by the individual but are drawn from what society allots him. He frees himself from one group, not to be free, but because there is another hold on him. While actively participating in an activity system, he is, nevertheless, also obliged to engage in other matters, in relationships, in multi-situated systems of activity, in sustaining norms of conduct that crosscut many particular activity systems. I want now to try to look more closely at some of the cultural influences that seem to be at work determining the expression of role-irrelevant identifications during role performance – influences that are broadly based in the society at large, in spite of the narrow arena in which they are given their due.

Given the fact that a man in the role of surgeon must act at times during surgery like a male, the question arises as to what capacity he is active in, what role he is playing, when he decides how to allocate his time and action between these two roles.

We find a clue when we examine the rules for beginners, whatever is being learned. When an individual is first working into his role, he will be allowed to approach his tasks diffidently, an excuse and apology ready on his lips. At this time he is likely to make many otherwise discreditable mistakes, but for this time he has a learner's period of grace in which to make them – a period in which he is not yet quite the person he will shortly be, and, therefore, cannot badly damage himself by the damaging expression of his maladroit actions. In the medical world, of course, this temporary licence is institutionalized in the statuses of intern and

G

junior resident. Here, incumbents have sufficiently little face to allow of their being scolded by senior staff and twitted by nurses, in that important arrangement by which children and others in training are permitted to pay for their mistakes in cash on the spot, thereby avoiding certain kinds of liens on their future.

While it is possible to say that the surgeon's role makes allow-and for maladroitness in beginners, we might just as economically argue that in our society there is a general appreciation that the individual, as a role-performer, ought to be given time to learn, and that the time thus given young surgeons expresses our conception of role-taker, not surgeon. If the sociologist can see past the particularities of a specific occupation to the general theme of the learner's plight, then perhaps society can too.

Roles certainly differ according to how seriously and fully the performers must stick to the script. Even in the most serious of roles, such as that of surgeon, we yet find that there will be times when the fully-fledged performer must unbend and behave simply as a male. In the same way, we have strict rules about how lightly the individual can treat an occupational role, and we know that boxers and baseball players who mock their role may be seriously sanctioned. Given a range of occupations, then – the professions, say – we find general understandings as to how stiff and how loose the performer may be. I think we can argue that these norms of seriousness do not always attach to our image of particular callings and persons performing in them, but rather to wider groupings of roles and even to role-enactment as such. To generalize, then, one could say that a role-performer in our society has a right to some learner's licence and a limit to formality of obligation – by sheer virtue of being a role-taker.

Since norms regarding the management of one's multiple identifications derive in part from the general culture, we should expect differences in this regard from society to society, and this is certainly the case. Throughout Western society, segregative tendencies as regards role are strong, and it is often expected that a person active in a given occupational or organizational role will not subvert his responsibilities there in favour of other ties, such as familial ones, while in Eastern societies there is less of this kind of compartmentalization.

Even within Western society we may expect some differences.

In British society, for example, in the recent past, the ideology of influential classes focused on the amateur player – the gentleman politician, the gentleman scholar, and the gentleman explorer. There was an anti-commercial hope that the individual would become a 'rounded person', not given over in a warped, constraining way to one calling. The ideal, apparently, was to exert high skill diffidently, a shark got up in bumbler's clothing. American society, by contrast, seems to have licensed a great bustling in one's occupational role – anger, haste, sleeves rolled up, and other signs of full engagement in the moment's task. (Perhaps we can even point to changes in style in this regard: the Madison Avenue complex seems to be associated with a decline in role segregation, accompanied by the soft sell and by very friendly office relations across status levels.) But even in our own society, role distance abounds, occurring in many contexts, with many functions, and in response to many motives.

There is other evidence that points in the direction of our having conceptions of role-taking as such. In every establishment where roles are institutionalized, some limitations on duty will also be institutionalized. Working conditions are regulated with a view to preservation of health; time off is given for eating, rest, and recreation. In some sense it is not a nurse or an orderly that warrants these privileges, but a person or citizen, and it is in part by virtue of this pervasive qualification that these rights are extended.*

Further, there is the extremely interesting institution of 'extenuating circumstances'. A man at work should tend to his job and forget about his family. Yet even in the most demanding of workplaces, it is recognized that the person who is a worker does have these other role concerns and that when he is in a state of crisis regarding them he should be allowed some time off from the legitimate work claims which ordinarily can be made on him. A soldier whose wife is having a child may be given some leave, as may an executive. I suggest that it is not as a soldier or an executive that the person gets leave, nor merely as a husband and father, but rather in part as a multiple-role-player who can compartmentalize himself within limits but who cannot, according to our conceptions of him, be asked to go too far in this compartmentalization.

* T. H. Marshall, *Citizenship and Social Class* (Cambridge: C.U.P., 1950), pp. 1–85.

In all these cases we see that the individual limits the degree to which he embraces a situated role, or is required to embrace it, because of society's understanding of him as a multiple-role-performer rather than as a person with a particular role. This view of the individual which empties his particular role of all content and conceives of him, formally, as a person of many identifications, whatever these particular identifications are, is expressed in still other ways.* Just as the surgeon is expected to remember today what happened at the clinic yesterday, so also, should he meet his wife in the hospital, he may be excused from operating on her, but nothing will excuse him from greeting her. In fact, we have extensive institutions of greeting whereby two individuals who are not then going to be involved together in an undertaking acknowledge that they will, or may, be so involved at other times. Finally, in a dim way we have conceptions of the limited and compensatory character of human attachment, and, whether justifiably or not, we try to understand the distance a man seems to maintain from his job by the closeness of his attachment to a hobby.

In summary, then, it may be stated that, given a situated system as a point of reference, role distance is a typical, not normative, aspect of role. But the lightness with which the individual handles a situated role is forced upon him by the weight of his manifold attachments and commitments to multi-situated social entities. Disdain for a situated role is a result of respect for another basis of identification.

When we shift our point of reference from the situated system, then, to these wider entities, role distance can again be seen as a response to a normative framework. As far as merry-go-round riding is concerned, the role distance exhibited by an eight-year-old boy is a typical, not obligatory, part of the situation; for the boy's manhood, however, these expressions are obligatory. A statistical departure in the first case would be a moral departure in the second.

* Much of our legal framework, which imputes individual responsibility, deals with the individual as an historically continuous, uniquely identifiable entity, and not as a person-in-role or a person as a set of role-slices. A financial debt incurred in one sphere of life while active in one capacity will have to be paid by monies drawn from what is due to others.

CONCLUSIONS

Much role analysis seems to assume that once one has selected a category of person and the context or sphere of life in which one wants to consider him, there will then be some main role that will fully dominate his activity. Perhaps there are times when an individual does march up and down like a wooden soldier, tightly rolled up in a particular role. It is true that here and there we can pounce on a moment when an individual sits fully astride a single role, head erect, eyes front, but the next moment the picture is shattered into many pieces and the individual divides into different persons holding the ties of different spheres of life by his hands, by his teeth, and by his grimaces. When seen up close, the individual, bringing together in various ways all the connexions that he has in life, becomes a blur. Hence many who have analysed roles have stood across the street from the source of their data, oriented by William James's abstract view of human action instead of by the lovingly empirical view established by his younger brother.*

One can limit oneself to a particular category of persons in a particular context of life – a situated role in a situated activity system – but no matter how narrow and specific these limits, one ends up by watching a dance of identification. A surgeon does not bring his wife to the operating table and is not in a husbandly relation to the body that is his patient, but it does not follow that while in the surgical theatre he acts solely in the capacity of a surgeon. I suppose one might want to ask what a salesgirl does in a store by virtue of her being a salesgirl. The test of close analysis, however, is to study what a person who is a salesgirl does in a store that persons who are not salesgirls do not do, for much of what only salesgirls do in stores is not done by them *qua* salesgirls and has nothing to do with sales. Thus, as a student† has recently

---

* Instances of microscopic analysis are to be found in R. G. Barker and H. F. Wright, *One Boy's Day* (New York: Harper, 1951), and, sometimes beautifully, in the occasional pieces of Ray Birdwhistell. See also the remarkable paper by Donald Roy, ' "Banana Time": Job Satisfaction and Informal Interaction', *Human Organization*, 18 (Winter, 1959–60), pp. 158–68. 'Small group' experimenters have certainly stood up close to their data but have used a considerable amount of this opportunity to adjust their equipment.

† E. M. Mumford, 'Social Behaviour in Small Work Groups', *The Sociological Review*, n.s., 7 (1959), pp. 137–57.

shown, waitresses in British dock canteens can find that self-applied norms on the job refer to extra-work relations with male customers, these norms being finally understandable only in terms of the general values of the community in which the canteens are located. What is necessitated here, then, is a fundamental shift from Linton's *stated* point of view: we do not ask how a chief surgeon, *qua* surgeon, is expected to act during surgery, but how those individuals who are designated chief surgeon are expected to act during surgery.

Further, a broadened version of Linton's role conceptions allows us to distinguish typical role from normative role and to treat role distance as something that can be typical and not normative. We can then, for example, deal with the pin-ups that workers and soldiers attach to their locker doors, noting that these posters introduce a thin layer of sex between what the men define themselves as and what the institutional scene has defined them as. We can see that not only a sexual stimulus is involved but also a moral wedge, the same kind that is employed by middle-class boys who separate themselves from their familial environment by hanging purloined 'Stop' signs and other emblems of civic irreverence in their bedrooms.

Furthermore, once role is broadened and attention is directed to role distance, we can deal with ranges of data that were ill-suited to traditional role analysis. I provide some graduated examples.

Starting with an individual's situated role in a situated system of activity, we can proceed to the domain traditionally handled by role analysis by assuming that his situated role is entirely characteristic of (and a reflection of) his role in a social establishment, an occupational system, a formal organization in which the situated system has its institutional setting. As suggested earlier, the terms needed in order to deal with the facts of behaviour within a situated system can then be extended *pari passu* to roles in any kind of multi-situated setting.

But this movement from situated systems to social establishments need no longer take us to the limits of the domain to which role concepts can be applied. So-called 'diffuse' or conditioning roles, such as age-sex roles, can now be considered, too, even though we can only point to modulations they introduce in the performance of other roles and can point neither to social establishments in which they have their principal jurisdiction nor to any bundle of tasks allocated to the performer. So also we can now include even more loosely structured roles arising in connexion with such items as physical appearance, attainments of skill and education, city of residence, relations to particular others, group affiliations of many kinds. Their inclusion is important, for each of these facts can place the individual in a life situation from which he might draw an identification of self and from which he might seek some distance, even though no coherent set of obligations and expectations – no social role in the traditional sense – may be involved.

Clothing patterns provide a systematic example for analysis with a broadened conception of role and illustrate the way in which the phenomenon of role distance requires our adopting this view. Young psychiatrists in state mental hospitals who are sympathetic to the plight of patients sometimes express distance from their administrative medical role by affecting shirts open at the collar, much as do socialists in their legislative offices. House-maids willing to wear a uniform but not to confine their hair by a cap provide a parallel example, partially rejecting their occupation in favour of their femininity.* (What we have in these cases is a special kind of status symbol – a disidentifier – that the individual hopes will shatter an otherwise coherent picture, telling others not what he is but what he isn't quite.) However, it is not only organizational roles which are handled in this way. Age-sex roles are dealt with in the same manner, as when a girl dresses in a tomboy style, or a sixty-year-old man wears the brim of his hat turned up or affects a crewcut. A vivid example of this kind of disidentifier may be cited in regard to 'race' groupings, taken from a novelistic description of the functions of clothing for a New York Negro, very hip, by name of Movement:

---

* Sexual attractiveness provides an exemplary means of role distance for females in the work world and is certainly not restricted to females in the meaner callings. For example, there is a tacit understanding in the medical world that female physicians on hospital staffs will mute their attractiveness (where they have any). A highly placed, good-looking female physician is therefore in a position, sometimes utilized, to bring a little pleasant uneasiness to an entire hospital.

The tension had got bad right after he left Kiefer. It had been all right in Harlem – there he had been staging his own entrances and exits, no involvement, it was an elaborate game, like most of existence up there. But at the tailor's, when he found the shoulder pads had not been removed from his jacket, he began to tighten up, his gut establishing dangerous liaison with his face.

'To know what kind of shoulders I want,' he said, his voice twice as colourless as usual, 'you would have to know who I am, or who I want to be. Who would know that better, you or me?'

'So who are you?' the tailor said. 'Jimmy Stewart? Anthony Eden?'

'You do not understand. What is this suit you make over and over, with the padded shoulders and the extreme drape and the pegged trousers? A uniform, Sam. I do not want to wear a uniform. Uniforms are for people who want to show themselves, not for those who want to hide.' . . .

'Movement, you're crazy. You don't like uniforms, all right. But you think this pogo-stick garment ain't a uniform? You look at those advertising guys marching on Madison, all look-alikes with button-down collars, all they need is a top sergeant yelling the march orders at them. It's a uniform like Cab Calloway's white gabardine reet-pleat is a uniform, only it's thin and up-and-down and the other one it's wide and sideways and curvy more.'

'It is a uniform,' Movement said, 'to those who wear it as a uniform. To the Madison Avenue people. For me, it is a disguise, to get the eyes off me.'

'Disguise, schmisguise. So you wear also a gold earring? That's a disguise too?'

'Between the earring and the Brooks Brothers suit,' Movement said, lips fighting to keep down the shout that was accumulating, 'is where I am. Where they stop crowding me. I have some elbow room there and that is my freedom.'*

But of course we cannot stop with organizational, age-sex, and

---

* Bernard Wolfe, *The Late Risers* (New York: Random House, 1954), pp. 217–18. The expressive significance of wearing only *one* earring is developed in the section called 'grandfather was an authentic field hand', pp. 136–42. For an interesting statement regarding the sartorial role distance of young drug users, see Harold Finestone, 'Cats, Kicks, and Color', *Social Problems*, 5 (1957), pp. 3–13, especially p. 3. See also T. H. Pear, *Personality, Appearance and Speech* (Allen & Unwin, 1957), p. 66: 'In World War I, an attempt to compel subalterns to grow a moustache, resulted at times in a defiant cultivation of a dot of hair under each nostril . . .'

ethnic group roles. A person of wealth may affect poor and worn clothing for many reasons, one of which is to demonstrate that he is something apart from what his wealth allows him to be. And what his wealth allows him is not a situated role in any full sense of the term, but rather a human situation in which certain contingencies are likely. In the same way, we would have to deal with the appearance pattern affected among bohemians, through which they expressively take a stand against that quite amorphous social entity – middle-class society.

The move from closely meshed situated systems to loose bases for roles is not the only one we must make. The role distance exhibited even in a situated system cannot always be handled as I have so far suggested. In some cases, as with the antics of merry-go-round riders and surgeons, role distance clearly seems to express a measure of disidentification relative to the identification available to anyone in the given situated position. It is soon apparent, however, that this distance may be meant to be seen as symbolic of distance from something different to position in the situated activity circuit. The individual may actually be attempting to express some disaffiliation from his position in a different kind of entity – a social relationship that he has to a fellow participant; the social establishment* or the social occasion in which the activity system occurs; the professional or occupational world to which the individual belongs.

For example, meal-taking in domestic establishments provides a situated system from which a member of the household may show distance by sitting down late, putting his nose in a book, talking to no one while eating, making 'unmannerly' noises, rejecting all food, or, as in the case of some persons at the onset of what is called a psychotic break, smearing the food or stealing it from the plates of others. Now, while such a person is clearly showing distance from the situated role of family meal-taker in a family meal, he may be motivated by an irritation not with the

---

* Very nice instances of this may be found in the language of derision that amputees and brain-surgery cases employ in regard to the hospital and staff involved in their treatment. See Edwin Weinstein and Robert Kahn, *Denial of Illness* (Springfield, Ill.: Charles Thomas, 1955). For similar joking by patients in mental hospitals, see Rose Coser, 'Some Social Functions of Laughter', *Human Relations*, 12 (1959), pp. 171–82.

eater's role but with quite different matters – a spouse or parent, his job, the educational system, his girl friend, the middle-class way of life, and so forth. Another clear example is provided again by surgeons. Often, surgeons make use of a hospital through a staffing arrangement by which they bring in paying patients in exchange for use of surgical facilities and hospital beds. In this bargain, surgeons often seem to feel that the hospital is not providing them with adequate staffing and equipment. During surgery, humorous and sarcastic remarks will thus be passed by surgeons, often to the permanent hospital staff such as nurses and anaesthetists, through which the physicians give evidence that while they must accept hospital conditions they are not happy with what they must tolerate.

> CHIEF SURGEON (*using the nurse as a target to express joking, hectoring hostility towards management for the inadequacies of the services they lay on*): Are all my instruments here, Nurse? Is everything I need here, eh? They don't have everything here, I have to bring my own, you know, and I want them back.

And, as implied in the quotation, in order to convey this attitude, surgeons sometimes draw on their store of conduct that is slightly unbecoming to a surgeon.

Given the fact that an individual may employ his role in a situated system to express distance from a basis of self-identification not officially at issue, we can appreciate that a situated role may be selected with this in mind. Participation in the situated activity may be made a convenience of, carried on not for its own sake but for what can be expressed through it about something else. At the same time, the individual may mobilize so much of his talk, appearance, and activity to exhibit distance from a particular role that the role itself may cease to be visible. All these elements seem to be illustrated in an interview quoted in a recent paper on the self-hate of intellectual academics:

> When I'm away from the university, I usually have plenty of dirt under my nails, or I'm getting a harvest. Some of us fool ourselves into believing that the stain of our profession doesn't follow us. I can work

with a carpenter for several weeks, and he has no notion I'm a university professor. I take a foolish pride, I suppose, in this.*

I suggest, then, that a single framework of analysis must cover the situation of the person with a traditional, well-focused, task-oriented role, like that of surgeon, and persons in the situation of being a rich widower of fifty, a fat girl of bad complexion, a stutterer, and so forth. And I imply that our actual interest in persons with well-focused roles has often been such as to render this broader treatment easy and natural. In cases of both focused and unfocused roles, the basic interest is in what befalls an individual by virtue of his being in a position, and whether this position is a part of a tightly encircled system of situated activity or merely the common feature of a heterogeneous class of social situations is not the first issue. Further, even when we deal with an apparently well-focused role, such as that of nurse or surgeon, we find that some of the most significant features of the position arise not while 'on the job' but at times when the individual is officially active in another role, such as that of fellow guest or motorist. Source of identification is one thing, an audience for this self-identification is another. Occupational roles with the firmest grasp on their performers are often ones which carry identifying implications for the performer when he is off duty and away from the immediate arena of his role. Often, it is precisely these unfocused consequences of a focused role that carry much of the reward and punishment of playing it – the situations of the policeman, the country nurse, and the minister are examples. One might almost argue that role-formation occurs to the degree that performance of a situated task comes to have significance for the way the performer is seen in other situations, and that the social psychology of identification moves always from a situated system in which a situated role is performed to wider worlds in which the mere fact of this performance comes to carry significance. This is so even though as one moves outward and away

* Melvin Seeman, 'The Intellectual and the Language of Minorities', *American Journal of Sociology*, 64 (1958), p. 32. A recent novel by Mark Harris, *Wake Up, Stupid!* (New York: Knopf, 1959), provides a rather full catalogue of role-distance fantasies for college teachers. The *genre* was, of course, established by Kingsley Amis's *Lucky Jim*.

from the situated system and its immediate audience of participants, the role term by which the individual is identified may become more and more abstract, a chest man becoming a surgeon, a surgeon a doctor, a doctor a professional man.

I have argued that the individual manifests role distance and less 'counter-oriented' role-irrelevant acts because of the commitments and attachments that he possesses and that these are a heterogeneous lot: his organizational roles, his diffuse roles, the situated system of activity itself. And now I am arguing that another complication is involved. For just as the individual manifests distance (in whatever name) from his situated role, so, too, he spends some of his moments and gestures manifesting distance from some of his non-situated, non-relevant connexions.*

As regards embracement, then, a person's conduct is complex indeed. Should he happen to be engaged, at the moment of analysis, in a situated role, then this will provide a focus, but rarely a sharp one. The substance of task activity can be more or less restricted to a situated role, but the style, manner, and guise in which this task is performed cannot be thus restricted. Individuals are almost always free to modulate what they are required to do, being free, thus, to give way to the wider constraints of their multiple self-identifications.†

* For a similar view of interaction, see Anselm Strauss, *Mirrors and Masks* (London: Collier-Macmillan, 1959), pp. 56–7.

† Role distance, Edward Sapir might have suggested, is to role as fashion is to custom:

Fashion is a custom in the guise of departure from custom. Most normal individuals consciously or unconsciously have the itch to break away in some measure from a too literal loyalty to accepted custom. They are not fundamentally in revolt from custom but they wish somehow to legitimize their personal deviation without laying themselves open to the charge of insensitiveness to good taste or good manners. Fashion is the direct solution of the subtle conflict. The slight changes from the established in dress or other forms of behaviour seem for the moment to give the victory to the individual, while the fact that one's fellows revolt in the same direction gives one a feeling of adventurous safety. . . .

The endless rediscovery of the self in a series of petty truancies from the official socialized self becomes a mild obsession of the normal individual in any society in which the individual has ceased to be a measure of the society itself.

'Fashion', *Encyclopedia of the Social Services* (London: Collier-Macmillan, 1937), 6, pp. 140–41.

One great theme of social organization is the scheduling of roles: the individual is allowed and required to be one thing in one setting and another thing in a different setting, the role that is given primacy at one occasion being dormant on another. In acclaiming this role-segregation, however, sociologists have neglected another basic theme. A situated system of activity and the organization in which this system is sustained provide the individual with that one of his roles that will be given principal weight on this occasion. But even while the local scene establishes what the individual will mainly be, many of his other affiliations will be simultaneously given little bits of credit.

A final comment is to be added. There is a vulgar tendency in social thought to divide the conduct of the individual into a profane and sacred part, this version of the distinction strangely running directly contrary to the one Durkheim gave us. The profane part is attributed to the obligatory world of social roles; it is formal, stiff, and dead; it is exacted by society. The sacred part has to do with 'personal' matters and 'personal' relationships – with what an individual is 'really' like underneath it all when he relaxes and breaks through to those in his presence. It is here, in this personal capacity, that an individual can be warm, spontaneous, and touched by humour. It is here, regardless of his social role, that an individual can show 'what kind of a guy he is'. And so it is, that in showing that a given piece of conduct is part of the obligations and trappings of a role, one shifts it from the sacred category to the profane, from the fat and living to the thin and dead. Sociologists *qua* sociologists are allowed to have the profane part; sociologists *qua* persons, along with other persons, retain the sacred for their friends, their wives, and themselves.

The concept of role distance helps to combat this touching tendency to keep a part of the world safe from sociology. For if an individual is to show that he is a 'nice guy' or, by contrast, one much less nice than a human being need be, then it is through his using or not using role distance that this is likely to be done. It is right here, in manifestations of role distance, that the individual's personal style is to be found. And it is argued in this paper that role distance is almost as much subject to role analysis as are the core tasks of roles themselves.

Where the Action Is

Where the Action Is

'To be on the wire is life;
the rest is waiting.'*

A decade ago among those urban American males who were little given to gentility the term 'action' was used in a non-Parsonian sense in reference to situations of a special kind, the contrast being to situations where there was 'no action'. Very recently this locution has been taken up by almost everyone, and the term itself flogged without mercy in commercials and advertisements.

This paper, then, deals with a term that points to something lively but is itself now almost dead. Action will be defined analytically. An effort will be made to uncover where it is to be found and what it implies about these places.

CHANCES

Wheresoever action is found, chance-taking is sure to be. Begin then with a simple illustration of chance, and work outwards from there.

Two boys together find a nickel in their path and decide that one will toss and the other call to see who keeps it. They agree, then, to engage in a *play* or, as probabilists call it, a *gamble* – in this case one go at the *game* of coin-tossing.

A coin can be used as a decision machine, much as a roulette wheel or a deck of cards can. With this particular machine it is plain that a fully known set of *possible outcomes* is faced: heads or tails, obverse or reverse. Similarly with a die: in ordinary manufacture and use,† it presents six different faces as possible outcomes.

* Attributed to Karl Wallenda, on going back up to the high wire after his troupe's fatal Detroit accident.
† A die can be used like a coin if, for example, 1, 2, or 3 is called tails, and 4, 5, or 6 is called heads. Among the types of unsporting dice are mis-spotted ones variously called tops and bottoms, horses, tees, tats, soft rolls, California

H

Given the two outcomes possible when a coin is tossed, the probability or *chance* can be assessed for each of them. Chances vary from 'sure' to 'impossible' or, in the language of probability, from 1 to 0.

What a player has in hand and undergoes a chance of losing is his stake or *bet*. What the play gives him a chance of winning that he doesn't already have can be called his *prize*. The *payoff* for him is the prize that he wins or the bet that he loses. Bet and prize together may be called the *pot*.*

In gaming, *theoretical odds* refers to the chances of a favourable outcome compared to those of an unfavourable one, the decision machine here seen as an ideal one; *true odds* are a theoretical version of theoretical ones, involving a correction for the physical biases found in any actual machine – biases never to be fully eliminated or fully known.† *Given odds* or *pay*, on the other hand, refers to the size of the prize compared to that of the bet.‡ Note that outcomes are defined wholly in terms of the game equipment, payoffs in terms of extrinsic and variable resources currently committed to particular outcomes. Thus, with theoretical odds and given odds, somewhat the same term is employed to cover two radically different ideas.

Weighting the pot by the chance on the average of winning it, gives what students of chance call the *expected value* of the play. Subtracting the expected value from the amount bet gives a measure of the price or the profit on the average for engaging

---

fourteens, door pops, Eastern tops, etc. These dice do not have a different number on each of the six sides, and (as with a two-headed coin) allow a player to bet on an outcome that is not among the possibilities and therefore rather unlikely to occur. Note that dice, much more frequently than coins, do land on their edges (by virtue of coming to rest against objects) and do roll out of bounds. The management of these regrettable contingencies is one of the jobs of the members of a craps crew, especially the stickman, in the sense that their very quick verbal and physical corrections are designed to make perfect a very imperfect physical model.

* The track has a word for it, 'extension'.

† Here and elsewhere in matters of probability I am indebted to Ira Cisin. He is responsible only for the correct statements.

‡ To increase the apparent attractiveness of certain bets some crap-table lay-outs state winnings not in terms of given odds but in terms of the pot; thus, a bet whose given odds are 1 *to* 4 will be described as 1 *for* 5.

in the play. Expressing this measure as a proportion of the bet gives the *advantage* or percentage of the play. When there is neither advantage nor disadvantage, the play is said to be *fair*. Then the theoretical odds are the reciprocal of the given odds, so that he who *gives* or *lays* the odds, gambling a large sum in the hope of winning a small one, is exactly compensated by the smallness of his chance of losing to the individual who *takes* the odds.

There are plays that allow a multitude of possible outcomes to choose among, each of which pays differently and may even provide the bettor with differing disadvantage. Casino craps is an example. Still other plays involve a set of favourable possible outcomes that pay differently so that the expected value of the play must be calculated as a sum of several different values: slot machines and keno provide examples.

In the degree to which a play is a means of acquiring a prize, it is an *opportunity*; in the degree to which it is a threat to one's bet, it is a *risk*. The perspective here is objective. A subjective sense of opportunity or risk is quite another matter since it may, but need not, coincide with the facts.

Each of our coin tossers can be defined as having a life course in which the finding of a nickel has not been anticipated. Without the find, life would go forward as expected. Each boy can then conceive of his situation as affording him a gain or returning him to what is only normal. A chance-taking of this kind can be called opportunity without risk. Were a bully to approach one of the boys and toss him for a nickel taken from the boy's own pocket (and this happens in city neighbourhoods), we could then speak of a risk without opportunity. In daily life, risks and opportunities usually occur together, and in all combinations.

Sometimes the individual can retract his decision to pursue a line of activity upon learning of likely failure. No chances, whether risky or opportune, are taken here. For chanciness to be present, the individual must ensure he is in a position (or be forced into one) to let go of his hold and control on the situation, to make, in Schelling's sense, a commitment.* No commitment, no chance-taking.

A point about determination – defining this as a process, not

* T. C. Schelling, *The Strategy of Conflict* (Oxford: O.U.P., 1963), esp. p. 24.

an accomplished event. As soon as the coin is in the air, the tosser will feel that deciding forces have begun their work, and so they have. It is true, of course, that the period of determination could be pushed back to include the decision to choose heads or tails, or still further back to include the decision to toss in the first place. However, the outcome (heads or tails) is fully determined during the time the coin is in the air; a different order of fact, such as who will select heads or how much will be chanced, is determined before the toss. In brief, an essential feature of the coin-tossing situation is that an outcome undetermined up to a certain point – the point of tossing the coin in the air – is clearly and fully determined during the toss. A *problematic* situation is resolved.

The term problematic is here taken in the objective sense to refer to something not yet determined but about to be. As already suggested, the subjective assessment of the actor himself brings further complication. He may be quite unaware that something at hand is being determined. Or he may feel that the situation is problematic when in fact the matter at hand has already been determined and what he is really facing is revealment or disclosure. Or, finally, he may be fully oriented to what is actually happening – alive to the probabilities involved and realistically concerned over the consequences. This latter possibility, where a full parallel is found between objective and subjective situation, will be our main concern.

The causal forces during the period of determination and prior to the final result are often defined as ones of 'mere chance', or 'pure luck'. This does not presume some kind of ultimate in-determination. When a coin is tossed its fall is fully determined by such factors as the prior state of the tosser's finger, the height of the toss, the air currents (including ones that occur after the coin has left the finger), and so forth. However, no human influence, intended and legitimate, can be exercised to manipulate the relevant part of the result.*

There *are* to be sure chancy situations where relevant orders of humanly directed determination are involved by virtue of skill,

---

* See the argument by D. MacKay, 'The Use of Behavioural Language to Refer to Mechanical Processes', *British Journal of the Philosophy of Science*, XIII, 50 (1962), 89–103; 'On the Logical Indeterminacy of a Free Choice', *Mind*, 69 (1960), 31–40.

knowledge, daring, perseverance, and so forth. This in fact, marks a crucial difference between games of 'pure' chance and what are called contests: in the former, once the determination is in play, the participants can do nothing but passively await the outcome; in the latter, it is just this period that requires intensive and sustained exercising of relevant capacities. None the less, it is still the case that during contests something of value to be staked comes up for determination; as far as participants are concerned, the intended and effective influences are insufficiently influential to render the situation unproblematic.

A crucial feature of coin-tossing is its temporal phases. The boys must decide to settle the matter by tossing; they must align themselves physically; they must decide how much of the nickel will be gambled on the toss and who will take which outcome; through stance and gesture they must commit themselves to the gamble and thereby pass the point of no return. This is the bet-making or *squaring off phase*. Next there is the in-play or *determination phase*, during which relevant causal forces actively and determinatively produce the outcome.* Then comes the revelatory or *disclosive phase*, the time between determination and informing of the participants. This period is likely to be very brief, to differ among sets of participants differently placed relative to the decision machinery,† and to possess a special suspensefulness of its own. Finally there is the *settlement phase*, beginning when the outcome has been disclosed and lasting until losses have been paid up and gains collected.

The period required by participants in a given play to move

---

* In coin-tossing this phase begins when the coin goes into the air and terminates when it lands on the hand – a second or two later. In horse-racing, determination begins when the starting-gates are opened and terminates when the finishing-line is crossed, a little more than a minute in all. In seven-day bicycle races, the determination phase is a week long.

† Horse-racing con games have been based on the possibility of convincing the mark that the period between an outcome at the track and its announcement at distant places is long enough to exploit for post-finish sure betting, that is, 'past-posting' – a condition that can in fact occur and has been systematically exploited. It might be added that friendly 21 dealers in Nevada, after completing a deal, will sometimes look at their hole card and josh a player about a destiny which has been determined and read but teasingly delayed in disclosure.

through the four phases of the play – squaring off, determination, disclosure, and settlement – may be called the *span* of the play. The periods between plays may be called *pauses*. The period of *a* play must be distinguished from the period of playing, namely, the *session*, which is the time between making the first bet and settling up the last one on any one occasion perceived as continuously devoted to play. The number of completed plays during any unit of time is the *rate* of play for that time.* Average duration of the plays of a game sets an upper limit to rate of play, as does average length of pauses; a coin can be tossed five times in half a minute; the same number of decisions at the track requires more than an hour.

Given these distinctions in the phases of play, it is easy to attend to a feature of simple games of chance that might otherwise be taken for granted. Once a play is undertaken, its determination, disclosure, and settlement usually follow quickly, often before another bet is made. A coin-tossing session consists, then, of a sequence of four-phase cycles with pauses between cycles. Typically the player maintains a continuous stretch of attention and experiencing over the whole four or five seconds course of each play, attention lapsing only during the pauses, that is, after the settlement of one play and before the making of another. Everyday life is usually quite different. Certainly the individual makes bets and takes chances in regard to daily living, as when, for example, he decides to take one job instead of another or to move from one state to another. Further, at certain junctures he may have to make numerous vital decisions at the same time and hence briefly maintain a very high rate of bet-making. But ordinarily the determination phase – the period during which the consequences of his bet are determined – will be long, sometimes extending over decades, followed by disclosure and settlement phases that are themselves lengthy. The distinctive property of

---

* For example, assume that the nickel-finders are engaged in a sudden-death game, one toss determining who gets the nickel. If the two boys are together on this occasion for one hour, their rate of chance-taking is once per hour. Should they change the nickel into pennies and toss these one at a time, each penny only once, then the rate of chance-taking is five times greater than it was before although the resulting swing in fortune no more and probably less.

games and contests is that once the bet has been made, *outcome is determined and payoff awarded all in the same breath of experience.* A single sharp focus of awareness is sustained at high pitch during the full span of the play.

CONSEQUENTIALITY

We can take some terms, then, from the traditional analysis of coin-tossing,* but this framework soon leads to difficulties.

The standard for measuring the amount of a bet or prize is set by or imputed to the community, the public at large, or the prevailing market. An embarrassment of game analysis is that different persons can have quite different feelings about the same bet or the same prize. Middle-class adults may use a nickel as a decision machine, but will hardly bother tossing just to decide who keeps the machine. Small boys, however, can feel that a co-finder's claim to a nickel is a big bet indeed. When attention must be given to variations in meaning that different persons give to the same bet (or the same prize), or that the same individual gives over time or over varying conditions, one speaks of subjective value or *utility*. And just as expected value can be calculated as the average worth remaining to a nickel pot, so *expected utility* can be assessed as the utility an individual accords a nickel pot weighted by the probability of his winning it.

The expected utility of a nickel pot must be clearly distinguished from the expected utility of tossing for this pot; for individuals regularly place a subjective value – positive or negative – on the excitement and anxiety generated by tossing. Further, after the toss, the displeasure at losing and the pleasure at winning are not likely to balance each other off exactly; the difference, on whichever side, must also be reckoned on the average as part of the expected utility of the play.† Objective standards can be used in getting at the meaning of bets; but we must use the murky notion of utility to get at the meaning of betting.

* A sound, if popular, treatment may be found in R. Jeffrey, *The Logic of Decision* (New York: McGraw-Hill, 1965).

† In gambling, these factors are not independent. No doubt part of the experience obtained from the toss derives from the difference between the satisfaction at contemplating winning and the displeasure at the thought of losing.

When we move from the neat notion of the expected value of a pot to one that will be relevant for our concerns, namely, the expected utility of playing for the pot, we move into almost hopeless complexities. When an individual asserts that a given period of play involves a big gamble, or when he feels that it is chancier than another, a whole set of considerations may be involved: the scale of betting; the length of the odds (and whether he is giving them or getting them); the brevity of the span of play; the smallness of the number of plays; the rate of play; the percentage paid for playing; the variation of size regarding prizes associated with favourable outcomes. Further, the relative weight given each of these considerations will vary markedly with the absolute value of each of the others.*

For us this means that different individuals and groups have somewhat different personal base-lines from which to measure risk and opportunity; a way of life involving much risk may cause the individual to give little weight to a risk that someone else might find forbidding.† Thus, for example, attempts to account for the presence of legalized gambling in Nevada sometimes cite the mining tradition of the state, a type of venturing that can be defined as very chancy indeed. The argument is that since the economy of the state was itself founded on gambles with the ground, it is understandable that casino gambling was never viewed with much disapproval.

In simple, literal gambling, then, the basic notion of 'chanciness' is shot through with a multitude of half-realized, shifting meanings. When we turn from gaming to the rest of living, matters get worse.

In coin tossing, there are *a priori* and empirical reasons for assessing the chances of either outcome in effect as fifty-fifty. The ultimate validity of this assessment need not concern those who toss coins. That's the nice thing about coins. In many ordinary situations, however, the individual may have to face an outcome

---

* Recent work, especially by experimental psychologists, has added appreciable knowledge to this area by a design which obliges individuals to show a preference among gambles involving various mixes of elements. See, for example, J. Cohen, *Behaviour in Uncertainty* (London: Allen & Unwin, 1964), Ch. 3, 'Making a Choice', pp. 27–42; and W. Edwards, 'Behavior Decision Theory', *Annual Review of Psychology*, 12 (1961), 473–98.

† For this and other suggestions, I am grateful to Kathleen Archibald.

matrix that cannot be fully defined. (This could arise, for example, were our two boys to pause before a deep, multi-tunnelled cave, trying to decide what might befall them were they to try to explore it.) Further, even when the full set of outcome possibilities is known, the chances that must be attached to each of them may be subject to only rough assessment based on vague appeals to empirical experience.* Moreover, the estimator will often have little appreciation of how very rough his assessment is. In most life situations, we deal with *subjective probability* and hence at best a very loose overall measure, *subjectively expected utility*.†

Further, while coin tossers typically face a 'fair' game, and casino gamblers a slightly disadvantageous one, wider aspects of living present the individual with much less balance in this regard; there will be situations of much opportunity with little risk and of much risk with little opportunity. Moreover, opportunity and risk may not be easily measurable on the same scale.‡

There is an important issue in the notion of value itself – the

* Reputable firms specializing in crooked gambling devices sell variously 'shaped' dice that provide the customer with a choice among five or six degrees of what is called 'strength'. Probably the ranking is absolutely valid. But no company has tested dice of any alleged strength over a long enough series of trials to provide confidence levels concerning the favourable percentage these unfair dice afford their users.

† In the literature, following F. Knight (*Risk, Uncertainty and Profit* [Boston: Houghton Mifflin, 1921], esp. Ch. 7 and 8) the term 'risk' is used for a decision whose possible outcomes and their probabilities are known, and the term 'uncertainty' where the probabilities across the various outcomes are not known or even knowable. Here see R. Luce and H. Raiffa, *Games and Decisions* (London: Wiley, 1957), pp. 13 ff. Following John Cohen, B. Fox (*Behavioral Approaches to Accident Research* [Association for the Aid to Crippled Children, New York, 1961], p. 50), suggests using the term hazard for objective dire chances, and risk for subjective estimates of hazard. Fox equates this with a slightly different distinction, that between risk as perceived to inhere in a situation and risk perceived as something intentionally taken on. See also Cohen, *op. cit.*, p. 63.

‡ The concept of utility, and the experimental techniques of a forced-choice between singles and pairs probabilistically linked, can attempt to reduce these variabilities to a single scheme. However, these efforts can be questioned. Many actual plays are undertaken in necessary conjunction with the player remaining unappreciative of the risk (while focusing on the opportunity), or unaware of the opportunity (while attending to the risk). To place a utility on this unappreciativeness in order to balance the books seems hardly an answer.

notion that bets and prizes can be measured in amounts. A nickel has both a socially ratified value and a subjective value, in part because of what its winning allows, or losing disallows, the tosser *later on* to do. This is the gamble's *consequentiality*, namely, the *capacity of a payoff to flow beyond the bounds of the occasion in which it is delivered and to influence objectively the later life of the bettor*. The period during which this consequentiality is borne is a kind of post-play or *consequentiality phase* of the gamble.

A tricky matter must be considered here. 'Objective value' and 'utility' are both means of establishing instantaneous equivalents for consequences that are to be actually felt over time. This is achieved by allowing either the community or the individual himself to place an appraisal on this future, and to accept or to give a price for it now. I want to avoid this sophistication. When, for example, a man proposes matrimony, it is true that the payoff is determined as soon as the girl makes up her mind, reported as soon as she gives her answer, and settled up when the marriage is consummated or the rejected suitor withdraws to court elsewhere. But in another sense, the consequence of the payoff is felt throughout the life remaining to the participant. Just as a 'payoff' is the value equivalent of an outcome, so 'consequentiality' is the human equivalent of a payoff. We move then from pots and prizes, neatly definable, to protracted payoffs, which can be described only vaguely. This is a move from pots to consequentiality, and from circumscribed gambles to wider arenas of living.

In addition to all these limitations on the coin-tossing model, there is another quite central one that we can only begin to consider now. The subjective experience enjoyed by small boys who toss a coin for keeps develops from the feel of light-heartedly exercising will. A decision to gamble or not gamble is made under conditions where no alien pressure forces the decision, and not gambling would be an easy, quite practical choice. Once this decision is made affirmatively, a second one is made as to possible outcome to bet on – here an illusory right, but fun none the less, and certainly not illusory in games involving skill. Once the result is in, this can be treated as a possibility that was foreseen and the gamble taken anyway. In consequence, the whole situation can easily come to be seen prospectively as a chance-taking occasion, an occasion generated and governed by the exercise of self-determination, an occasion for *taking* risk and *grasping* opportunity. In daily life, however, the individual may never become aware of the risk and opportunity that in fact existed, or may become alive to the gamble he was making only after the play is over. And when the situation *is* approached with its chanciness in mind, the individual may find that the cost of not gambling is so high that it must be excluded as a realistic possibility, or, where this decision is a practical one, that no choice is available as to which of the possible outcomes he will be betting on. Some freedom of choice, some self-determination is present here, but often not very much. The coin-tossing model can be applied to all of these situations, but only by overlooking some important differences between recreational chance-taking and real-life gambles. Apart from the question of the amount at stake, our two boys who toss a coin are not engaged in quite the same type of chance-taking as is employed by two survivors who have mutually agreed that there is no other way than to toss to see who will lighten the raft; and they, in turn, are subject to chance differently than are two sick passengers who are forced by their well companions to submit to a toss decision to see which of the two will no longer share the lifeboat's supply of water.

FATEFULNESS

An individual ready to leave his house to keep an engagement finds he is thirty minutes early and has some 'free time' to use up or put in. He could put the time to 'good' use by doing now an essential task that will have to be done sometime. Instead he decides to 'kill' this time. He picks up a magazine from the ones at hand, drops into a comfortable chair, and leafs through some pages until it is time to go.

What are the characteristics of this activity used to kill time with? Approach this question through another: What are the possible effects of this little piece of the individual's life on the whole of the rest of it?

Obviously, what goes on during killed time may have no bearing at all on the rest of the individual's life.* Many alternative lines of

* Although, of course, his choice of means of killing time can be expressive of him.

activity can be pursued and still his life will go on as it is going. Instead of reading one magazine, he can read another; or he can while away the time by watching TV, cat-napping, or working a puzzle. Finding he has less time to put in than he had thought, he can easily cut his dawdling short; finding he has more time, he can dawdle more. He can try to find a magazine that interests him, fail, and yet lose little by this failure, merely having to face the fact that he is temporarily at loose ends. Having nothing to kill time with, or to kill enough time with, he can 'mark' it.

Killed moments, then, are inconsequential. They are bounded and insulated. They do not spill over into the rest of life and have an effect there. Differently put, the individual's life course is not subject to his killed moments; his life is organized in such a way as to be impervious to them. Activities for killing time are selected in advance as ones that cannot tie up or entangle the individual.*

Killing time often involves the killer in problematic activity. The decision as to magazine or TV may be a close one whose determination is not begun until the individual is about to sit down. Here then is problematic behaviour that is not consequential. (Interestingly, this is exactly the case in tossing for a nickel. Our youthful gamblers may subjectively place great value on winning the toss, yet the payoff can hardly be consequential.)

In contrast to time off we have time on and its world of collectively organized serious work, which gears the individual's efforts into the needs of other persons who count on him for supplies, equipment, or services in order to fulfil their own obligations. Records are kept of his production and deliveries, and penalties given if he fails to perform. In brief, the division of labour and

---

* Time off comes in all sizes, a few seconds to a few years. It comes between tasks on the job; in transit between home and work; at home after the evening meal; weekends; annual vacations; retirement. (There is also – largely in fantasy – the time away from ordinary life that Georg Simmel calls 'the Adventure'.) When time off is killed, presumably this is done with freely chosen activity possessing a consummatory end-in-itself character. Whether the individual fills his time off with consequential or inconsequential activity, he usually must remain on tap at the place where serious, scheduled duties are located; or he must be within return-distance to his station. Note that time off to kill is to be distinguished from a close neighbour, the time that unemployed persons are forced to mark and cannot justify as an earned respite from past duties or imminent ones.

the organization of work-flow connect the individual's current moments to other persons' next ones in a very consequential manner.

However, the consequentiality of properly attending to one's duties on any one occasion is very little noted. Results are, to be sure, more or less pictured in advance, but the probability of their occurrence is so high that little attention seems required in the matter. Nothing need be weighed, decided, or assessed; no alternatives have to be considered. This activity is indeed consequential, but it is well managed; it is not problematic. Incidentally, any moment, whether worked or killed, will have this element. It is a matter of total consequentiality that our coin tossers continue to inhale and exhale and do not run their heads against a concrete wall; any failure in the first and any success in the second can have very far-reaching effects on all a boy's moments to come. However, continuing to breathe and not beating one's head against the wall are objectives so continuously and unthinkingly sought and so assuredly and routinely realized, that the consequentiality of lapse need never be considered.

Time-off activities, then, can be problematic but are likely to be inconsequential, and time-on activities are likely to be consequential but not problematic. Thus both types of activity can easily be uneventful: either nothing important happens or nothing important happens that is unexpected and unprepared for.

However, an activity *can* be problematic *and* consequential. Such activity I call *fateful*, although the term eventful would do as well, and it is this kind of chanciness that will concern us here.

It must now be admitted that although free time and well-managed work time tend to be unfateful, the human condition is such that *some* degree of fatefulness will always be found. Primordial bases of fatefulness must be reckoned with.

First, there is the adventitious or literary kind of fatefulness. An event that is ordinarily well managed and un-noteworthy can sometimes cast fatefulness backwards in time, giving to certain previous moments an uncharacteristic capacity to be the first event in a fateful conjunction of two events. Should one of our youthful gamblers need a nickel to make a crucial telephone call with at the moment the nickel is found, then the chance to win the toss can become fateful. Similarly, our time-killing individual can become

so caught up in a magazine story that he loses all track of time*
and does not surface until too late – an irritation, merely, unless
the appointment that is missed happens to be important. Or,
leafing through the magazine, he can come upon an article on
intelligence tests containing sample questions. His appointment is
an examination in which one of these questions appears. A moment
to fritter away is not totally cut off from the moments to come;
it *can* have unexpected connexions with them.

Although individuals and their activities are always subject to
some adventitious fatefulness, there are some enterprises whose
vulnerability in this regard is marked enough to serve as a
characterization of them. Where co-ordination and concealment
are vital, a whole range of minor unanticipated hitches lose their
usual quality of correctability and become fateful. Stories of near-
perfect crimes and nearly exposed commando raids enshrine this
source of fatefulness as do tales of strategic goofs:

Maidstone, England: A gang of masked men wielding blackjacks and
hammers ambushed a car carrying $28,000 to a bank here yesterday but
they grabbed the wrong loot – a bag of sandwiches.
  The cash was locked in the trunk of the car and the bag containing
the bank official's lunch was on the car seat.†

Three robbers who completely botched what was supposed to be a
simple little bank robbery in Rodeo were sentenced in Federal Court
here yesterday. . . .
  All three were nabbed by some 40 police officers Jan. 7 as they
struggled to make off with $7,710 stuffed into a laundry sack they had
just taken out of the United California bank, the only bank in Rodeo . . .
  Pugh walked in with a sawed off shotgun and lined up the 13 employees and two customers, while Fleming, carrying a pistol, went to the
vault and started filling the laundry bag with currency and, alas, coins.
  'The coins can't be traced,' he said cleverly. He kept piling in coins

* In our urban society the individual is likely to check up on the time
periodically and can almost always estimate the time closely. Light sleepers
may even orient themselves constantly in time. Struck on some occasion how
'time has flown', the individual may in fact mean only one or two hours.
Finding that his watch has stopped, he may find in fact that it stopped only
a few minutes ago, and that he must have been checking himself against it
constantly.
  † *San Francisco Chronicle*, 10 March 1966.

until the bag weighed about 200 pounds. Then he dragged the bag across the floor to the door – and the frayed rope snapped.

Both men then lugged the bag through the door, but it caught and ripped a hole, letting coins trail behind them as they dragged the bag to the get-away car, with Duren at the wheel.

Duren though, had parked too close to the high curb, so the three could not open the door to get the loot inside. Finally they did, by moving the car, and raced away – around the corner. There the car stopped when the three saw the clutter of sheriff, Highway Patrol and police cars.*

These mistakes are everyday ones and would ordinarily be easily absorbed by the reserve for correction that characterizes most undertakings. What is special about criminal enterprise (and other military-like operations) is the narrowness of this reserve and hence the high price that must be paid for thoughtlessness and bad breaks. This is the difference between holding a job down and pulling a job off; here an act becomes a deed.†

Second, no matter how inconsequential and insulated an individual's moment is and how safe and well managed his place of consequential duties, he must be there in the flesh if the moment is to be his at all, and this is the selfsame flesh he must leave with and take wherever he goes, along with all the damage that has ever occurred to it. No matter how careful he may be, the integrity of his body will always be in jeopardy to some degree. While reading, he may slip in his chair, fall to the floor and injure himself. This is unlikely to be sure, but should he kill time by taking a bath or earn his living by working at a lathe, in a mine, or on construction jobs, the possibility of injury would be considerably more likely, as actuarial data show. Physical danger is a thin red thread connecting each of the individual's moments to all his others. A body is subject to falls, hits, poisons, cuts, shots, crushing, drowning, burning, disease, suffocation, and electrocution. A body is a

---

* *Ibid.*, 6 May 1966.

† In fictional vicarious worlds, criminal jobs (as well as the structurally similar undercover operations of various government agents) are realized in the teeth of a long sequence of threatened and actual hitches, each of which has a high probability of ruining everything. The hero manages to survive from episode to episode, but only by grossly breaking the laws of chance. Among young aspirants for these roles, surely the probabilistically inclined must be subtly discouraged.

piece of consequential equipment, and its owner is always putting it on the line. Of course, he can bring other capital goods into many of his moments too, but his body is the only one he can never leave behind.

A third pertinent aspect of the human condition concerns co-presence. A *social situation* may be defined (in the first instance) as any environment of mutual monitoring possibilities that lasts during the time two or more individuals find themselves in one another's immediate physical presence, and extends over the entire territory within which this mutual monitoring is possible.

By definition, an individual's activities must occur either in social situations or solitarily. Does which it will be, make a difference for the fatefulness of his moments?

For the special kind of consequentiality we are concerned with, the fateful kind involving the significant problematic bearing of one moment's activity upon the next, it should not matter whether the event is socially situated or not. Our concern, after all, is with the later effects of an action, not its current condition. None the less, the difference between solitary and socially situated activities has a special relevance of its own.

Just as the individual always brings his body into every occasion of his activity and also the possibility of a fortuitous linking of an already consequential event to one that would otherwise be innocuous, so he brings himself as an upholder of conduct standards like physical adoptness, honesty, alertness, piety, and neatness. The record of an individual's maintenance of these standards provides a basis others use for imputing a personal make-up to him. Later they employ this characterization in determining how to treat him – and this is consequential. Of course, most of these standards are unthinkingly and consistently maintained by adults; they are likely to become aware of these norms only when a freak accident occurs or when, in their mature and ritually delicate years, they essay for the first time to ride a horse, skate, or engage in other sports requiring special techniques for the maintenance of physical aplomb.

In some cases solitary misconduct results in a record of damage that can later be traced to the offender. In many other cases, however, no such responsibility is found; either the effects of the misconduct are ephemeral (as in gestured acts of contempt) or they cannot be traced to their author. Only the conscience of the individual can make such activity consequential for him, and this kind of conscience is not everywhere found. However, when the conduct occurs in a social situation – when, that is, witnesses are present – then these standards become immediately relevant and introduce some risk, however low.

A similar argument can be made about opportunities to display sterling personal qualities. With no witnesses present, the individual's efforts may have little identifiable lasting effect; when others are present, some kind of record is assured.

In social situations, then, ordinary risks and opportunities are confounded by expressions of make-up. Gleanings become available, often all too much so. Social situations thus become opportunities for introducing favourable information about oneself, just as they become risky occasions when unfavourable facts may be established.

Of the various types of object the individual must handle during his presence among others, one merits special attention: the other persons themselves. The impression he creates through his dealings with them and the traits they impute to him in consequence have a special bearing on his reputation, for here the witnesses have a direct personal stake in what they witness.

Specifically, whenever the individual is in the presence of others, he is pledged to maintain a ceremonial order by means of interpersonal rituals. He is obliged to ensure that the expressive implications of all local events are compatible with the status that he and others present possess; this involves politeness, courtesy, and retributive responses to others' slighting of self. And the maintenance of this order, whether during time off or time on, is more problematic than might first appear.

A final word about social situations: The ceremonial order sustained by persons when in one another's presence does more than assure that each participant gives and gets his due. Through the exercise of proper demeanour, the individual gives credit and substance to interaction entities themselves, such as conversations, gatherings, and social occasions, and renders himself accessible and usable for communication. Certain kinds of misconduct, such as loss of self-control, gravely disrupt the actor's usability in face-to-face interaction and can disrupt the interaction itself. The

I

concern the other participants have for the social occasion, and the ends they anticipate will be served through it, together ensure that some weight will be given to the propriety of the actor's behaviour.

I have argued that the individual is always in jeopardy in some degree because of adventitious linkings of events, the vulnerability of his body, and the need in social situations to maintain the proprieties. It is, of course, when accidents occur – unplanned impersonal happenings with incidental dire results – that these sources of fatefulness become alive to us. But something besides accident must be considered here.

The physical capacities of any normal adult equip him, if he so wills it, to be immensely disruptive of the world immediately at hand. He can destroy objects, himself, and other people. He can profane himself, insult and contaminate others, and interfere with their free passage.

Infants are not trusted to forgo these easy opportunities (which in any case they are insufficiently developed to exploit fully) and are physically constrained from committing mischief. Personal development is the process by which the individual learns to forgo these opportunities voluntarily, even while his capacity to destroy the world immediately around him increases. And this forgoing is usually so well learned that students of social life fail to see the systematic desisting that routinely occurs in daily living, and the utter mayhem that would result were the individual to cease to be a gentleman. Appreciation comes only when we study in detail the remarkable disruption of social settings produced by hypomanic children, youthful vandals, suicidals, persons pathologically obsessed by a need for self-abasement, and skilled saboteurs. Although our coin tossers can be relied upon not to hold their breath or run their heads up against a concrete wall, or spit on each other, or besmear themselves with their own faecal matter, inmates of mental hospitals have been known to engage in exactly these behaviours, nicely demonstrating the transformation of unproblematic consequential activity into what is fateful.

PRACTICAL GAMES

The human condition ensures that eventfulness will always be a possibility, especially in social situations. Yet the individual ordinarily manages his time and time off so as to avoid fatefulness. Further, much of the eventfulness that does occur is handled in ways that do not concern us. There are many occasions of un-avoided fatefulness that are resolved in such a way as to allow the participants to remain unaware of the chances they had in fact been taking. (The occurrence of such moments, for example while driving, is itself an interesting subject for study.) And much of the fatefulness that occurs in consequence of freakish, improb-able events is handled retrospectively; only after the fact does the individual redefine his situation as having been fateful all along, and only then does he appreciate in what connexion the fateful-ness was to occur. Retrospective fatefulness and unappreciated fatefulness abound, but will not be considered here.

And yet of course there are extraordinary niches in social life where activity is so markedly problematic and consequential that the participant is likely to orient himself to fatefulness pros-pectively, perceiving in these terms what it is that is taking place. It is then that fateful situations undergo a subtle transformation, cognitively reorganized by the person who must suffer them. It is then that the frame of reference employed by our two small boys is brought into serious life by serious men. Given the practical necessity of following a course of action whose success is problem-atic and passively awaiting the outcome thereof, one can discover an alternative, howsoever costly, and then define oneself as having freely chosen between this undesirable certainty and the un-certainty at hand. A Hobson's choice is made, but this is enough to allow the situation to be read as one in which self-determination is central. Instead of awaiting fate, you meet it at the door. Danger is recast into taken risk; favourable possibilities, into grasped op-portunity. Fateful situations become chancy undertakings, and exposure to uncertainty is construed as wilfully taking a practical gamble.*

* Decision theorists currently demonstrate that almost any situation can be usefully formulated as a payoff matrix enclosing all possible outcomes, each outcome designated with a value that is in turn weighted by the probability of occurrence. The result is that conduct that might be construed as un-problematical and automatic or as an obligatory response to inflexible and traditional demands, can be recast as a rational decision voluntarily taken in regard to defined alternatives. Further, since the choice is among outcomes

Consider now the occupations where problematic consequentiality is faced and where it would be easy to define one's activity as a practical gamble voluntarily taken:

1. There are roles in commerce that are financially dangerous or at least unsteady, subjecting the individual to relatively large surges of success and failure over the short run; among these are market and real estate speculators, commercial fishermen,* prospectors.

2. There are roles in industry that are physically dangerous: mining, high construction work,† test piloting, well-capping.

3. There are the 'hustling' jobs in business enterprise where salesmen and promoters work on a commission or contract-to-contract basis under conditions of close competition. Here income and prestige can be quickly gained and lost due to treacherous minor contingencies: a temporary let-up in effort, the weather, the passing mood of a buyer.

4. There are performing jobs filled by politicians, actors, and

---

that have only a probability of coming out, or, if certain, then only a probability of being satisfactory, the decision can be seen as a calculated risk, a practical gamble. (Characteristically, the payoff matrix equally handles a possible outcome whose probability is a product of nature, as when an invasion decision considers the probability of good or bad weather across the several possible landing points, or whose probabilistic features have been intentionally introduced by means of gambling equipment, as when one of the available alternatives involves dicing for a specified prize.) Resistance to this sort of formulation can be attributed to a disinclination to face up to all the choosing implied in one's act. Acceptance of this formulation involves a certain amount of consorting with the devil; chance taking is embraced but not fondled. Whatever the social and political consequence of this decision-theory perspective, a purely cultural result might be anticipated, namely, a tendency to perceive more and more of human activity as a practical gamble. One might parenthetically add that the Bomb might have a somewhat similar effect – the transformation of thoughts about future society into thoughts about the chances of there being a future society, these chances themselves varying from month to month.

* See F. Barth, 'Models of Social Organization', *Royal Anthropological Institute Occasional Paper, No. 23* (Glasgow: The University Press, 1966), p. 6.

† A recent description is G. Talese, *The Bridge* (New York: Harper & Row, 1965).

other live entertainers who, during each stage appearance, must work to win and hold an audience under conditions where many contingencies can spoil the show and endanger the showman's reputation. Here, again, any let-up in effort and any minor mishap can easily have serious consequences.

5. There are the soldier's calling* and the policeman's lot – stations in public life that fall outside the ordinary categories of work, and make the incumbent officially responsible for undergoing physical danger at the hands of persons who intend it. The fact that these callings stand outside civilian ranks seems to reinforce the notion of self-determination.

6. There is the criminal life, especially the lesser non-racketeering varieties, which yields considerable opportunity but continuously and freshly subjects the individual to gross contingencies – to physical danger, the risk of losing civil status, and wide fluctuations regarding each day's take.† 'Making it' on the street requires constant orientation to unpredictable opportunities and a readiness to make quick decisions concerning the expected value of proposed schemes – all of which subject the individual to great uncertainties. As already seen, getting to and getting away from the scene of a crime subjects the participants to the fateful play of what would ordinarily be minor incidents.

7. A further source of fatefulness is to be found in arenas, in professional spectator sports whose performers place money, reputation, and physical safety in jeopardy all at the same time: football, boxing, and bullfighting are examples. Stirling Moss's vocation is another:

. . . motor-racing on the highest level, in the fastest, most competitive company, *grand prix* driving is the most dangerous sport in the world. It is one of the riskiest of man's activities. Motor-racing kills men. In

---

* Which features, of course, an interesting dilemma: in battle a tradition of honour and risk-taking must be maintained, yet behind the lines the organization needs steady men in grey-flannel uniforms. See M. Janowitz, *The Professional Soldier* (London: Collier-Macmillan, 1964), pp. 35–6.

† A useful autobiographical portrait of the chance-taking continuously involved in the life of a slum hustler specializing in mugging may be found in H. Williamson, *Hustler!* (New York: Doubleday, 1965). See also C. Brown, *Manchild in the Promised Land* (New York: Macmillan, 1965), for the Harlem version.

one recent year the mortality rate was twenty-five percent, or one out of four. These are odds to be compared with those cited for fighter pilots and paratroopers.*

8. Finally, there are the recreational non-spectator sports that are full of risk: mountain climbing, big-game hunting, skin diving, parachuting, surfing, bob-sledding, spelunking.

ADAPTATIONS

Uneventful moments have been defined as moments that are not consequentially problematic. They tend to be dull and unexciting. (When anxiety is felt during such moments it is felt for eventful ones slated to come later.) Yet there are many good reasons to take comfort in this uneventfulness and seek it out, voluntarily forgoing practical gambles along with risk and opportunity – the opportunity if only because it is so often related to the risk. The question is one of security. In uneventful situations, courses of action can be managed reliably and goals progressively and predictably realized. By such self-management the individual allows others to build him into their own plans in an orderly and effective way. The less uncertain his life, the more society can make use of him. It is understandable then that the individual may make realistic efforts to minimize the eventfulness – the fatefulness – of his moments, and that he will be encouraged to do so. He engages in *copings*.

One basic technique is physical care. The individual handles himself so as to minimize the remote danger of accidental injury to his body. He does not tip his chair too far back or daydream while crossing a busy intersection.† In both the matter of exercising physical care and the need for doing so, idle pursuits make the same claims as obligated, serious ones. *Some* care must always be exerted. Taking care is a constant condition of being. Thus it is

* S. Moss (with K. Purdy), *All But My Life* (London: Kimber, 1963), p. 10.
† Much of this case, of course, is built into the environment by safety design. Chairs are constructed to limit the possibility of their breaking, stools of their tipping, etc. Even cars are coming to be designed to minimize possible injuries.

one of the central concerns that parents in all societies must impress upon their young,* the injunction being to 'take care' and not become unnecessarily involved in avoidable fatefulness.

Another means of controlling eventfulness, and one almost as much employed as physical care, is sometimes called providence; an incremental orientation to long-range goals expressed through acts that have a very small additive long-term consequence. The work of building up a savings account is an example; the acquisition of seniority at a workplace and working one's way up by the gradual acquisition of training are two others. The raising of a large family might also qualify. The important point here is that any one day's effort, involving as it does only a small increment, can be sacrificed with little threat to the whole. Here is the Calvinistic solution to life: once the individual divides his day's activities into ones that have no effect and others having a small contributive consequence, nothing can really go wrong.

Another standard means of protecting oneself against fatefulness is insurance in whatever form, as when householders invest in candles and spare fuses, motorists in spare tyres, and adults in medical plans. In this way the cost of possible trouble can be easily spread over the whole course of the individual's life, a 'converting of a larger contingent loss into a smaller fixed charge'.†

Systems of courtesy and etiquette can also be viewed as forms of insurance against undesired fatefulness, this time in connexion with the personal offence that one individual can inadvertently give to another. The safe management of face-to-face interaction is especially dependent on this means of control.

Note that the availability and approval of risk-reducing measures create a new contingency, a new basis for anxiety. When an untoward event occurs during a moment meant to be uneventful, and the event spills over the boundary of the moment and contaminates parts of the individual's life to come, he faces a double loss: the initial loss in question plus that of appearing to himself and others as having failed to exercise the kind of intelligent control, the kind of 'care', that allows reasonable persons to minimize danger and avoid remorse.

* Suggested by Edward Gross.
† Knight, *op. cit.*, p. 246.

These, then, are some of the means – largely avoidant – by which the individual realistically copes with situations of fatefulness. Another issue must now be considered, which is easy to confuse with this – defensive behaviour.

Anticipated fateful activity creates anxiety and excitement. This is implied in the notion that the utility of what is bet is likely to be quite different from the utility of betting it. Also, as suggested, the individual often feels remorse when something undesirable happens, the chance of which he had failed to reduce, and disappointment when something desirable does not, the occurrence of which he had failed to assure. Any practice that manages the affective response associated with fatefulness – affects such as anxiety, remorse, and disappointment – may be called a *defence*.*

When we shift consideration from the management of fatefulness to the management of an affective state associated with it, we are required to review again the phases of a play. For in fact there are situations in which objectively inconsequential phases of play are responded to with a sense that they are fateful. Our individual, about to open the letter containing examination results, may feel excited and anxious to the point of engaging in little rituals of propitiation and control before casting his eyes on the awful news. Or, when the nurse approaches him with information about the condition of his wife and gender of his child, he may feel that the moment is fateful; as he may when the hospital staff returns with news gleaned from a biopsy performed on him to see whether a growth is malignant or benign. But it should be plain that these moments are not really fateful, merely revelatory. In each case the individual's fate has been determined before he entered the news-acquiring situation; he is simply apprised of what is already in force, of something that, at this late date, he can do nothing about. Opening a letter or analysing a bioptic section

* The distinction between coping and defence is borrowed from D. Mechanic, *Students Under Stress* (London: Collier-Macmillan, 1962), p. 51. A somewhat similar distinction is employed by B. Anderson in 'Bereavement as a Subject of Cross-Cultural Inquiry: An American Sample', *Anthropology Quarterly*, XXXVIII (1965), 195: 'Stressor-directed behavior is oriented toward removing, resolving, or alleviating the impinging circumstances themselves; strain-directed behavior, toward the assuagement of the physical or psychological discomfort that is a product of these happenings.'

cannot generate or determine a condition, but only reveal what has already been generated.*

Just as disclosures can create the excitement and concern of fate being generated, so can settlements, that is, occasions when crucial matters known to have been determined in a particular way are finally executed. Thus, in modern times, a condemned man's last walk has not been fateful even though each step has brought him closer to death; his execution was merely dramatic, it was his trial that was fateful. In the eighteenth century, when many death sentences were passed and most of these commuted, the trial was not as fateful as the period following it. Very recently, of course, with the agitation against capital punishment, the post-trial period has again become appreciably fateful.

Now we can return to consider defences, if only in a passing manner, in order to bring a much discussed topic into relationship with the subject-matter of this paper.

The most obvious type of defence, perhaps, is the kind that has no objective effect on fate at all, as in the case of ritualistic superstitions. The behaviour said to be true of boxers will serve as an example:

Since most bouts are unpredictable, boxers usually have superstitions which serve to create confidence and emotional security among them. Sometimes the manager or trainer uses these superstitions to control the fighter. One fighter believed that, if he ate certain foods, he was sure to win, because these foods gave him strength. Others insist on wearing the same robe in which they won their first fight; one wore an Indian blanket when he entered the ring. Many have charm pieces or attribute added importance to entering the ring after the opponent. . . . Some insist that, if a woman watches them train, it is bad luck. One fighter, to show he was not superstitious, would walk under a ladder before every fight, until this became a magical rite itself. Consistent with this attitude, many intensify their religious attitudes and keep

* Of course, where the fate is not a matter of immediate life or death, mere apprisal of what has befallen can begin the work of adjusting to the damage, so that a *failure* to learn *now* about an eventual loss can itself be fateful. Here disclosure of fate cannot affect what is disclosed but can affect the timing of reconstitutive efforts. Similarly, if the quickness of the individual's response to the situation is of strategic significance in his competition with another party, then the *timing* of his learning about the outcome can be fateful, even though the disclosure of the outcome cannot influence that particular outcome itself.

Bibles in their lockers. One fighter kept a rosary in his glove. If he lost the rosary, he would spend the morning before the fight in church. Although this superstitious attitude may be imported from local or ethnic culture, it is intensified among the boxers themselves, whether they are white or Negro, preliminary fighters or champions.*

Gamblers exhibit similar, if less religious, superstitions.†

Clearly, any realistic practice aimed at avoiding or reducing risk – any coping – is likely to have the side effect of reducing anxiety and remorse, is likely, in short, to have defensive functions. A person who coolly resorts to a game theory matrix when faced with a vital decision is reducing a painful risk to a calculated one. His frame of mind brings peace of mind. Like a competent surgeon, he can feel he is doing all that anyone is capable of doing, and hence can await the result without anguish or recrimination. Similarly, a clear appreciation of the difference between the determinative phase of a play and the disclosure and settlement of the play can help the individual deal with the anxiety produced during the span of the activity; such discriminations can have defensive functions.

It is not surprising, then, that when a causal basis is not readily found for discounting the determinativeness of the current situation, it may be sought out; and where it can't be found, imagined. Thus, for example, we find that events determined locally may be interpreted as a consequence of prior determination. A version of this 'defensive determinism' is found in the belief in fate, predestination, and kismet – the notion that the major outcomes regarding oneself are already writ down, and one is helpless to improve or worsen one's chances. The soldier's maxim is an illustration: 'I won't get mine 'til my number's up so why worry.'‡

* K. Weinberg and A. Arond, 'The Occupational Culture of the Boxer', *American Journal of Sociology*, LXVIII (1952), 463–4.

† In modern society such practices tend to be employed only with appreciable ambivalence and are no doubt much on the decline. For the changing situation with respect to one traditionally superstitious group, commercial fishermen, see J. Tunstall, *The Fishermen* (London: MacGibbon & Kee, 1962), pp. 168–70.

‡ See W. Miller's discussion of fate in 'Lower Class Culture as a Generating Milieu of Gang Delinquency', *Journal of Social Issues*, XIV (1958), 11–12. The religious roots, of course, are to be found in John Calvin and ascetic Puritanism.

Just as causality can be sought outside the situation, so it can be sought in local forces that similarly serve to relieve one's sense of responsibility. A type of scapegoating is involved, pointing to the function of lodging causal efficacy within what is seen as the enduring and autonomous parts of the individual's personality, and thereby transforming a fateful event into something that is 'only to be expected'. Suffering an accident because of carelessness, the individual can say, 'That's just like me; I do it all the time.' About to take a crucial examination the individual can ease matters by telling himself that the exam will be fair, and so everything depends on how much work he has or has not long since done.

Further, belief in pure, blind luck can protect the individual from the remorse of knowing that something could have and should have been done to protect himself. Here is the opposite tack to defensive determinism – a kind of defensive indeterminism – but the consequences are much the same. 'It's nobody's fault', the individual says. 'It was just a question of bad luck'.*

Obviously, then, a traditional statement of coping and defence can be applied in connexion with fatefulness. But this neglects a wider fact about adaptation to chance-taking. When we look closely at the adaptation to life made by persons whose situation is constantly fateful, say that of professional gamblers or front-line soldiers, we find that aliveness to the consequences involved comes to be blunted in a special way. The world that is gambled is, after all, only a world, and the chance-taker can learn to let go of it. He can adjust himself to the ups and downs in his welfare by discounting his prior relation to the world and accepting a chancy relation to what others feel assured of having. Perspectives seem to be inherently normalizing: once conditions are fully faced, a life can be built out of them, and by reading from the bottom up, it will be the rises not the falls that are seen as temporary.

---

* An example is cited in Cohen, *op. cit.*, p. 147: 'The possibility of a falling back on "luck" may also be a great comfort in other circumstances. In 1962, British universities rejected some 20,000 applicants for entry. Many of them reconciled this rejection with their pride by saying that the offer of a university place depends as much on luck as on merit. The rejects are described as "submitting applications, like a gambler putting coins into a fruit-machine, sure that the jackpot must come up at last".'

ACTION

Although fatefulness of all kinds can be handled both by coping and by defence, it cannot be avoided completely. More important, there are, as suggested, some activities whose fatefulness is appreciable indeed if one combines the amount chanced, the rate of chance-taking, and the problematicalness of the outcome. It is here, of course, that the individual is likely to perceive the situation as his taking of a practical gamble – the wilful undertaking of serious chances.

Given the claims of wider obligation that commit some individuals to what they can perceive as chancy undertakings, virtue will sometimes be made of necessity. This is another defensive adjustment to fatefulness. Those with fateful duties sometimes hold themselves to be self-respecting men who aren't afraid to put themselves on the line. At each encounter (they claim) they are ready to place their welfare and their reputation in jeopardy, transforming encounters into confrontations. They have a more or less secret contempt for those with safe and sure jobs who need never face real tests of themselves. They claim they are not only willing to remain in jobs full of opportunity and risk, but have deliberately sought out this environment, declining to accept safe alternatives, being able, willing, and even inclined to live in challenge.*

Talented burglars and pickpockets, whose skill must be exercised under pressure, look down, it is said, on the petty sneak thief, since the only art he need have for his calling is a certain low cunning.† Criminals may similarly disesteem fences as being

* Ernest Hemingway, *Death in the Afternoon* (New York: Scribners, 1932; London: Jonathan Cape), p. 101, suggests that men of this stamp, being disinclined to calculate too closely, have their own disease: 'Syphilis was the disease of the crusaders in the middle ages. It was supposed to be brought to Europe by them, and it is a disease of all people who lead lives in which disregard of consequences dominates. It is an industrial accident, to be expected by all those who lead irregular sexual lives and from their habits of mind would rather take chances than use prophylactics, and it is a to-be-expected end, or rather phase, of the life of all fornicators who continue their careers far enough.' Penicillin has undermined this route to manliness.

† C. Shaw, 'Juvenile Delinquency – A Group Tradition', *Bulletin of the State University of Iowa*, No. 23, N.S. No. 700 (1933), p. 10, cited in R. Cloward and L. Ohlin, *Delinquency and Opportunity* (London: Routledge & Kegan Paul, 1961), p. 170.

'thieves without nerve'.* So, too, Nevada casino dealers may come on shift knowing that it is they who must face the hard intent of players to win, and coolly stand in its way, consistently blocking skill, luck, and cheating, or lose the precarious reputation they have with management. Having to face these contingencies every day, they feel set apart from the casino employees who are not on the firing line. (In some casinos there are special dealers who are brought into a game to help nature correct the costly runs of good luck occasionally experienced by players, or to remove the uncertainty a pit boss can feel when a big bettor begins to play seriously. These dealers practise arts requiring delicacy, speed, and concentration, and the job can easily be visibly muffed. Morever, the player at this time is likely to be heavily committed and searching openly and even belligerently in a small field for just the evidence that is there. Skilled card and dice 'mechanics' understandably develop contempt not only for *non*-dealers but also for *mere* dealers.)† The small-scale fishermen I knew on the Shetland Islands had something of the same feeling; during each of the five or six runs of a day's fishing they subjected themselves to a serious gamble because of the extreme variability of the catch.‡ Peering into the net as the winch brought the bag and its fish into view was a thrill, known by those who experienced it to be something their fellow islanders would not be men enough to want to stomach regularly. Interestingly, Sir Edmund Hillary, who came to practise a truly chancy calling, provides us with the following view of the work he and his father lived by, namely, beekeeping:

It was a good life – a life of open air and sun and hard physical work. And in its way it was a life of uncertainty and adventure; a constant fight against the vagaries of the weather and a mad rush when all our 1,600 hives decided to swarm at once. We never knew what our crop

* S. Black, 'Burglary', Part Two, *The New Yorker*, 14 December 1963, p. 117.

† With some reverence, dealers cite as a reference model the blackjack mechanics in New York who worked next door to the hang-out of the Murder Incorporated mob, and daily 'dealt down' to customers likely to be demonstrably intolerant of dealers caught cheating them. Surely those who could survive such work must have known themselves to be men of considerable poise, a match in that department for anyone they could imagine.

‡ Field Study, 1949–50.

would be until the last pound of honey had been taken off the hives. But all through the exciting months of the honey flow the dream of a bumper crop would drive us on through long hard hours of labour. I think we were incurable optimists. And during the winter I often tramped around our lovely bush-clad hills and learned a little about self-reliance and felt the first faint stirrings of interest in the unknown.*

When we meet these stands we can suspect that the best is being made of a bad thing – it is more a question of rationalizations than of realistic accountings. (It is as if the illusion of self-determinancy were a payment society gives to individuals in exchange for their willingness to perform jobs that expose them to risk.) After all, even with chancy occupational roles, choice occurs chiefly at the moment the role itself is first accepted and safer ones forgone; once the individual has committed himself to a particular niche, his having to face what occurs there is more likely to express steady constraints than daily re-decidings. Here the individual cannot choose to withdraw from chance-taking without serious consequence for his occupational status.†

However, there are fateful activities that *are* socially defined as ones an individual is under no obligation to continue to pursue once he has started to do so. No extraneous factors compel him to face fate in the first place; no extraneous ends provide expediential reasons for his continued participation. His activity is defined as an end itself, sought out, embraced, and utterly his own. His record during performance can be claimed as the reason for participation, hence an unqualified, direct expression of his true make-up and a just basis for reputation.

By the term *action* I mean activities that are consequential, problematic, and undertaken for what is felt to be their own sake. The degree of action – its seriousness or realness – depends on how fully these properties are accentuated and is subject to the same ambiguities regarding measurement as those already described

* Edmund Hillary, *High Adventure* (New York: Dutton, 1955), p. 14.

† Dean MacCannell has suggested that there are jobs that holders gamble with, as when a night watchman takes time off to go to a movie during time on and enjoys the gamble as much as the movie. However, these jobs are characteristically 'mere' ones, taken up and left rapidly by persons not specifically qualified for them and not qualified for anything better. When these jobs are subjected to only spot supervision, gambling with the job seems to occur.

in the case of chanciness. Action seems most pronounced when the four phases of the play – squaring off, determination, disclosure, and settlement – occur over a period of time brief enough to be contained within a continuous stretch of attention and experience. It is here that the individual releases himself to the passing moment, wagering his future estate on what transpires precariously in the seconds to come. At such moments a special affective state is likely to be aroused, emerging transformed into excitement.

Action's location can easily and quickly shift, as any floating crap game attests; indeed, should a knife fight develop next to a crap table, the action may shift in location even while it is shifting in kind, and yet participants will apply the same word, as if the action in a situation is by definition the most serious action in that situation at the moment, regardless of its content.* In asking the famous question, 'Where's the action?' an individual may be more concerned with the intensity of the action he finds than its kind.

Whoever participates in action does so in two quite distinct capacities: as someone who hazards or chances something valuable, and as someone who must perform whatever activities are called for. In the latter capacity the individual must ordinarily stand alone,† placing in hazard his reputation for competence in play.‡ But in the former he can easily share his gamble with others or even let them 'take' all of it. Action, then, is usually something one can obtain 'a piece' of; the performer of the action is typically a single individual, but the party he represents can contain a

---

* Thus, Ned Polsky in 'The Hustler', *Social Problems*, XII (1964), 5–6, suggests that a pool game between skilled players for a small bet will take second place to one between lesser players who are gaming for higher stakes.

† The capacity to perform tends to be imputed to the individual, but there are situations, as in gang molestations, where this capacity clearly derives from the visible backing he can readily call on. Further, there are some situations whose action arises because a set of actors have committed themselves to closely co-ordinated acts – as in some current robberies. The sheer working out of the interdependencies in the face of various contingencies becomes a source of action.

‡ It is quite possible for an individual to be more concerned about his reputation as a performer than for the objective value of the pot at stake. For example, casino dealers, especially in the 'break-in' phase, can find it more difficult to manage dealing to a big bet during the shift than to manage the placing of the same bet as a customer after work.

quickly shifting roster of jointly committed members. For analysis, however, it is convenient to focus on the case where the performer takes all his own action and none of anyone else's.

It is, of course, in the gambling world that the term action had its slang beginning, and gambling is the prototype of action. In the casinos of Nevada, the following usages can be found: 'dollar action' refers to light bettors and their effect on the day's take; and 'good (or real or big) action' refers to heavier takes. Dealers who get flustered by heavy bettors are said to be unable 'to deal to the action', while cool dealers are said to be 'able to handle the action'. Naturally, new dealers are 'pulled out of the action', and when bets get heavy and multitudinous at a crap table, the better of the base men may be 'put on the action side'. Casinos that try to avoid high-limit games are said 'not to want the action', while houses that can face heavy bettors without becoming nervous are said 'to be able to take the action'. A 'high roller' known to 'drop' a lot of money may find himself warmly welcomed at a casino because 'we like his action'. Pit bosses, ever concerned to show that they are somehow earning their keep, will, from a tactful distance, 'keep their eye on the action'. Someone known to cheat, or to be able to 'count cards' in 21, may be asked to leave the casino permanently with the statement, 'We don't want your action'. Players who are indecisive 'hold up the action', and one who fails to cover all of what is considered a good bet may cause another player to ask if he can 'take the rest of the action'. Deserving casino managers may be rewarded by being 'given a piece of the action', that is, a share of ownership ('points'). In casinos with only one cluster of tables (one 'pit') there is likely to be one table that because of location or special maximum is called the 'action table', just as in large casinos there will be a high minimum 'action pit'.*

Although action is independent of type and concerned with amount, amount itself cannot be taken as a simple product of the size of each bet and the number of players betting. This is most evident in craps. A table whose sole player is making hundred-dollar bets can be seen as having more action than another table

---

* Similarly Polsky, *op. cit.*, p. 5, reports that certain pool halls are nationally identified as 'action rooms', and within one hall there will be one or two tables informally reserved for the action.

whose twenty players are making five- and ten-dollar bets. A table 'jam up' with players, all of whom are making many different kinds of bets, can be seen as having more action than another table where ten players are betting a higher aggregate by means of simple line and field bets. Correspondingly, to say that a dealer can 'handle the action' may mean, either, that he can deal coolly to a very large bettor, or that he can deal accurately and rapidly when a large number of calculations and payoffs must be made quickly.

Another aspect of the gambler's use of the term action arises from the fact that action and the chance-taking it involves may constitute the source of the gambler's daily livelihood. Thus, when he asks where the action is he is not merely seeking situations of action, but also situations in which he can practise his trade. Something similar is found in the thief's and the prostitute's conception of where the action is – namely, where the risks to earn one's living by are currently and amply available.* Here, compressed pridefully into one word, is a claim to a very special relationship to the work world.

No doubt it was gamblers who first applied their term to non-gambling situations, thus initiating a diffusion of usage that non-gamblers have recently extended still further. Yet almost always the use seems apt. Underlying the apparent diversity in content is a single analytical property that can be sensed with sureness by persons who might be unable to define closely what it is they sense.

This diffusion of use is nowhere better seen than in the current touting of action in our mass media. In fact, contributors to the media have recently helped to clarify the inner meaning of the term and to show its applicability to new ranges of situation, giving a special accent to current popular culture. Thus a newspaper advertisement for 'Teenage Day' at Whiskey à Go Go (no liquor, live music), declares:

Dance to the Big Beat music of the original Whiskey à Go Go – WHISKEY A GO GO WHERE THE ACTION IS!†

* Suggested by Howard Becker, *The Dictionary of American Underworld Lingo*, ed. H. Goldin, F. O'Leary, and M. Lipsius (New York: Twayne Publishers, 1950), defines action: Criminal activity. 'Shape up (be present) tonight, Joe, there's action – a Brooklyn score (robbery).'

† *San Francisco Chronicle*, 7 August 1965.

K

Herb Caen, reporting on East Bay doings, states that:

M. Larry Lawrence, Pres. of Hotel del Coronado, and Stockbroker Al Schwabacher Jr. huddled at the P'Alto Cabana the other day, which is why the rumor's around that Al might buy a piece of the Coronado's historic action.*

Similarly, Caen writes:

You know where the action is these nights? In Oakland, that's where. Or so it seemed early yesterday, in a go-go spot at Jack London Square, where Oakland Mayor John Houlihan and Millionaire Bernie Murray got into a pushing and shoving contest that ended with Hizzoner flat on his honor in the middle of the dance floor – as the dancers Frugged around and over his reclining figure. . . .†

The *Las Vegas Sun*, underneath a picture of the contest, reports:

BRIDGE ACTION – Women spectators closely watch bridge experts in competition at Riviera Hotel.‡

During another tournament, a column heading in the *Sun* reads:

Gin Action Goes Into 2nd Round.§

And the same paper's columnist reports:

Shirley Jones' sexy dance from the 'Elmer Gantry' movie at the Flamingo these nights is the most explosive bit of action since Juliet Prouse . . .||

Newsweek titles a cover story:

SINATRA: Where the Action Is.¶

A colour-page advertisement in *Look*:

7-UP . . . WHERE THERE'S ACTION! Seven-up is a real natural for the

* *Ibid.*, 22 July 1965.
† *Ibid.*, 24 September 1965.
‡ *Las Vegas Sun*, 10 February 1965.
§ *Ibid.*, 4 December 1965.
|| *Ibid.*, 20 April 1965.
¶ *Newsweek*, 6 September 1965.

action crowd! It's got the sparkle that swings . . . and the quick-quenching action to make thirst quit. Look for it. 7-UP . . . where there's action!*

And an advertisement in *California Living*, showing a girl applying lipstick, and suggesting that 'A girl's mouth is always moving', titles the half-page:

Where the Beauty Action Is†

A full-page cover picture in the same magazine features two models in a section of a department store organized as a teenage hang-out, above a title saying:

Check the Fashion Action.‡

And a feature article on the San Francisco Police Department sale of unclaimed articles recovered from burglaries reports that the auctioneer 'keeps the pace lively for hundreds of bidding buyers':

If there is no honor among thieves, neither is there a common denominator of thievery. Check the action at the police auction to see why.§

Financial columnists, of course, also have recourse to the term:

If it was panic selling that gripped the market in October, 1929, and May, 1962, then today we're surely in the throes of panic buying. Least that's how Shearson, Hammill & Co. view the current free-for-all.
'Apparently the major motivation at the moment is fear of missing or having missed a major buying opportunity,' the brokerage firm observes.
'To a greater extent every day, stock buyers – we won't use the term "investors" – are going where the action is, and it is not hard to find.'

---

* *Look*, 24 August 1965.
† *California Living*, 7 November 1965. Action figures in other unexpected parts of the body too. My liquor merchant, pushing a cheap Dutch imported beer, opens a trial bottle for me, puts the bottle near my face and says:'Taste that action'.
‡ *Ibid.*, 13 February 1966.
§ *San Francisco Sunday Examiner and Chronicle, California Living*, 17 April 1966.

For anyone desiring a piece of the action, Shearson has this advice: . . .*

Heavy selling developed during the first hour and stock tickers began to lag behind the action.†

Those who report on government contracting can employ the term, evoking an image of occasions when decisions, allocations, and very nice opportunities are in the very process of determination:

Powerful lobbyist Tom Gray's investment firm got a $40,000 cut of the action when the Board of Supervisors approved a $2 million extension of the Fifth and Mission Garage, The Chronicle learned yesterday.‡

These journalistic accents have significance. The cult of cars provides a case in point. One support for this world is found in professional racing and the spectator sport organized around it. Another support is found in advertising, two examples of which I cite from a recent colour brochure printed by Buick:

Think of a car that's loaded with action, classic in line, agile as a cat, and luxurious beyond belief. The car you're thinking about is the Riviera by Buick. Here's a unique blend of blazing performance (325 h.p.) and solid roadability that sets the Riviera apart from all other cars. In other words, it's a car that might be equally at home on the track as on the road.

THE ACCENT'S ON ACTION! A car doesn't really come alive until you turn the key to start the engine. This is the greatest moment in owning a Buick. With any one of Buick's six engines and four transmissions you've bought yourself a piece of action that just won't quit.

These two sources of publicity contribute support for the manufacture, sale and use of sports cars and fast sedans, and this in turn provides official equipment for transforming the highways into scenes of action, places where skill, impatience, and costly

---

* Lloyd Watson in *San Francisco Chronicle*, 23 April 1966.
† *Boston Traveler*, 22 August 1966.
‡ *San Francisco Chronicle*, 4 August 1966, front page, under the lead 'A $40,000 Piece of The Action'.

equipment can be displayed under seriously chancy conditions.*
In this essay action will be considered chiefly in the context of
American society. Although every society no doubt has scenes of
action, it is our own society that has found a word for it. Interestingly enough, we have become alive to action at a time when –
compared to other societies – we have sharply curtailed in civilian
life the occurrence of fatefulness of the serious, heroic, and dutiful
kind.

A final word about the spread of words. In casino gambling
when a player makes a large bet and loses it he sometimes speaks
of what he did as 'blowing it'. Thus, to engage in action unsuc-
cessfully is to 'blow it'. The implication is that a desirable stake
(in this case monetary) that had been possessed has now been lost,
and that neither possession of the stake nor its loss was particularly
justified or legitimate. Blowing a big bet reflects badly on oneself,
but not so badly that one can't fairly easily accuse oneself of
having done so. It is this complex that has come to be general-
ized.

Casino personnel 'breaking in' on a job feel there is much
profit if they 'make it' but no practical way of ensuring that they
will. During this difficult phase there will be many minor infractions of rules, which can serve as sufficient grounds for being
fired: coming on shift a few minutes late; declining an undignified
task; mishandling chips; being irreverent concerning a house loss;
expressing impatience with one's rate of progress, and so forth.

* Driving often becomes a form of action, and the relation of everyday
driving practices to the ideally dangerous world of track racing and the ideal-
pushing world of car advertising is an important social topic, perhaps
sufficiently appreciated only by those who have a professional interest in
decreasing the accident rates. See, for example, Mervyn Jones's article, 'Who
Wants Safe Driving', in the *Observer*, 16 August 1964, p. 17; Cohen, *op. cit.*,
Ch. 5, 'Gambling with Life on the Road'; and J. Roberts, W. Thompson and
B. Sutton-Smith, 'Expressive Self-Testing in Driving', *Human Organization*,
25, 1 (1966), 54–63.
  Driving so as to 'make time' saves a remarkably small amount of time
but does generate a current of underlying action; often it seems that time
is being saved so that risk can be experienced. Some persons enjoy air travel
for the same reason. They time their departure for the airport so as to minimize
wait when they get there, and incidentally ensure some danger of missing
the flight, and once on the plane they welcome for the duration of the flight
a sense of slight danger to life.

Once skill and reputation have been acquired, tenure is only somewhat more secure: runs of ill luck; ill-founded suspicion of theft; change in owner-sponsorship; all can provide grounds for sudden dismissal.

Loss of a job due to what can, in fact, be seen as a meaningless lapse is also 'blowing it'. In contrast to the middle-class perspective that tends to define occupational position as something only deservedly acquired and deservedly lost, occupational situation for the casino worker tends to oscillate very rapidly between 'having it made', and 'blowing it', neither of which state is seen as particularly warranted. This perspective has extended to other areas of life, and a dealer may speak of having blown his marriage or his chance at a college education.

The logic of this racy attitude to the fundamentals of life, which implies a defence in depth to living with action, can be understood in reference to social organization in Nevada: the relative ease of divorce and marriage; the presence of a very large number of persons who have failed occupationally or maritally; a frontier tradition of asking no questions about a person's history or current livelihood; the clear possibility of getting an equivalent job across the street after being fired; the high visibility of a large number of casino employees known to have worked recently in better jobs in other casinos; the fact that sporadic bouts of big play mean sporadic realization of the ideal experience of a culture, such that however long and lean the days between bouts, this use of one's money may be the best that Nevada can offer. In any case, action is not the only term that appears to have spread outward from the gaming tables. A family of terms seems to be involved, and the entire family seems to be migrating.*

* Along with action and blowing it, we must count the phrase 'having it made', this being a source of income, whether deserved or undeserved, which allows a life of little work and considerable spending, and one sense of the phrase 'to have something going for oneself', namely, an edge of some kind, as when a casino employee says that he never plays 21 unless he's got something going for him with the dealer – a condition of play, incidentally, that is very hard to stop from developing. I will not consider here a term used by casino employees in many contexts: the term, 'to hustle'. This is an adopted member of the casino's family of terms, having originated in an older business.

WHERE THE ACTION IS

I have argued that action is to be found wherever the individual knowingly takes consequential chances perceived as avoidable. Ordinarily, action will not be found during the week-day work routine at home or on the job. For here chance-takings tend to be organized out, and such as remain are not obviously voluntary. Where, then, is action routinely to be found? Let me summarize the suggestions already made in passing.

First, contenders find action in commercialized competitive sport. Perhaps because this activity is staged for an audience and watched for fun, it is felt that no fully serious reason could exist for engaging in the activity itself. Also, the fact that amateurs perform these spectacular activities on their own, privately and without pay, as recreation, reinforces the notion that the professionals are engaged in a self-determined free-will calling. This is the case even though it is apparent that professional and commercial interests may be staked in a business-like way on the outcome of the spectacle. Although a sports car racer may make a living at the wheel, and the decision of a company to continue or discontinue a car model may hinge on a race outcome,* it is still felt that drivers could take other types of jobs or at least sit out the current race, and that this sort of chance-taking is somehow voluntary.

The next place of action to consider is non-spectator† risky sports. No payment is received for this effort; no publicly relevant identity is consolidated by it; and it incurs no obligations in the serious world of work. In the absence of the usual pressures to

* For example, the Corvette participation in the 1956 Sebring race, as described by the driver John Fitch (with C. Barnard) 'The Day That Corvette Improved the Breed', pp. 271–86 in C. Beaumont and W. Nolan, *Omnibus of Speed* (New York: Putnam, 1958): 'I knew that failure at Sebring would probably mean the end of Chevrolet's interest in racing sports cars' (p. 286).

† It is characteristic that risky recreational sports are 'worth watching', that they will often be watched, and that the performer must accept this watching. He should be able to perform while being watched; yet he should not perform just in order to be watched and should perform in spite of having no watchers. No matter how big a crowd a sportsman gets, nor how much he is enthralled by their enthralment, their role is unratified; they can't demand that he schedule his performance or complete it once begun. They have a right to have their watching overlooked by him, but a duty to accept his overlooking them.

engage in an activity, it is presumably easy to assume that self-determination is involved and that the chances incurred are brought on solely because of the challenge that results. Interestingly, some of these vigorous sports are dominated by solid young-minded citizens who can afford the time, travel, and equipment. These persons seem to get the best of both worlds, enjoying the honour of chance-taking without greatly threatening their routinized week-day involvements.

Next to consider are the more commercialized places of action – places, conveniently located, where equipment and the field for its use can be rented and a slight degree of action laid on. Bowling alleys, pool halls, amusement parks, and arcade streets provide arrangements where the cost of the play and the value of the prize generate a mildly fateful context for displaying competence. Public betting at race tracks and in casinos permits the gambler to demonstrate a variety of personal attributes, although at considerable cost. The 'vertigo' rides at fairs and amusement parks nakedly resolve our dilemma concerning action by providing danger that is guaranteed to be really not dangerous – what Michael Balint has nicely described as the safe excitement of thrills:

> In all amusements and pleasures of this kind three characteristic attitudes are observable: (*a*) some amount of conscious fear, or at least an awareness of real external danger; (*b*) a voluntary and intentional exposing of oneself to this external danger and to the fear aroused by it; (*c*) while having the more or less confident hope that the fear can be tolerated and mastered, the danger will pass, and, that one will be able to return unharmed to safety. This mixture of fear, pleasure, and confident hope in face of external danger is what constitutes the fundamental element of all *thrills*.*

* M. Balint, *Thrills and Regressions* (London: The Hogarth Press and the Institute of Psycho-Analysis, 1959), p. 23. Balint goes on to make this interesting comment (pp. 23–4): 'Let us briefly examine in what way other thrills resemble those offered in funfairs. Some are connected with *high speed*, as in all kinds of racing, horse-riding and jumping, motor racing, skating, skiing, tobogganing, sailing, flying, etc. Others are connected with *exposed situations*, like various forms of jumping and diving, rock-climbing, gliding, taming wild animals, travelling into unknown lands, etc. Lastly, there is a group of thrills which are connected with *unfamiliar* or even *completely new forms of satisfaction*, either in the form of a new object or of an unfamiliar method of pleasure. The obvious new object is a virgin, and it is amazing

There is a final type of commercialized action involving direct participation, which I will call 'fancy milling'.* Adults in our society can obtain a taste of social mobility by consuming valued products, by enjoying costly and modish entertainment, by spending time in luxurious settings, and by mingling with prestigeful persons – all the more if this occurs at the same time and in the presence of many witnesses. This is the action of consumption. Further, mere presence in a large, tightly packed gathering of revelling persons can bring not only the excitement that crowds generate, but also the uncertainty of not quite knowing what might happen next, the possibility of flirtations, which can themselves lead to relationship formation, and the lively experience of being an elbow away from someone who does manage to find real action in the crowd.

When these various elements of fancy milling are combined, and the individual views the prestige and the brevity of participation against the cost of getting to the scene and the rate of expenditure necessitated during each moment of participation, a kind of diffuse action – or rather a flavour of action – results, however limited the fatefulness.† The individual brings into himself the role of performer and the role of spectator; he is the one who engages in the action, yet he is the one who is unlikely to be permanently affected by it.

Here hotel casinos provide an extreme example. Not only are money gambles made available, this type of action is overlaid with the consumption kind. A brief penetration into high living is laid

---

how many thrills claim this adjective. One speaks of virgin land, a virgin peak, or a virginal route to a peak, virgin realms of speed, and so on. On the whole, any new sexual partner is a thrill, especially if he or she belongs to another race, colour or creed. The new forms of pleasure include among others: new food, new clothes, new customs, up to new forms of "perverse" sexual activities. In all these phenomena we find the same three fundamental factors described above: the objective external danger giving rise to fear, the voluntary and intentional exposure of oneself to it, and the confident hope that all will turn out well in the end.'

* The necessity of considering this mode of action was recommended by Howard Becker.

† Services in such places *must* be priced high if this kind of action is to be facilitated. Proprietors accommodate, but for other reasons.

on. Attendant-parked limousines are cluttered at the entrance. Beyond the entrance, the setting is luxurious. Liquor is served at the tables, often at no cost to the consumer. A quality buffet may be provided, allowing for discriminative gorging. A gratuity system is encouraged that elevates its users and provides scantily clad waitresses, selected for their looks, to be somewhat accessible. A 'pit' operated signal system enables these girls to deliver drinks, cigarettes, and aspirin anywhere on the premises upon request. Keno 'runners' and change girls are similarly organized to be at beck and call. Table contact is facilitated with the nationally known and with big spenders. Proximity to what some might consider the gangster element is also provided. Easy access to nationally famous entertainment is assured, and even some physical closeness to the entertainers themselves. The lounge bar is 'dressed' with chorus girls clothed in their off-stage costumes. Female customers feel they can experiment with sports high-fashion, claiming an age and style they might be too modest to try out at home. In brief, the opportunity for ephemeral ennoblement abounds. However, should the consumer want to sit down during this ennoblement, he will very likely have to sit at a gaming table. There is a rich ambience, then, but each minute of it is likely to cost the risking of considerable money.

Other public service establishments, too, are coming increasingly to overlay their services with indulgence choices heretofore considered irrelevant. Thus, our cross-country jets have added pretty girls, goodish food, movies, and free liquor.* Filling stations can

---

* In a feature article on 'The "Secrets" of Air Hostesses' (*San Francisco Chronicle*, 4 April 1966), under the heading 'Those Cupcakes in the Sky', we read: 'What we want in our hostesses is understated sexiness,' says Nancy Marchand, a statuesque blonde in charge of PSA girls. 'In choosing a hostess, we play particular attention to her figure.'

Passengers, said Lawrence [the President of Braniff, and a current leader in airline merchandising] are entitled to more than a safe, comfortable journey. They are entitled to a little fun.

Lawrence's definition of fun aloft included painting Braniff's fleet of jet-liners a variety of Easter-egg colours and wildly redecorating the aircraft interiors, ticket offices and waiting-rooms. But he reserved the company's hostesses for the most fun of all. He hired famed Italian dress designer Milio Pucci, the inventor of stretch pants, to create a hostess costume with 'flair, excitement and surprise'.

now provide not only gas but a moment's company with a 'bumper bunny'. And, of course, there is the current 'topless' trend, which brings, along with food, waitresses who are assuredly attractive.*

Certain segments of each community seem more responsive than others to the attraction of this kind of action. It is worth noting that individuals respond not as members of a local community but as like-minded, otherwise unrelated members of the great society. Strangers in town can ask the local cabby where the action is and probably gain entry when they get there. A freemasonry of individuals who would otherwise be strangers is involved, a temporary coalition against the society of the respectable in which an action seeker is likely to have friends and relations. The traditional mechanisms of acquaintanceship and personal invitation are not needed to restrict participation; the risks of participation serve instead.

Although it is possible and desirable to look for where the action is by broadly examining social organization, a much more specific effort concerns me here. I want to consider the actual social arrangements through which action is made available.

The social world is such that any individual who is strongly oriented to action, as some gamblers are, can perceive the potentialities for chance in situations others would see as devoid of eventfulness; the situation can even be structured so that these possibilities are made manifest.† Chance is not merely sought out but carved out. It should be added that the form of chance likely to be found here is appreciable risk to bodily welfare in exchange

* No clearer case of the indulgence overlay is to be found, I think, than The Harry's Shoeshine Palace, San Francisco (as reported in the *San Francisco Chronicle*, 26 July 1966), which provides topless shoeshines for $2.00 and an ID card. De Sade would have been impressed by this merchandising of his principles.

† Suggested by Sheldon L. Messinger. The garden variety, as popularized by Damon Runyon, is the small-time Broadway gambler who perceptually reconstitutes the immediate environment into a continuous series of soon-to-be-determined bettable outcomes on which propositions can be offered. The culture hero here is John W. 'Bet-a-Million' Gates, the barbed-wire king, who, in 1897 on a train between Chicago and Pittsburgh, apparently won $22,000 by betting on raindrop races, a windowpane serving as a course. (See H. Asbury, *Sucker's Progress* [New York: Dodd Mead, 1938], p. 446.)

for the opportunity of trifling gain. Some version of 'Russian roulette' is the one scene of fatefulness that almost everyone is in a position to construct, and a scene that nicely illustrates chance-taking as an end in itself. Interestingly, there is currently available through LSD and other drugs a means of voluntarily chancing psychic welfare in order to pass beyond ordinary consciousness. The individual here uses his own mind as the equipment necessary for action.* Persons who gesture with suicide use their bodies in a gamble, but here, as with drugs, chance-taking as such does not seem to be the main purpose of the undertaking.† The current widespread interest in the deleterious effects of smoking and of cholesterol provide a milder example of the same possibility; to various flavours can be added the extra flavour of not-giving-a-damn.‡

In the cases so far considered, chance lies in the attitude of the individual himself – his creative capacity to redefine the world around him into its decisional potentialities. Turn now to the action possibilities that place greater demands upon the environment and are more directly facilitated by organization.

A simple beginning can be found in casino gambling, since these are places, first of all, whose physical and social organization is designed to facilitate the occurrence of action. The efficiency of these arrangements must be understood and appreciated. A player need only stride into a casino (off-street casinos are not likely to require even the opening of a door) and put money on a squaring-off or commitment area. If the dealer is not already in play, he will immediately initiate it, a momentary pause that is itself avoided in many casinos by employing skills to keep dead games going. In a matter of seconds, the player can plug himself into quite meaningful activity; sockets are available.

Further, casino plays have a remarkably short span, permitting a very high rate of play. A slots play takes only four or five seconds. A hand at 21 may take as little time as twenty seconds, by virtue of card management practices that dealers are uniformly trained

* Suggested by Nancy Achilles.
† The various kinds of gambles with life indulged by the suicidally inclined are considered in N. Farberow and E. Schneidman, *The Cry for Help* (Maidenhead: McGraw-Hill, 1961), esp. pp. 132–3.
‡ Suggested by Dean MacConnell.

to employ.* In all casino games it is possible, also, to engage in more than one play at a time, and, in the case of slots and craps, to phase the multiple betting so that a commitment is made and determination begun in regard to one bet while another is in the later phases of the determination process. One game, keno, available in most casinos, is specifically organized so that in almost all regions of the casino bets can be made and determination followed. Keno display boards are posted at various places and simultaneously scored electrically. Keno runners collect bets and deliver payoffs everywhere in the casino except the bathrooms. The phasing of play coincides with no other activities in the casino. Thus, whatever an individual is doing, and wherever he is doing it, he can overlay his activity with keno play and always have at least a keno number 'going for him'.†

A player can engage in all manner of calculation and divination regarding how to manage his bet, whether this involves copings, defences, or both. But he also may, if he wants, merely push an uncounted pile of money or chips in the general direction of the commitment area and the dealer will scrupulously do the rest. (I have seen a dealer assist a blind man to play, and one too arthritic to handle his own cards.) A great range of player effort is thus managed neatly by the same organization of play. This means that a player can start out very attentively watching all that happens and making elaborate calculations, find himself getting weary beyond measure after eight or nine hours of play, or drunk to the point where attendants must prop him up to prevent his falling out of his chair, and yet by merely making a few relevant gestures remain active in his gambling capacity. The organization of play in casinos is designed to service with action not only persons of widely different social status, but also those in widely differing physiological states.

---

* Polsky, *op. cit.*, p. 6, suggests that in 'action rooms' billiard games are selected and even modified in order to increase the action rate, which might otherwise be too low. However, five-minute plays still seem to be the shortest time except when individual shots are bet on.

† In American society at large, horse-racing, 'the numbers', and the stock market provide means by which an individual can have one or two things 'going for him' every day. Keno has a somewhat similar overlay character, but each play takes only a few minutes.

Beyond these various organizational arrangements, there is the central fact that casinos, within very broad limits, routinely cover bets of any size. The player can therefore put his capital in jeopardy regardless of its size. He is assured of the opportunity of facing the excitement of a little more financial risk and opportunity than most persons of his means would be at ease with. Casinos concretely embody arrangements for allowing the individual to press himself to the margin of his own tolerance for loss or gain, thereby ensuring a real and close test, at least in his own eyes.

Some specific arrangements outside of casinos for efficiently generating opportunities for action might be mentioned. A good example can be found in the conventions associated with bullfighting. Here, the style and grace of movement and posture, the knowledge of the work, and the domination of the bull, three central qualities exhibited in bullfighting, are scored according to the danger to self that is voluntarily introduced by oneself during the movements. The extreme limits to safety must therefore be pressed:

> In modern bullfighting it is not enough that the bull be simply dominated by the muleta so that he may be killed by the sword. The matador must perform a series of classic passes before he kills if the bull is still able to charge. In these passes the bull must pass the body of the matador within hooking range of the horn. The closer the bull passes the man at the man's invitation and direction the greater the thrill the spectator receives.*

> Bullfighting is the only art in which the artist is in danger of death and in which the degree of brilliance in the performance is left to the fighter's honour. In Spain honour is a very real thing. Called pundonor, it means honour, probity, courage, self-respect and pride in one word.†

A somewhat similar set of arrangements can be found as the basis of action in car racing. Typically, difference in mere capacity for speed of cars similarly classed is not relevant enough to win races. A driver wins by more frequently approaching the limits where speed will take his car out of control than the other drivers

---

* Ernest Hemingway, 'The Dangerous Summer', *Life*, 5 September 1960, p. 86.

† Hemingway, *Death, op. cit.*, p. 91.

are competent or daring enough to approach.* In fact, it is the possibility of restructuring routine activity so as to allow limits-pressing that transforms routine activity into a field of action. For example, on the highway cars often spread themselves out in a pattern whose stability is produced by each driver assessing what other drivers would not dare to do, and then, in effect, patrolling these limits; one's place in the traffic is therefore sustained. To 'make time' on the road when traffic is heavy is to press beyond the point other drivers have judged as protecting their position.†

If margin-pressing effort is to be possible, the equipment the actor uses may have to be restricted appropriately. After all, bull-fighting could hardly test a man if a Weatherby 460 were used instead of cape and sword. Similarly, if a challenge is to be made out of crossing the ocean, one must forgo liners in favour of rafts. If a fish is to be constituted into a fighting opportunity, then line, hook, and rod must be selected with the nicest of self-limitation, and often are.‡ If big-game hunting is to be risky as well as costly, then telescopic sights seem hardly 'fair'; in fact, the rifle itself might better be given up for bow and arrow.

Arrangements that call forth marginal effort generate the possibility of action. One further action arrangement might be considered. It is found when a series can be created by consecutive winning turns, such that each further turn adds the same additional probability of terminating the series while adding more than the previous turn's value to the series as a whole. For example, in bowling, an individual's reputation as a bowler is related to his maximum attained score. And score is dependent on number of 'strikes' during any one series or string of shots, with the score

* Moss, *op. cit.*, p. 22. 'The fastest driver is the one who can come closest to the point at which the car's tyres will break adhesion to the road and let the machine go into an uncontrolled slide. ("Uncontrolled" is the key word. Much of the time, the driver has deliberately broken the car loose, and is allowing it to slide, but under control.)'

† Improvement in roads and in driving qualities of cars of course merely allows the driver to be 'expressive' at higher speeds; whatever the conditions of road traffic, the other's territory will always be there to be pressed.

‡ B. Gilbert, 'The Moment-of-Truth Menace', *Esquire*, December 1965, p. 117. Gilbert's article is a description of how far sportsmen go to find a piece of nature that can be transformed, with proper equipment limitation, into a challenge. Cave-searching and rapids-running are described as examples.

mounting more than linearly with the number of strikes made in sequence. Further, a full-scoring next shot tends to be mentally assimilated to what the individual already has achieved, so failure to achieve it constitutes a 'blowing' of a scoring sequence that the player 'had going'. As the gain to be made with each bowl mounts, the difficulty of maintaining skill does likewise. Something similar is to be found in casino gambling in connexion with the practice of 'letting it ride', namely, betting all the previous win on the next play, and continuing to do this for a sequence of plays. He who manages to 'parlay' or pyramid his wins in this way is often given respect as someone who has 'nerve', is 'hot', and 'knows when to bet'. And since the bet is being doubled each time, the fifth or sixth straight win will be very much heavier than the second or third. And so the player finds that money and psychic gain increase more than arithmetically, while at the same time ever new opportunities for total loss must be faced.

A final issue must be raised concerning the organizational basis of action. Earlier I suggested that persons present in a social situation can serve not only as witnesses but also as the very objects upon which the individual acts, and that his record in this regard will be of special significance. When these other-involving acts entail fateful chances intentionally created just so they can be taken, then a special type of action results in which the persons who are present to the actor themselves provide the field for his action. Hemingway provides a wonderfully crude illustration, one that is also provided by circus performers who throw knives, and small boys who throw snowballs:

One of the attractions Mary had set up in the park was a shooting booth she had hired from a traveling carnival. Antonio had been a little shocked in 1956 when Mario, the Italian chauffeur, had held up cigarettes in his hands in a gale of wind for me to cut off their lighted ends with a .22 rifle. At the party Antonio held cigarettes in his mouth for me to shoot the ashes off. We did this seven times with the shooting gallery's tiny rifles and at the end he was puffing the cigarettes down to see how short he could make them.

Finally he said, 'Ernesto, we've gone as far as we can go. The last one just brushed my lips.'

The Maharaja of Cooch-Behar became another addict of this light-hearted amusement. He started conservatively using a cigarette holder but abandoned it immediately for the puffing school. I quit while I was still ahead and refused to shoot at George Saviers because he was the only doctor in the house and the party was just under way. It went a long way.*

While one person is providing a field of action for another, that other can in turn use the first individual as his field of action. When this reciprocity of use is found and the object is to exercise a skill or ability of some kind, we speak of a contest or duel. What occurs at these scenes might be called *interpersonal action*.†

Interpersonal action seems occasionally merely to duplicate the ordinary kind. In a pistol duel, for example, one individual is the passive target field for the other, while at the same time the other is the passive target field for the first – excepting, of course, the minor stratagems of standing at an angle to present the least surface to the opponent, and using the arms as shield for the heart. In fact, a pistol duel can be analysed as an arrangement for collapsing together two separable functions: target competition and a pay-off scheme for winners and losers. More often, however, reciprocality is more intimate and more interesting. The very act by which one participant exercises his capacities in the face of the other can itself provide the field for the other's competing or countering action. The figure one participant cuts will be cut out of the figure the other participant cuts. Even in Hemingway's target amusements there is a flavour of this: the coolness exhibited by

---

* Hemingway, 'Summer', *op. cit.*, 12 September, p. 76.

† Typically, contest arrangements require contestants to be face to face, but there are, for example, courtship contests between two suitors for the same hand wherein the opponents never meet; there are contests in the letters-to-the-editor column, and there are others (as Hemingway suggests) where the record of one party, who may be absent at the time, becomes the context of action of the other ('Summer', *op. cit.*, 5 September, pp. 91–2): 'Bullfighting is worthless without rivalry. But with two great bullfighters it becomes a deadly rivalry. Because when one does something, and can do it regularly, that no one else can do and it is not a trick but a deadly dangerous performance only made possible by perfect nerves, judgment, courage and art and this one increases its deadliness steadily, then the other, if he has any temporary failure of nerves or of judgment, will be gravely wounded or killed if he tries to equal or surpass it. He will have to resort to tricks and when the public learns to tell the tricks from the true things he will be beaten in the rivalry and he will be very lucky if he is still alive or in business.'

L

Antonio in submitting to the target role requires for its field of action the marksman efforts of Hemingway.

Just as there are social arrangements for ensuring action, so there are arrangements for ensuring interpersonal action. An important example is the widespread practice of handicapping in contests.* This device ensures that however badly matched the contestants may be, each will have about the same chance of winning or losing and each will have to depend on pushing himself to the limit. The outcome is thus guaranteed to be not only unpredictable and therefore attention-sustaining, but also a matter of *marginal effort*, the win going to the contestant who pushes himself closer to his limits than the others push themselves to theirs. The last extra bit of effort determines outcome. A handicap contest, then, is an arrangement nicely calculated to transform two individuals into fields of action for each other, with the additional bite that one person's success must be balanced by the other person's failure. It might be added that self-imposed equipment limitation in hunting and fishing can also be seen as a type of handicapping; the prey is transformed into an opponent and a 'fair' (or rather, almost fair) contest results. Fair games require fair game.

In various games and sports, then, individuals may use one another as fields of action, usually, in a segregated arena, physically and temporally cut off from serious life. But obviously the mutual use of one another as a field of action is more general. As a bridge from games to the world let us glance at dealings between the sexes.

All of the situations of action described so far are much more the scene of male activity than of female; indeed, action in our Western culture seems to belong to the cult of masculinity – in spite of lady bullfighters, female aerialists, and a preponderance of females in the slot machine pits of casinos.† There are records

---

* E. Goffman, 'Fun in Games', p. 67 in *Encounters* (Indianapolis: Bobbs-Merrill, 1961).

† Masculinity seems especially important as a value in Latin society, and as a value can hardly be dissociated from its basis in the biological aspects of sex. See 'Honour and Social Status', by J. Pitt-Rivers, Ch. 1, p. 45, in *Honour and Shame* (Chicago: University of Chicago Press, 1966), ed. J. Peristiany: 'Thus restraint is the natural basis of sexual purity, just as masculinity is the natural basis of authority and the defence of family honour. The ideal or

of a few duels fought by European women, but these encounters seem to be held up as a perversion of the fair sex, not its ornament.* But, of course, females are involved in one kind of action in a special way; they are the fields of play for sexual and courtship action. Adult males may define a female as an object to initiate a sexually potential relationship with. The risk is rebuff, misalliance, responsibility, betrayal of prior relationships, or displeasure of other males; the opportunity is for the kind of confirmation of self that success in this area alone can bring. This action is sometimes called 'making out'.

In our society there are special times and places set aside for making out: parties, bars,† dances, resorts, parks, classrooms, public events, association meetings, office coffee-breaks, church gatherings, and public streets of ill repute. Making out itself is of two kinds, according to whether the circle in which it occurs contains persons who are acquainted or unacquainted. Among the acquainted we find flirtatious exchanges and the initiation of affairs; among the unacquainted, interchanges of signs of interest and pickings-up.

Among the unacquainted, organizational facilitation of making out takes many forms: the institution of social hostess at resorts; telephone bars; bartender mediation in the buy-you-a-drink routine; etc. I cite at length the situation in Nevada casinos.

Casino tables are by definition open to any adult with money to

---

the honourable man is expressed by the word *hombria*, "manliness". . . . Masculinity means courage whether it is employed for moral or immoral ends. It is a term which is constantly heard in the *pueblo*, and the concept is expressed as the physical sexual quintessence of the male (*cojones*). The contrary notion is conveyed by the adjective *manso* which means both tame and also castrated. Lacking the physiological basis, the weaker sex cannot obviously be expected to possess it, and it is excluded from the demands of female honour.' Presumably the female counterparts of the classic male virtues involve modesty, restraint and virginity, whose display would seem to comprise anything but action.

* Robert Baldick, *The Duel* (London: Chapman & Hall, 1965), Ch. 11, 'Women Duellists', pp. 169–78.

† A close statement is found in Sherri Cavan, *Liquor License* (Chicago: Aldine Press, 1966). See also J. Roebuck and S. Spray, 'The Cocktail Lounge: A Study of Heterosexual Relations in a Public Organization', *American Journal of Sociology*, January 1967.

spend. In spite of the apparent impersonality of the operation, strangers at the same table find that a slight camaraderie is generated by a joint and mutually visible exposure to fate. Big bettors, with an implied involvement because of the size of their bets, and the implied status of the visibly moneyed, render themselves somewhat accessible to fellow players and even to watchers. Imputed mutual responsibility for outcome (in the limited but constant sense in which this is imputed) adds to mutual exposure and relatedness. And between the sexes additional openness prevails. Males can almost always give a little free advice to neighbouring females, gradually joining with them into a coalition of hope against the dealer. Further, if a female happens to play in a way that can be interpreted as profitable to all, a bet can easily be 'put up' for her and mutual involvement heightened. Similarly, when acquaintance with a female is struck up, she can be treated to play without obviously compromising her position. Her keeping all or some of her wins can then seem natural. Tables thus provide the first move in the acquaintance game and also a very graceful cover under which cash payment can be made in advance for social and sexual favours granted later in an uncommercial manner. Thus is making out organizationally facilitated.

It should be noted that there are many males who shy away from actively involving themselves in making out, even when attending places established for the purpose. There are many others who are everywhere on the lookout for these opportunities, whether in the home, at places of work, or in service contacts. And they face each day with such potentialities in mind.* These chronically oriented males must be classed with those who are ready to transform any event into a betting proposition, or any task into a contest of strength, skill, or knowledge.

Attempts to initiate a sex-potential relationship are, of course, only one variety of the interpersonal action that occurs in the community at large. Another important type occurs when the individual serves as a field for action by virtue of his capacity to

---

* Although the notion of action is certainly relevant to heterosexual contacts, it seems even more relevant to homosexual ones. Gay society apparently features the one-night stand (or rather, part-of-the-night stand), much more so than straight society, with a correspondingly high rate of contingency and chance-taking regarding relationship formation.

receive and give injury of both a physical and a verbal kind. To find those who indulge in this sport we are likely to look to 'outsiders' who, like adolescents, have not been tightly woven into organizational structures. Presumably among them these fateful activities will be least disruptive and the most tolerable; it is a case of having little to lose, or little to lose yet, a case of being well organized for disorganization. The study of corner gangs of aggressive, alienated youth provides an illustration:

> The quickened tempo of the testing of relationships on corners, in contrast with, for example, work groups, arises in part because leaders do not control important amounts of property, because there are few privileges or immunities they can bestow, and because there are no external institutional pressures that constrain members to accept the discipline of the gang.*

Among such youths the notion of 'kicks' has its fullest bearing. Here the culture and cultivation of recognized sports is not present to mask the gratuitousness of the chance-taking; the community itself is transformed into a field for action, with special use made of peers, unprotected adults, and persons perceived as symbols of police authority. Walter Miller provides a good statement:

> Many of the most characteristic features of lower class life are related to the search for excitement or 'thrill'. Involved here are the highly prevalent use of alcohol by both sexes and the widespread use of gambling of all kinds – playing the numbers, betting on horse races, dice, cards. The quest for excitement finds what is perhaps its most vivid expression in the highly patterned practice of the recurrent 'night on the town'. This practice, designated by various terms in different areas ('honky-tonkin' ', 'goin' out on the town', ' 'bar hoppin' '), involves a patterned set of activities in which alcohol, music, and sexual adventuring are major components. A group or individual sets out to 'make the rounds' of various bars or night clubs. Drinking continues progressively throughout the evening. Men seek to 'pick up' women, and women play the risky game of entertaining sexual advances. Fights between men involving women, gambling, and claims of physical prowess, in various combinations, are frequent consequences of a night of making the rounds. The explosive potential of this type of adventuring

---

* J. Short and F. Strodtbeck, *Group Process and Gang Delinquency* (Chicago: Chicago University Press, 1965), p. 196.

with sex and aggression, frequently leading to 'trouble', is semi-explicitly sought by the individual. Since there is always a good likelihood that being out on the town will eventuate in fights, etc., the practice involves elements of sought risk and desired danger.*

A student of lower-class Boston Italians provides another statement:

> For the action-seeker, life is episodic. The rhythm of life is dominated by the adventurous episode, in which heights of activity and feeling are reached through exciting and sometimes riotous behaviour. The goal is action, an opportunity for thrills, and for the chance to face and overcome a challenge. It may be sought in a card game, a fight, a sexual interlude, a drinking bout, a gambling session, or in a fast and furious exchange of wisecracks and insults. Whatever the episode, the action-seeker pursues it with a vengeance, and lives the rest of his life in quiet – and often sullen – preparation for this climax, in which he is usually said to be 'killing time'.†

CHARACTER

Beginning with a boy's chance-taking, we moved on to consequentiality; from there to fatefulness of the dutiful kind (noting that this could lead to construing the situation as a practical gamble voluntarily undertaken); and from there to action – a species of

---

* Miller, *op. cit.*, p. 11. An early statement of the excitement theme in delinquency is to be found in F. Thrasher, *The Gang* (University of Chicago Press [London], 1963), Ch. 5, 'The Quest for New Experience'. A more current version is to be found in H. Finestone, 'Cats, Kicks, and Color', *Social Problems*, 5 (1957), esp. p. 5, who describes a group that combines disdain for the work world with a strong concern for the expression of coolness in the face of trouble. Similarly, the 'focal concerns' that Miller imputes to lower-class urban culture (trouble, toughness, smartness, excitement, fate, autonomy) seem very suited to support involvement in action.

† H. Gans, *The Urban Villagers* (London: Collier-Macmillan, 1962), p. 29. He presents a further discussion of the appeals of action on pp. 65–9. In the literature the argument is often made that adolescent males must develop and demonstrate manliness and that the search for action serves this end. It is argued in this paper that manliness is a complex of qualities better called 'character', and that it is this that must be considered in the analysis of adolescent 'acting out'. In any case, as Bennett Berger points out ('On the Youthfulness of Youth Culture', *Social Research*, 30 [1963], 326–7), action orientation involves a concern not only for maleness but also for youth.

activity in which self-determination is celebrated. And we saw that the fatefulness, which many persons avoid, others for some reason approve, and there are those who even construct an environment in which they can indulge it. Something meaningful and peculiar seems to be involved in action. Hemingway's description of the human situation of one of his favourite bullfighters provides a hint of what we must look for:

We had spoken about death without being morbid about it and I had told Antonio what I thought about it, which is worthless since none of us knows anything about it, I could be sincerely disrespectful of it and sometimes impart this disrespect to others, but I was not dealing with it at this time. Antonio gave it out at least twice a day, sometimes for every day in the week, traveling long distances to do it. Each day he deliberately provoked the danger of it to himself, and prolonged that danger past the limits it could normally be endured, by his style of fighting. He could only fight and he did by having perfect nerves and never worrying. For his way of fighting, without tricks, depended on understanding the danger and controlling it by the way he adjusted himself perfectly to the bull's speed, or lack of it, and the control of the bull by his wrist which was governed by his muscles, his nerves, his reflexes, his eyes, his knowledge, his instinct and his courage.

If there was anything wrong with his reflexes he could not fight in this way. If his courage ever failed for the smallest fraction of a second, the spell would be broken and he would be tossed or gored. In addition, he had the wind to contend with which could expose him to the bull and kill him capriciously at any time.

He knew all these things coldly and completely and our problem was to reduce the time that he had to think about them to the minimum necessary for him to prepare himself to face them before entering the ring. This was Antonio's regular appointment with death that we have to face each day. Any man could face death but to be committed to bring it as close as possible while performing certain classic movements and do this again and again and then deal it out yourself with a sword to an animal weighing half a ton, which you love, is more complicated than just facing death. It is facing your performance as a creative artist each day and your necessity to function as a skillful killer. Antonio had to kill quickly and mercifully and still give the bull one full chance at it when he crossed over the horn at least twice a day.*

* Ernest Hemingway, 'The Dangerous Summer', *Life*, 12 September 1960, pp. 75–6.

If one examines moments when an individual undergoes these chances, whether as part of serious work or dangerous play, certain capacities, certain properties of his make-up, appear to be of intrinsic or 'primary' relevance: in high construction work, care and balance; in mountain climbing, 'condition', and stamina; in bullfighting, timing and perceptual judgement; in game hunting, aim; in gambling, a knowledge of the odds; and in all cases, memory and experience. Often these primary capacities can be created by training. Significantly, the same capacities can be exercised during unconsequential circumstances, when the chancy features of actual occasions are avoided altogether or merely simulated. Thus one finds dry runs, target practice, trial effort, war games, and stage rehearsals. Organized training uses this kind of simulation extensively. Here a good or bad showing need not be fateful in itself nor in its effect on the reputation of the actor. Similarly, primary capacities can often be exercised on occasions when effective performance is easily and unthinkingly achieved, when, in brief, the results are consequential but not problematic.

Under perceivedly fateful circumstances – consequential and problematical – and *only* a close connexion with them, a second set of capacities or properties appear. An individual's sudden sense of what might shortly occur can have a marked effect on his behaviour, with respect to both social ties and task performance. In the case of relations to others, the principled behaviour he manages to exhibit during ordinary occasions may break down. The quick consciousness of what his principles are costing him at the moment may cause his wonted decency to falter, and in the heat and haste of the moment, naked self-interest may obtrude. Or, contrariwise, the sudden high cost of correct behaviour may serve only to confirm his principledness. Similarly, in the matter of task performance, his imagining to himself the consequence of failing or succeeding can work strongly upon his capacity to exercise the primary capacities in question. The imminent possibilities may make him nervous, incapable of drawing on what he knows, and incapable of organized action;* on the other hand,

* J. L. Austin, in his 'Pleas for Excuses' (*Philosophical Papers*, ed. J. Urmson and G. Warnock [Oxford: O.U.P., 1961]), p. 141, discussing the various 'departments into which the business of doing actions is organized', suggests: 'There is for example the stage at which we have actually to *carry out* some

the challenge may cause him to mobilize his energies and perform above himself. In contrast to Hemingway's friend Antonio, there is Jose Martinez who, upon his début as a matador at Murcia, on entrance of the bull, fainted.*

These capacities (or lack of them) for standing correct and steady in the face of sudden pressures are crucial; they do not specify the activity of the individual, but how he will manage himself in this activity. I will refer to these maintenance properties as an aspect of the individual's *character*. Evidence of incapacity to behave effectively and correctly under the stress of fatefulness is a sign of *weak* character. He who manifests average, expected ability does not seem to be judged sharply in terms of character. Evidence of marked capacity to maintain full self-control when the chips are down – whether exerted in regard to moral temptation or task performance – is a sign of *strong* character.

Primary properties and those of character both contribute to the reputation an individual acquires; both are therefore consequential. But there are important differences between the two. As suggested, primary qualities can be expressed in a situation that is not fateful; qualities of character – in the aspects considered here – emerge only during fateful events, or at least events subjectively considered to be fateful. One may approve of, disapprove of, or be morally neutral towards primary qualities. Properties of character, however, are always judged from a moral perspective, simply because a capacity for mobilizing oneself for the moment is always subjected to social evaluation. And, in contrast to primary properties, character traits tend to be evaluated in the extremes, referring to failures in no way expected or successes out of the ordinary; mere conformance with usual standards is not the issue. Finally,

---

action upon which we embark – perhaps we have to make certain bodily movements or to make a speech. In the course of actually *doing* these things (getting weaving) we have to pay (some) attention to what we are doing and to take (some) care to guard against (likely) dangers; we may need to use judgement or tact: we must exercise sufficient control over our bodily parts: and so on. Inattention, carelessness, errors of judgement, tactlessness, clumsiness, all these and others are ills (with attendant excuses) which affect one specific stage in the machinery of action, the *executive* stage, the stage where we *muff* it.'

* Reported by Charles McCabe, *San Francisco Chronicle*, 2 June 1966.

unlike primary traits, those of character tend to be 'essentializing,' fully colouring our picture of the person so characterized, and (as we will see later) a single expression tends to be taken as an adequate basis for judgement.

Consider some of the major forms of character that bear on the management of fateful events.

First, there are various forms of *courage*, namely, the capacity to envisage immediate danger and yet proceed with the course of action that brings the danger on. The variations are established by the nature of the risk, for example, whether physical, financial, social, or spiritual. Thus, among professional gamblers, there is respect for a quality called 'gamble', namely, a willingness to submit to the rules of the game while chancing a major portion of one's current capital – presumably with the grace to carry off the win or loss circumspectly. Note that the interests served by courageous actions may be quite selfish; the issue is the actor's readiness to face great risk.

There is *gameness*, the capacity to stick to a line of activity and to continue to pour all effort into it regardless of set-backs, pain, or fatigue, and this not because of some brute insensitivity but because of inner will and determination. Boxers provide a version:

There is also a cult of a kind of persevering courage, called a 'fighting heart', which means 'never admitting defeat'. The fighter learns early that his exhibited courage – his ability, if necessary, to go down fighting – characterizes the respected, audience-pleasing boxer. He must cherish the lingering hope that he can win by a few more punches.*

It should be added that persons are not alone, and perhaps not even first, in this matter of showing heart. Bulls, properly bred, wonderfully have it; that is why they accept the matches made for them and continue to fight from an increasingly weakening position, and that is why there can be bullfights. Race horses, under a special reading of the term 'class', can have it too.†

A fundamental trait of personal character from the point of view of social organization is *integrity*, meaning here the propensity to resist temptation in situations where there would be much

---

* Winberg and Arond, *op. cit.*, p. 462.
† See M. Scott, *The Racing Game* (Chicago: Aldine Books, 1968).

profit and some impunity in departing momentarily from moral standards. Integrity seems especially important during fateful activity that is not witnessed by others. Although societies differ widely in the kinds of character they approve, no society could long persist if its members did not approve and foster this quality. Everyone tends to claim a high standard of integrity, however rarely realized; excellence in this regard is taken for granted, and it is persons who fall short who are the ones to be designated, in this case, as having weak characters.* (We can find examples of integrity therefore in the littlest corners of life: when a salesperson touts an unsuitable product with less persuasion than he could have mustered; when a girl does not break a date that sudden opportunity has made disadvantageous; when a school child admits to an offence others would have been thought guilty of; when a cab driver or barber gives back three dollars *in bills* when a two-dollar debt is paid with a five.) Somewhat similar comments can be made about 'self-discipline', the capacity to refrain from excessive involvement in the easy pleasures of the table – whether in a bar, restaurant, or casino.

Earlier it was suggested that social situations carry in themselves some reputational implications, especially in connexion with the standards that participants are obliged to maintain in their dealings with one another. It was said that this consequentiality was usually not problematic. However, here we must see that circumstances can sometimes render it so.

For example, the continued maintenance of the ceremonial order can occasionally become very costly, producing the questionable privilege of displaying a special version of integrity. At these times the individual will have to decide whether or not to give in under pressure, whether or not to let standards lapse. *Gallantry* refers to the capacity to maintain the forms of courtesy when the forms are full of substance. It is shown when Douglas Fairbanks, in the middle of a cinematic duel to the death, retrieves his opponent's fallen sword and hands it to him with a polite bow, the better to prevent a meaningless advantage from cutting short the opportunity for valid expression. Other competitions provide similar opportunities:

* I am grateful to Marvin Scott for suggestions concerning the specia place of integrity as a property of character.

It was in 1902 that the British then-champion, Selwyn F. Edge, driving in the Paris–Vienna race, punctured an inner tube and was forced to stop for repairs. He soon discovered, however, that the tire pump which his car carried would not work. Without it, the tube could not be inflated and the car could not continue.

At this moment, the colorful Count Louis Zborowski came along the road in a Mercedes, took in the situation at a glance, pulled up next to Edge's car and tossed his own tire pump to his rival. Edge went on to win the Gordon Bennett cup. Zborowski was second.*

It is interesting that examples of gallantry are usually of the kind I have cited, and neglect the place of this property in everyday life. In fact, a shopkeeper is gallant when he unnecessarily and politely refunds a large sale for a tourist who suddenly has had misgivings. Certainly a stand-by passenger is gallant when he voluntarily gives up the second last seat so that a youthful pair next in line can stay together and yet not be stranded.†

Gallantry, of course, is not the only quality of character that is found in connexion with the costly and problematic maintenance of the ceremonial order. Just as the individual owes others courtesies, so they owe courtesies to him, and should they fail to treat him properly he may find he must risk retaliatory acts in order to show that advantage cannot be taken of him. In contemporary times the police provide excellent illustrations of this theme, since sometimes they feel they must pledge their fists, their clubs, and even their guns to ensure a nice deference from those they arrest or otherwise accost.‡

* S. Davis, 'Chivalry on the Road', pp. 32–3, in Beaumont and Nolan, eds., *op. cit.*

† In casinos, gallantry is institutionalized and made the special right and obligation of the pit boss. Bets whose outcome is disputed are adjudicated by him, and the traditional, preferred style is gently to suggest to the customer how the fault could be or is his, and then when the dealer has been cleared, to graciously allow the decision to go against the house. I have seen pit bosses thus conduct themselves when the bet was large enough to appreciably count in the table's take for the shift. Here of course the casino itself is concerned to acquire and sustain a reputation for what in this context is called 'class', the opposite of being 'cheap'. (A general treatment of organizational character is provided in P. Selznick, *Leadership in Administration* [London: Harper & Row, 1957], especially pp. 38–42.)

‡ See W. Westley, 'Violence and the Police', *American Journal of Sociology*, LIX (1953), 39–40.

Retaliatory acts of this sort assume, of course, that the offended person has ample authority and resources. When this is not the case then he may feel obliged to sacrifice his own substance to maintain the forms. Gallantry in reverse results: not costly courtesy but costly contempt. In the mythic extreme, dutifully employed in many action novels, the hero, stripped and bound to a chair, spits or at least sneers into the face of the villain who threatens death and torture; the hero voluntarily exacerbates a precarious situation in order to show distaste for the villain's presumption and style. More realistically, we find that servers of all kinds know that if the value of their service or of their selves is disputed, they can with majesty decline any payment or can even ask the customer to take his patronage elsewhere – a matter of cutting off one's nose in order to destroy the other's face. These pyrrhic victories are often disapproved of, along with the quality of character felt to be responsible for exacting them. And no doubt such incidents do not actually occur frequently. Yet stories of their occurrence are everywhere and seem to play a significant role in maintaining the self-respect of servers and the self-restraint of those they serve.

Of all the qualities of character associated with the management of fatefulness, the one of most interest for this essay is *composure*, that is, self-control, self-possession, or poise. This attribute is doubly consequential, for it directly affects the functioning of a primary property and is a source of reputation in its own right.

Composure has a behavioural side, a capacity to execute physical tasks (typically involving small muscle control) in a concerted, smooth, self-controlled fashion under fateful circumstances. Money-making at pool provides an example:

On the other hand, the hustler must have 'heart' (courage). The *sine qua non* is that he is a good 'money player', can play his best when heavy action is riding on the game (as many non-hustlers can't). Also, he is not supposed to let a bad break or distractions in the audience upset him. (He may pretend to get rattled on such occasions, but that's just part of his con.) Nor should the quality of his game deteriorate when, whether by miscalculation on his part or otherwise, he finds himself much further behind than he would like to be.*

* Polsky, *op. cit.*, p. 10.

One example of what this capacity is *not* might be cited:

> A nervous man wearing a trench coat and dark glasses stood at the check-cashing booth of the Safeway store at 4940 Mission Street last night.
> Reaching in his pocket, he pulled out a .32 caliber blue steel automatic. Or at least he tried. The gun caught on the pocket, firing a shot into the baseboard of the cashier's booth.
> Some fifteen customers and ten clerks stared at the man. He licked his lips nervously.
> 'This is a holdup,' he blurted to cashier Rose Catelli, 30, of 579 Naples Street. 'I want all the money in the safe.'
> Whereupon he turned and bolted from the store, with manager Val Andreacchi and clerk Tom Holt in pursuit.
> Without even a glance back, the gunman wildly fired three or four more shots as he sprinted half a block up an alley to London Street, jumped into his car and sped away.*

Composure also has what is thought of as an affective side, the emotional self-control required in dealing with others. Actually what seems to be involved here is physical control of the organs employed in discourse and gesture. Sir Harold Nicolson, reviewing the qualities required of the professional diplomat, provides illustrations:

> A third quality which is essential to the ideal diplomatist is the quality of calm. Not only must the negotiator avoid displaying irritation when confronted by the stupidity, dishonesty, brutality or conceit of those with whom it is his unpleasant duty to negotiate, but he must eschew all personal animosities, all personal predilections, all enthusiasms, prejudices, vanities, exaggerations, dramatizations, and moral indignations. . . .
> The quality of calm, as applied to the ideal diplomatist, should express itself in two major directions. In the first place he should be good-tempered, or at least he should be able to keep his ill-temper under perfect control. In the second place he should be quite exceptionally patient.
> The occasions on which diplomatists have lost their tempers are remembered with horror by generations of their successors. Napoleon

---

* *San Francisco Chronicle*, 17 November 1963.

lost his temper with Metternich in the Marcolini Palace at Dresden on 26 June 1813, and flung his hat upon the carpet with the most unfortunate results. Sir Charles Euan Smith lost his temper with the Sultan of Morocco and tore up a treaty in the imperial presence. Count Tattenbach lost his temper at the Algericas Conference and exposed his country to a grave diplomatic humiliation. Herr Stinnes lost his temper at Spa.*

These men 'flooded out', ceased to be their own masters, becoming, along with their principles, subject to control by others.

Along with the value of smooth movements and unruffled emotions, we can consider that of mental calmness and alertness, that is, *presence of mind*. This competency is important for the proper execution of many impersonal tasks, as, for example, examinations. These are meant to be a sampling device for uncovering a just and only-to-be-expected outcome. But, in fact, one's test score depends on mobilizing memory and knowledge under pressure and then fashioning an orderly comprehensive answer in less than comfortable time; the opposite of what is sometimes called 'blocking'.† Presence of mind is also important in tasks that involve other persons directly. This kind of presence of mind is what people known as wits have and the self-conscious person does not. Books of famous *mots*, brilliant statements of tact, and effective 'squelches' and 'put-downs' attest to the general interest in this mindedness.

Composure has still another side, the capacity to contemplate abrupt change in fate – one's own and, by extension, others' – without loss of emotional control, without becoming 'shook up'.‡

* H. Nicolson, *Diplomacy* (New York: Oxford University Press, Galaxy Books, 1964), p. 62.

† As part of socialization, school tests may be important not because of what pupils must learn to take them but what they may learn in the taking of them. For here, at least in our society, is perhaps the most important early training in performing difficult tasks under time-limited conditions, such that lack of mental composure is likely to use up limited time and to further increase its own production. Interestingly, in our society formal tests requiring *physical* composure under difficult circumstances seem to come much later in life, when at all.

‡ A consideration of this issue is given in B. Glaser and A. Strauss, *Awareness of Dying* (Chicago: Aldine, 1965), Ch. 13, 'Awareness and the Nurse's Composure', pp. 226–56.

Composure also has a bodily side, sometimes called *dignity*, that is, the capacity to sustain one's bodily decorum in the face of costs, difficulties, and imperative urges.* Here the sport of surfing (even more than ski-ing) is of special interest. Physical aplomb and the dignity of upright posture must be maintained on a flat narrow board against rumbling forces that press to the limit the human capacity for this kind of bodily self-control. Here the maintenance of physical poise is not merely a condition of effective performance but a central purpose of it.

A final aspect of composure might be considered: *stage confidence* – the capacity to withstand the dangers and opportunities of appearing before large audiences without becoming abashed, embarrassed, self-conscious, or panicky. Behind this is the special type of poise that pertains to dealing with the contingency of being under the observation of others while in an easily discredited role. An interesting variation is honoured in the undercover world of agents, plainclothesmen, and criminals, where it may be necessary to 'act natural' before a critical audience when one knows that in a few seconds the whole show may be up. It is written of one of New York's best burglars that, just after making a very big score on the tenth floor of an hotel:

He walked back down to the ninth floor and took the elevator to the lobby. With what police call 'the nerves of a burglar', he let the doorman call him a cab. 'It was the first time in my life I couldn't tip the doorman,' he told the police. 'My pockets were so full of jewelry that I couldn't reach for any change. It was very embarrassing.'†

Here an important set of assumptions is involved. Persons who have good reason to fear that they may be apprehended shortly are inclined to bolt for it or at least look out constantly for possible

---

* Dignity can make news. Thus a *Sun-Times* release (with picture) 17 April 1953: 'Viviane Romance, French screen star who refused to let actor spit in her face and curse her in movie scene, was fined $11,428 for breach of contract in Paris. Star said action was "beneath my dignity".' A nice example of conduct some would think undignified may be found in Lillian Ross's *Picture* (New York: Dolphin Books, 1962), wherein she describes the menial tasks that Albert Band apparently performed as the assistant to John Huston and Gottfried Reinhardt. See especially pp. 32–57, 91–7.

† Black, *op. cit.*, p. 118.

danger. These quite natural tendencies can be held in check but rarely without leaving some trace of agitation. Authorities, seeking among the apparently innocent for the actually guilty, will therefore be rightly inclined to check up on persons who appear wary, or anxious without visible cause. To look self-conscious, then, is to break the cover of 'looking like anyone else'. But in addition, should the individual sense that his appearance is giving him away, he will feel he has further cause to be fearful. Suppressing the urge to leave the field that this new fear creates will generate still further signs of unnaturalness, and these in turn will have their circular effect.

Composure in all its different dimensions has traditionally been associated with the aristocratic ethic. In recent years, however, a version of this quality has been strongly touted by raffish urban elements under the label 'coolness'. Sir Harold might be disinclined to the locution but his advice to an errant diplomatist could be accurately expressed by saying, 'Baby, don't blow your cool'.* The significant point here is that we find composure a concern and a value in many different cultures and across many different strata. There appear to be two major reasons for this.

First, whenever an individual is in the immediate presence of others, especially when he is co-operatively involved with them – as in, for example, the joint maintenance of a state of talk – his capacity as a competent interactant is important to them. The social order sustained in the gathering draws it ingredients, its substance, from disciplined small behaviours. His contribution of proper demeanour is melded in with the contribution of the others

* Yet contemporary coolness seems to have shading all its own. The phrasing employed assumes that although coolness is a personal trait, the possessor is in an estranged relation to it, since retaining it will always be problematic. Just as a wallet can be lost, so can one's cool. Also, the term is extended to cover not merely involvement in disruptive matters but involvement in anything at all – on the assumption apparently that for those whose social position is vulnerable, any concern for anything can be misfortunate, indifference being the only defensible tack. Finally, in the phrase 'to cool it', an injunction is conveyed against behaviour that might excite undesired response from others and hence, by extension, increase the threat to one's own situation and in consequence one's own cool. I might add that certain slum styles of discourse have so penetrated upwards that language Sir Harold abjures is no doubt being employed by his hippier colleagues as evidence of their connexion with the world.

M

to produce socially organized co-presence. He will have to maintain command of himself if he is to make himself available to the affairs at hand and not disrupt them. Discomposure will disqualify him for these duties and threaten the jointly sustained world that the others feel they have a right to be in.

Second, whether or not the individual is in the presence of others, any task he performs involves the practised easy use of human faculties – mind, limbs, and, especially, small muscles. Often this management must be acquired and sustained under very special circumstances: any temporary failure of control due to concern about the situation will itself provide a reason for still more self-consciousness and hence still further maladroitness and so on, until the individual is quite rattled and unable to handle the task. Sword swallowers provide a clear example. The touch and temperature of the blade make the unpractised gag, which certainly renders the task impossible. Once this response is effectively suppressed, the learner finds that the sword causes his throat to close quite tight. Still further practice is required before these muscles become relaxed and the sword can pass without touching. The more the sword touches, the more likely an involuntary spasm, which will, of course, further increase the amount of touching.* (Correspondingly, of course, the more composed the swallower, the less the sword will touch and the less constrictive the passage will be, and so forth.) As has been suggested, a similar predicament occurs under limited time conditions. Maladroitness can waste time, which further tightens the situation, which in turn gives still greater cause for discomposure.

Because persons in all societies must transact much of their enterprise in social situations, we must expect that the capacity to maintain support of the social occasion under difficult circumstances will be universally approved. Similarly, since individuals in all societies and strata must perform tasks, the composure that this requires will everywhere be of concern.

I have discriminated several bases of strong character: courage, gameness, integrity, composure. It should be apparent that these may be combined, producing decorations for the moral life of the community. A wireless operator who politely declines to leave

* See D. Mannix, *Memoirs of a Sword Swallower* (New York: Ballantine, 1964), pp. 94–8.

his sinking ship and goes down while coolly improvising repairs on the transmitter, gamely driving himself even though his hands are burned, combines in his deed almost all that society can ask of anyone. He transmits an important message even though his S.O.S. may not get through.

Now I want to return to the suggestion that although properties of character are typically found during fateful moments, they are also exhibited during times of mere subjective fatefulness, when a fate that is already determined is being disclosed and settled. The feelings generated during these moments may require powers of self-control if they are to be managed well. And, of course, this self-possession will be of special importance when others are immediately present, since the orderly interaction they sustain would be jeopardized by the discomposure of the fated one.

No better example can be found than the qualities exhibited by someone about to be hung, guillotined, shot, or gassed. Executions occur under conditions where the audience is quite labile, and where physical co-operation and psychic equanimity are required of the condemned man if things are to go smoothly. The lore of executions consequentially records persons who fought, twisted, spluttered, wailed, fainted, and were incontinent during the moments before their dispatch, proving thus to lack character:

> The people of York witnessed another unpleasant hanging when Joseph Terry fought, screamed and bit as the hangman tried to place the noose round his neck. Six men came on to the scaffold to hold him and eventually the rope was forced over his head, but in another struggle the cap fell off. At this moment the platform fell. Terry leaped and managed to get a foot on the edge of the scaffold, clinging to one of the corner-posts of the gallows with his arm. Here he managed to fight off the united efforts of the hangman and his assistants for a minute before they dislodged him. He died with his face uncovered in frightful contortions.*

* Atholl, *Shadow of the Gallows* (London: John Long, 1954), p. 77. The history of executions is typically written in evolutionary terms, starting with cruel deaths accorded for many crimes and moving to our time when humane death is administered for very few crimes, and there is much pressure to abolish the death penalty entirely. Actually, the history of executions could better be written in interaction terms, for the evolution of executionary

Conversely, the lore tells of other performers who exchanged pleasantries with the audience, maintained the social niceties, assisted the hangman in adjusting the noose, and generally made matters easier for everyone present. Gallows humour literally does occur, as when an aristocrat, about to be guillotined, declines the traditional glass of rum, saying, 'I lose all sense of direction when I'm drunk.'*

The procedural difficulties unwilling execution victims can cause, and their general tendency to go to their death co-operatively, demonstrate the desire persons have to exhibit strong character. The condemned man is usually co-operative; he is a good sport; he is not a child; he accepts his losing game without getting into a huff or bursting into tears,† and can even show a fighter's heart, disdaining with a sneer to hedge his final bet in the traditional way, that is, with piety, prayer, and a request that those who remain

---

techniques has largely to do with the development of devices and practices for ensuring a smooth social occasion. Given that the audience, the executioner, and the victim will all be on edge, how can the deed be managed so as to facilitate the self-containment of all three types of participants? The history of executionary practices is the story of the slowly accumulating answer. Take the art of hanging for example. Gallows came to be developed which could be erected silently overnight in the prison yard in order to minimize gruesome sights and sounds; a 'table of drops' according to weight and condition of the neck so that the length of the free fall would neither leave a man to wriggle nor tear off his head but nicely break his neck – a knot and type of cord being designed to facilitate this adjustment; arm pinions to prevent the man from obstructing the fall; and trap doors sure to hold until the cord was pulled, sure to open quickly once it had, and (in one of the nicest touches of all) designed not to bang back and forth in doleful reverberation of the fall.

It can be argued that the humaneness of the execution ought hardly to be significant for the victim, since the question of how one is shortly to be dispatched might well be considered of no importance compared to the fact that one *is* about to be dispatched. Only those who are left behind can take comfort that lasts in knowing that the end was practically painless and that no one enjoyed the terrible business of arranging it and witnessing it.

* A. Kershaw, *A History of the Guillotine* (London: Calder, 1958), p. 71.

† Of course it is not only children who can be poor sports and lose their equanimity and hence their character when a game is lost. As a female chess expert tells it: 'In one game, a player from the Netherlands suddenly had her queen snipped off the board by a Russian. She ran off the stage in tears.' (Miss Lisa Lane quoted in 'Talk of the Town', *The New Yorker*, 19 September 1964, p. 43.)

forgive him and be forgiven.* This kind of grace is the final and awful socialized act, for the condemned man smoothes out the social situation, supporting the most evanescent part of our social life – its social occasions – just at a time when he can very little longer share in what he is supporting. After all, others are present. Pass through the teeth of eternity if you must, but don't pick at them.

Understandably, during the days of public executions, the doomsday conduct of the condemned was closely watched and contributed importantly to his posthumous reputation. Heroes could thus be born, confirmed, and killed while dying. In communities where the possibility of execution is lively, this interest is still to be found, as Claude Brown suggests in his Harlem memoirs:

> It seemed like a whole lot of people in the neighborhood, cats that we'd come up with, gone to school with, were being cooked in Sing Sing. It had become a thing with people in the neighborhood to talk to these cats' mothers and relatives, cats who went to the electric chair in Sing Sing. I remember when I was younger, when I was at Warwick [prison] and right after I came out, I had heard about people I knew who had gone to the chair. We all wanted to know what they said because we wanted to find out something for ourselves. We wanted to find out if it was worth it at the last minute, if they felt it was worth it, now that they were going to die.
>
> When I was younger, a few years after Warwick, I wanted to know just whether these cats were really hard. I think most of the guys my age looked upon them as heroes when they were getting cooked at Sing Sing. We wanted to know their last words. Somebody told me that when they cooked Lollipop – Lollipop was a cat who was kind of crazy, and we called him Lollipop because he liked candy – just before he left, he said, 'Well, looks like Lolly's had his last lick.' That was it. Everybody admired him for the way he went out. He didn't scream or anything like that.†

* Correlated with the trend towards 'humane' dispatch there has been a decline in the demands for grace and character that we place upon the doomed. In the gas chamber in American prisons, the victim may be requested to breathe deeply soon after the cyanide drops, but no one would ask him to present a dying speech in the manner that was customary in the seventeenth and eighteenth centuries. (On dying speeches see Atholl, *op. cit.*, p. 56.)

† Brown, *op. cit.*, p. 211.

In viewing some of those personal qualities that influence the way an individual will perform on desperate occasions, I have suggested a connexion between action and character. The relationship should not be pressed too far. Those who support a morality are likely to feel that it can be carried too far, even though society may benefit from the example provided by extreme devotion. It must also be admitted that there are certain positively valued qualities of character earned by sticking to an undramatic task over a long period of time, and, consequently, conduct during any moment cannot contain a rounded expression of the trait. Morever, during dutiful fatefulness, as when men do battle, the self-distinguishing kind of intrepidity and grace exhibited by gamblers and race-track drivers will not be enough. As William James remarked in his praise of the military virtues, there is a need to surrender private interests and show obedience to command.* A crisis may call for not only those qualities of character that lead an individual to outdo others and set himself apart, but also for those that lead to his submerging himself into the immediate needs of the whole. Even self-interest may require the disciplined display of quite unheroic qualities. The money pool-player provides an example:

> The hustler must restrain himself from making many of the extremely difficult shots. Such restraint is not easy, because the thrill of making a fancy shot that brings applause from the audience is hard to resist. But the hustler must resist, or else it would make less believable his misses on more ordinary shots.†

Here the deeper quality of character is to be able to appear under pressure to have less grace than one has. Finally, as already suggested, there are the qualities of character traditionally associated with womanhood. These oblige the female to withdraw from all frays in order to preserve her purity, ensuring that even her senses will be unsullied. Where action is required to ensure this virtue, presumably her male protector undertakes it.

I have been suggesting that while the individual is in a social

---

* W. James, 'The Moral Equivalent of War', in his *Essays on Faith and Morals* (New York: Meridian, 1962), p. 323.

† Polsky, *op. cit.*, p. 9.

situation he is exposed to judgement by the others present, and that this involves their assessing him in regard to primary capacities and to qualities of character. No picture of these reputational contingencies would be complete without considering the folk-beliefs prevalent in society regarding the nature of persons, for these beliefs provide the frame of reference for the trait-judgements made regarding the witnessed individual.

First, with properties of character, unlike primary properties, a single expression tends to be taken as definitive. Since properties of character are called for only on those rare occasions when eventfulness has not been avoided, additional corroborative or corrective manifestations are not immediately likely. Reliance, perforce, will have to be put on a sample of one. More important, it is part of the imagery of these traits that no exceptions are allowed. It is just when he is most tempted to deviate that the individual has the most telling opportunity to be constant and thereby demonstrate his character; this constancy-in-spite-of-everything is, in fact, what character is all about. To say that lay imputations are impulsive and unsound, and that over time and across various situations the individual might not, in fact, maintain the character he currently manifests, is quite true but quite beside the point. I am here not concerned with whether a given individual does or does not possess a specified characteristic, but with how notions about character function in daily life. In our dealings with another we assume that his currently expressed character is a full and lasting picture of him, and in his dealings with us he makes the same assumption as to how he will be viewed. Of course, excuses are offered, accountings given, and exceptions made; but this work is done in relation to the prior assumption that the current showing is crucial, and in any case is often incompletely effective.

Second, once evidence of strong character has been established, it need not be intentionally re-established, at least not right away; for the moment the actor can stand on his record. He can rely on others assuming that should the right occasion arise he would bear out the implications of his manner and act with character. But this, of course, adds its own danger to moral life, since we tend to operate in terms of optimistic views of ourselves, which would be discredited if ever put to the test.

Third, there is the belief that once an individual has failed in a particular way he becomes essentially different from that moment on and might just as well give up. A soldier indoctrinated with the idea that he has a will and that wills stand up entirely or are utterly broken, may tend, because of this, to divulge everything he knows during enemy interrogation, once he has divulged something.* Similarly, a bullfighter may be described as having lost all his valour after his first goring.† So, too, in horse racing circles there is discussion of jockeys 'losing their nerve' and either riding poorly thereafter or refusing to ride at all. Exemplary stories tell of famous jockeys who, feeling they had lost their nerve, proclaimed this fact and retired for life from racing.‡ Like tales are told of deep-sea divers. And detective fiction often describes tough cops and hoods who receive a severe beating and thereafter never quite have their old spunk. And, of course, there is the common belief that once a man's price has been discovered and paid, he no longer has any reliability left and might just as well accept bribes that are small but frequent.

Coupled with the belief in the 'losability' of nerve, the destructibility of moral fibre and 'never-the-sameness', there is another: after long having no nerve or moral fibre, an individual can suddenly acquire 'guts' or 'heart', and from that point on continue to have it.

Cayetano Ordonez, Nino de la Palma, could manage the muleta perfectly with either hand, was a beautiful performer with a great artistic and dramatic sense of a faena, but he was never the same after he found the bulls carried terms in the hospital, inevitable, and death, perhaps, in their horns as well as five thousand peseta notes between their withers. He wanted the notes, but he was unwilling to approach the horns to get them when he found the forfeit that was collectable from their points. Courage comes such a short distance; from the heart to the head; but when it goes no one knows how far away it goes; in a hemorrhage, perhaps, or into a woman and it is a bad thing to be in bullfighting business when it is gone, no matter where it went.

---

* A. Biderman, 'Social-Psychological Needs and Involuntary Behavior as Illustrated by Compliance in Interrogation', *Sociometry*, 23 (1960), 138–9. A further statement is presented in E. Goffman, *Asylums* (New York: Doubleday, 1961), pp. 89–90.

† For example, Hemingway, *Death, op. cit.*, p. 89.

‡ J. Leach, 'Unseated by Nerves', *Observer*, 3 March 1963.

Sometimes you get it back from another wound, the first may bring fear of death and the second may take it away, and sometimes one woman takes it away and another gives it back. Bullfighters stay in the business relying on their knowledge and their ability to limit the danger and hope the courage will come back and sometimes it does and most times it does not.*

In fiction and myth, redemption is often achieved only in the act that gives the individual strength enough to die for his principles, the decease of the redeemed one serving to maintain the contradictory assumptions that a fall from grace is permanent and that a broken person can mend himself.

Given the belief that character can be dramatically acquired and lost, the individual will plainly have reason for going through with a chancy situation no matter what the likely material or physical cost to himself, thereby manifesting what is sometimes called pride. Interestingly, our beliefs about nerve allow a little outside help in this matter: it is generally felt that a quick drink of straight liquor will allow a man to carry off a difficult action easier and better, and a surprising number of situations allow for such fortification.†

Given these arguments about the nature of character, it is possible to understand better why action seems to have a peculiar appeal. Plainly, it is during moments of action that the individual has the risk and opportunity of displaying to himself and sometimes to others his style of conduct when the chips are down. Character is gambled; a single good showing can be taken as representative, and a bad showing cannot be easily excused or re-attempted. To display or express character, weak or strong, is to generate character. The self, in brief, can be voluntarily subjected to re-creation. No doubt this licence is practicable from society's viewpoint because, as clearly illustrated in connexion with gamblers' 'gamble', the price of putting on these shows is likely to provide an automatic check against those who might be over-inclined to stage them. In any case, here is the opportunity to be measured by Hemingway's measure of men.

* Hemingway, *ibid.*, p. 222.
† Execution practice is one illustration. See, for example, A. Keller, ed., *The Hangman's Diary* (London: Philip Allen, 1928), p. 8, under the phrase, *stärkenden Trunk*.

We can begin to see that action need not be perceived, in the first instance, as an expression of impulsiveness or irrationality, even where risk without apparent prize results. Loss, to be sure, is chanced through action; but a real gain of character can occur. It is in these terms that action can be seen as a calculated risk.* Statements (including mine) that action is an end in itself must be understood as locutions. The voluntary taking of serious chances is a means for the maintenance and acquisition of character; it is an end in itself only in relation to other kinds of purpose. To consider action literally as an end in itself would be to trivialize and truncate social explanation.

And now we begin to see character for what it is. On the one hand, it refers to what is essential and unchanging about the individual – what is *characteristic* of him. On the other, it refers to attributes that can be generated and destroyed during fateful moments. In this latter view the individual can act so as to determine the traits that will thereafter be his; he can act so as to create and establish what is to be imputed to him. Every time a moment occurs, its participants will therefore find themselves with another little chance to make something of themselves.

Thus a paradox. Character is both unchanging and changeable. And yet that is how we conceive of it.

It should be no less clear that our illogic in this matter has its social value. Social organization everywhere has the problem of morale and continuity. Individuals must come to all their little situations with some enthusiasm and concern, for it is largely through such moments that social life occurs, and if a fresh effort were not put into each of them, society would surely suffer. The possibility of affecting reputation is the spur. And yet, if society is to persist, the same pattern must be sustained from one actual social occasion to the next. Here the need is for rules and conventionality. Individuals must define themselves in terms of properties already accepted as theirs, and act reliably in terms of them.

To satisfy the fundamental requirements of morale and continuity, we are encouraged in a fundamental illusion. It is our

---

* This argument has recently been made in connexion with the risk entailed in extra-marital sexual relations and in gang fights. See F. Strodtbeck and J. Short, 'Aleatory Risks Versus Short-run Hedonism in Explanation of Gang Action', *Social Problems*, 12 (1964), 127–40.

character. A something entirely our own that does not change, but is none the less precarious and mutable. Possibilities regarding character encourage us to renew our efforts at every moment of society's activity we approach, especially its social ones; and it is precisely through these renewals that the old routines can be sustained. We are allowed to think there is something to be won in the moments that we face so that society can face moments and defeat them.

CHARACTER CONTESTS

Starting with the notion of fateful occupational duties, we can view action as a kind of self-oriented evocation in ritualized form of the moral scene arising when such duties are exercised. Action consists of chancy tasks undertaken for 'their own sake'. Excitement and character display, the by-products of practical gambles, of serious fateful scenes, become in the case of action the tacit purpose of the whole show. However, neither fateful duties nor action tell us very much about the mutual implications that can occur when one person's display of character bears upon another's, nor do we learn about the framework of understanding we possess for dealing with such occurrences. For this we must turn to interpersonal action.

During occasions of this kind of action, not only will character be at stake, mutual fatefulness will prevail in this regard. Each person will be at least incidentally concerned with establishing evidence of strong character, and conditions will be such as to allow this only at the expense of the character of the other participants. The very field that the one uses to express character may be the other's character expression. And at times the primary properties at play may themselves be openly made a convenience, pointedly serving merely as an occasion for doing battle by and for character. A *character contest* results; a special kind of moral game.

These engagements occur, of course, in games and sports where opponents are balanced and marginal effort is required to win. But character contests are also found under conditions less obviously designed for contesting, subjecting us all to a stream of little losses and gains. Every day in many ways we can try to score points, and every day in many ways we can be shot down.

(Perhaps a slight residue remains from each of these trials, so that the moment one individual approaches another, his manner and face may betray the consequences that have been usual for him, and subtly set the interaction off on a course that develops and terminates as it always seems to do for him.) Bargaining, threatening, promising – whether in commerce, diplomacy, warfare, card games, or personal relations – allow a contestant to pit his capacity for dissembling intentions and resources against the other's capacity to rile or cajole the secretive into readability. Whenever individuals ask for or give excuses, proffer or receive compliments, slight another or are slighted, a contest of self-control can result. Similarly, the tacit little flirtations occurring between friends and between strangers produce a contest of unavailability – if usually nothing more than this. And when banter occurs or 'remarks' are exchanged, someone will have out-poised another. The territories of the self have boundaries that cannot be literally patrolled. Instead, border disputes are sought out and indulged in (often with glee) as a means of establishing where one's boundaries are. And these disputes are character contests.

If the significance of character contests is to be appreciated, however, we must turn from games and skirmishes to constitutive features of social life. We must examine the investment an individual is obliged to make in legitimate expectations that happen to be his own, especially informal ones, and the means available in society for establishing authority, invidious position, dominance, and rank. In the interplay of righteousness and ranking, a code is to be found that cuts to the centre of the self and is worth attempting to formulate ideally.

When two persons are mutually present, the conduct of each can be read for the conception it expresses concerning himself and the other. Co-present behaviour thus becomes mutual treatment. But mutual treatment itself tends to become socially legitimated, so that every act, whether substantive or ceremonial, becomes the obligation of the actor and the expectation of the other. Each of the two participants is transformed into a field in which the other necessarily practises good or bad conduct. Morever, each will not only desire to receive his due, but find that he is obliged to exact it, obliged to police the interaction to make sure that justice is done him.

When a contest occurs over whose treatment of self and other is to prevail, each individual is engaged in providing evidence to establish a definition of himself at the expense of what can remain for the other. And this dispute will embarrass not only the desire for a satisfactory place in the definitions that prevail, but also the right to be given such a place and the duty to insist thereon. A 'matter of principle' is involved, that is, a rule whose sanctity derives not only from the actual conduct that is guided by it, but also from its symbolic implication as one of a whole set of rules, the system itself being in jeopardy.* Insisting on a desirable place is thus covered and strengthened by insisting on one's rightful place, and this is further hardened by the obligation to do so, lest the whole pattern of rules deteriorate. *Honour* can thus be engaged, namely, that aspect of personal make-up that causes the individual dutifully to enjoin a character contest when his rights have been violated – a course he must follow in the very degree that its likely costs appear to be high.†

The game typically starts with one player offending against a moral rule, the particular application of which the other player is pledged to maintain personally, usually because he or those he identifies with are the targets of the offence. This is the 'provocation'. In the case of minor infractions, the offender is likely to offer an immediate apology, which restores both the rule and the honour of the offended; the offended need only convey acceptance to abort the whole game – in fact, he may apologize himself at the same time, or accept apology before it is offered, demonstrating again the great concern of persons to stay out of this kind of action. (An important structural issue here is that it is easier to proffer an excuse and apology in one's capacity as guardian of the other's rights, when this is self-initiated, than it is to accept an affront in

---

* See the argument by C. Fried, 'Reason and Action', *Natural Law Forum*, vol. 11 (1966), 13–35.

† The leading case here is the sixteenth-century duel of honour. A gentleman stood by his honour, but only a small number of others were socially qualified to oblige him to satisfy his honour by means of a duel, and then, of course, the problems of arranging mutually satisfactory time, place, and equipment were so great that in countries like England few duels actually did get fought. See F. Bryson, *The Point of Honor in Sixteenth Century Italy: An Aspect of the Life of the Gentleman* (Publications of the Institute of French Studies, Inc., Columbia University, New York, 1935); Baldick, *op. cit.*

one's capacity as protector of one's own sanctity.) A similar termination of the game occurs when the offended conveys a mild challenge (enough to show he is not without honour), drawing the offender's attention to what has happened, which is followed by a sequence of apology and acceptance. 'Satisfaction' is asked for and given, and little character is generated, although each party can once again affirm that he is a properly socialized person with proper piety regarding the rules of the game. Even, however, where the offence is uncommon and deep, serious consequences can be avoided. The offended person can openly express his feeling that the offender is not the sort of person whose acts need to be taken seriously;* the offender, on being challenged, can back down with wit, so that while one part of him becomes defamed, it is another part of him that is doing the defaming – and doing it so well as to undercut the challenger's claim of having self-restorative work to do.

Since a challenge can be communicated and declined with the slightest of cues, one finds here a general mechanism of interpersonal social control. An individual who has moved slightly out of line is reminded of the direction he is taking and its consequences before any serious damage has been done. The same mechanism seems to be employed in the establishment of a pecking order regarding various kinds of rights.

If the contest is to begin in earnest, the challenge conveyed by the offended must be serious, and the other player must pointedly decline to give satisfaction. When both of these responses are present they together transform retrospectively the meaning of the initial offence, reconstituting it into the beginning of what is sometimes called a 'run-in'. This is always a two-party affair, unlike an 'incident', which may centrally involve only one person. Moral combat results, with properties of character brought into play as something to be lost and gained.† Run-ins involve the victim

---

* Tellers have foiled bank robberies by simply refusing to take seriously the threat-note to them by would-be armed robbers. Similarly policemen have countered pistol threats against themselves by simply turning their backs on the gunman, thereby removing the basis for contest. (See *San Francisco Chronicle*, 26 July 1965, p. 3, 'Cop Turns His Back – And Disarms a Gunman'.

† Traditional duels were more complex because of the choice-of-weapons rule. Were the offended party to challenge the offender to a duel the latter

himself in all the phases of the sanctioning process. In this court, the plaintiff must act as judge and executioner. As is characteristic of action in general, the unaided individual is here the efficacious unit of organization.

It should be apparent that the meaning of these various moves derives in part from the orientation the player brings to them and the readings he retrospectively makes of them.* Therefore there will be leeway in defining the situation, and a certain degree of mutual consent will be required before a full-fledged run-in can occur.

In today's world, when a run-in does happen, a character contest is likely to follow immediately, if indeed it is to occur. In myth and ritual, however, the parties often withdraw to meet again at a designated place, voluntarily keeping an appointment with fate, of both the corporeal and the characterological kind. In either case, bystanders are necessary and always must carefully refrain from interfering. (This ensures that the contest will be reputed as 'fair', a valid scene for the play of character.)

When the run-in has occurred and the contest begun, the characterological implications of the play can unfold in different ways, and not necessarily with 'zero-sum' restrictions.

One party can suffer a clear-cut defeat on the basis of properties of character: he proves to have been bluffing all along and is not really prepared to carry out his threatened deed; or he loses his nerve, turns tail and runs, leaving his opponent in the comfortable position of not having to demonstrate how seriously he was prepared to carry through with the contest; or he collapses as an opponent, abases himself and pleads for mercy, destroying his own status as a person of character on the tacit assumption that he will then be unworthy as an opponent and no longer qualify as a target of attack.

Both parties can emerge with honour and good character

---

would ordinarily have the choice of weapons, an unfair advantage for someone who had already done wrong. And so the offended party would openly insult the offender, 'giving him the lie', and with this provocation the original offender would then be forced to challenge the offended. Through this extensive co-operation, choice of weapon could be lodged on the right side.

* Suggested by P. Bourdieu, 'The Sentiment of Honour in Kabyle Society', p. 200, in Peristiany, *op. cit.*

affirmed – an outcome carefully achieved, apparently, in most formal duels of honour, a considerable achievement since injury was also usually avoided.

And presumably both parties can lose, just as one party may lose while the other gains little. Thus, that ideal character contest, the 'chicken run', may end with both vehicles swerving, neither vehicle swerving, or one swerving so early as to bring great dishonour to its driver but no particular credit to the opponent.*

Obviously, the characterological outcome of the contest is quite independent of what might be seen as the 'manifest' result of the fray. An overmatched player can gamely give everything he has to his hopeless situation and then go down bravely, or proudly, or insolently, or gracefully, or with an ironic smile on his lips.† A criminal suspect can keep his cool in the face of elaborate techniques employed by teams of police interrogaters, and later receive a guilty sentence from the judge without flinching. Further, a well-matched player can grimly suffer while his opponent stoops to dishonourable but decisive techniques, in which case a duel is lost but character is won. Similarly, an individual who pits himself against a weak opponent may acquire the character of a bully through the very act of winning the match. And a bully who ties is lost indeed, as this news story from Fresno, California illustrates:

A barmaid and a bandit played a game of 'chicken' with loaded pistols early yesterday and, although no shots were fired, the barmaid won.

---

* A fictionalized presentation of the vehicular chicken run may be found in G. Elliott, *Parktilden Village* (New York: Signet Books, 1961), pp. 42–3. An elegant analytical treatment is provided by T. C. Schelling, *Arms and Influence* (New Haven: Yale University Press, 1966), pp. 116–25. Note that before the game can be played, persons must know how the equipment accessible to them can be used for this purpose. Some middle-class boys don't know that a lit cigarette butt held between the sides of the hands of two different boys until it burns down to the flesh provides perfect facilities for the game. (The first one to draw his hand away loses, of course, and automatically terminates the trial for both of them.) The breath-holding contest seems more widely known.

† One of the reasons unexpected rescues are employed in action stories is that only in this way can the hero be given a chance to demonstrate that even in the face of quite hopeless odds he will not cry uncle. Second leads are allowed to prove this the hard way, being expendable in the plot.

The action took place at The Bit, a proletarian beer and wine oasis on the southern fringe of town, where lovely Joan O'Higgins was on duty behind the bar.

Suddenly a towering bandit walked into the establishment, ordered a beer, flashed a small pistol and commanded Miss O'Higgins to clean out the cash register.

The barmaid placed $11 on the bar, an amount that failed to satisfy the bandit, whose height was estimated at six feet five.

'Give me the rest,' he demanded.

Barmaid O'Higgins reached into a drawer for the main money bag and the .22 caliber pistol beneath it.

She pointed the gun at the man and asked:

'Now, what do you want to do?'

The bandit, realizing that he had met his match in The Bit, blinked at the sight of the gun and left, leaving his beer and the $11 behind.*

Just as a move is subject to interpretation, so a characterological outcome may be differently read by different participants. In negotiations between nations, for example, no unambiguous criteria may emerge for agreeing as to who won and who lost.† Scoring in some cases may be so flexible that each side can maintain its own view of the final outcome. Thus, some fights between rival street gangs end with both teams feeling that they won.‡ This sort of conceit is facilitated by a variable intermix of concern for the physical or manifest outcome, allowing one team to stress score in primary attributes, the other in properties of character.

The cowboy or slap-leather duel is especially instructive in pointing out the co-operativeness and regard for rules that are required on the part of all participants if the game is to be successful in generating and jeopardizing character, that is, bringing character into play. Both parties must take the game seriously: both, as suggested, must make themselves available, voluntarily giving themselves up to the game. During the combat that results, the hero, should he find himself with an easy advantage, must disdainfully give it up, restricting himself to a means of having it out that will leave the villain with no way of dodging the expres-

* *San Francisco Chronicle*, 14 July 1966.

† F. Iklé, *How Nations Negotiate* (New York: Harper & Row, 1964), p. 964 ff. See also Bourdieu, p. 207, in Peristiany, *op. cit.*

‡ J. Short and F. Strodtbeck, 'Why Gangs Fight', *Transaction*, I (1964), 26.

N

sions of character that result. And the hero, upon winning a challenge or a duel, can at that very moment turn his back on his opponent, knowing that superiority once established will not be immediately re-challenged, and that in any case constant care is not dignified.*

Given these suggestions about the dynamics of the character game, let us go on to consider briefly some of the implications.

He who would avoid fateful events must avoid run-ins or wriggle safely out of ones that have not been avoided – whether he be the offender or offended. Almost everyone does such wriggling, although the Kaiser's officers are said to have barely done so. Even Casanova who, according to his own account, was a formidable swordsman and gentleman of much character, admits to such avoidance, commenting on such during an occasion when honour had just forced him into a duel with a stranger:

We had a pleasant supper and talked cheerfully together without a word being said about the duel, with the exception that an English lady said, I forget in what connection, that a man of honour should never risk sitting down to dinner at an hotel unless he felt inclined, if necessary, to fight. The remark was very true at the time, when one had to draw a sword for an idle word and expose oneself to the consequences of a duel or else be pointed at, even by the ladies, with the finger of scorn.†

Another implication follows from the first. It has to do with ·contest contests'. The individual's tendency to avoid occasions when character is in jeopardy exposes him to being forced by someone else into a contest over whether or not there will be a contest.

---

* This strange fateful trust in the fair-play of the just-defeated enemy has an obvious social function. Without this trust, dominance and the pecking order would not provide a practical social mechanism for establishing temporary order. Were opponents to re-contest a run-in as soon as it had been played through, no order could be established. Everyone would always be engaged either in fighting or in carefully standing guard. In any case, one finds 'terminal self-exposure' on the part of the winner as a standard move in ending a wide variety of contests – wrestling matches, bullfights, cowboy duels, etc.

† *The Memoirs of Jacques Casanova*, tr. A. Machen (New York: Dover, 1961), vol. 2, p. 958.

The aggressor, knowing that his victim is likely to seek almost any means to avoid a show-down, can force him to face up to a display of this weakness before witnesses, while the aggressor displays his own bravery.

The aggressor in a contest can begin either by committing an offence that the other can scarcely overlook, or by responding to a minor or even microscopic offence in a way that draws the near-innocent offender into a fray.* If the victim still declines to join battle, the aggressor may goad him with increasingly unpalatable acts, in an apparent effort either to find his ignition point or to demonstrate that he doesn't have one. We speak here of 'baiting', 'ranking', 'sounding', or 'getting a rise'; when the aggressor is a subordinate, we speak of 'insolence'. It should be repeated that although this sort of aggression may not be common, at least in middle-class daily life, nonetheless, all face-to-face contacts between individuals are ordered by a multitude of anticipated signs of mutual respect, which ordering can easily be transformed by an aggressor into a perilous field of fateful interpersonal action. For example, everywhere the individual goes he implants a tacit demand that the others present will respectfully keep their eyes, their voices, and their bodies away from the circle immediately around him. Everywhere these territorial courtesies are sustained automatically and unthinkingly; yet everywhere they provide ample means at hand by which an aggressor (through the pointed, unhurried failure to accord these considerations) can test the individual's honour. Similarly, strangers in public places are bound

---

* L. Yablonsky (*The Violent Gang* [London: Collier-Macmillan, 1962], pp. 208–9), in describing types of gang members, describes the logical extreme: '. . . Other youths who may be included in the category of marginal gang membership are the sociopathic individuals almost *always* ready to fight with any available gang. They seek out violence or provoke it simply as they describe it: "for kicks or action". They are not necessarily members of any particular violent gang, yet are in some respects members of all. They join gangs because for them it is a convenient and easily accessible opportunity for violence. When the gang, as an instrument, is not appropriate they "roll their own" form of violence (for example, the three stomp slayers who kicked a man to death for "whistling a song we didn't like"). For example, in one typical pattern utilized by this type of gang boy, he will approach a stranger with the taunt, "What did you say about my mother?" An assault is then delivered upon the victim before he can respond to the question, which, of course, has no appropriate answer for preventing the attack.'

N*

together by certain minimal obligations of mutual aid, establishing the right, for example, to ask the time or directions, or even to request a cigarette or small coin. In granting such a plea, the individual may find that his entire package of cigarettes is calmly taken or all the change in his hand while his eye is held by the aggressor so that the affront is anchored in mutually recognized mutual awareness. Pushcart operators in slum streets may find a piece of fruit being taken in the same insolent manner.*

The mutual accommodation that orders human traffic can thus be seen to render vulnerable those who take it for granted. I would like to cite at length a novelistic illustration provided by William Sansom. The scene is a London drinking 'club'. The hero, and narrator, who plays the piano at the club, is suddenly addressed:

'As a voice above me says: "Ain't you gonna play s'more fellah?"'

It is a young man I have never seen before, a boy almost too young to be in a bar. His head sags like a pale knob of bone on a neck too thin to hold it. He wears exaggerated clothes, and a special sort of hairdress like a hedgehog's. He bunches his shoulders up to make them bigger. His eyes are dull as dead fish-scales. He grits his mouth thin as if he wants to be sick.

"In a moment," I tell him. His tone has been really insolent, but one dismisses a lot as youth.

"Not too long then, fellah," he says, still fixing me with his fishy dead eyes.

Behind him then, I started to see a kind of twin – but he was only another youth in the same cut of clothes. And then I saw that there were six or seven others standing at the bar or lounging legs stretched out from the tables. I caught Belle's [the proprietress] eye and she gave me a hopeless shrug across the room – as if this sudden phenomenon was beyond her.

"My," I said to Marie, ignoring the young man, who still stood there, looking down at me, "we've got company tonight."

"You have," said the boy sadly, "you certainly have," and he walked away, at a conscious stiff-legged strolling pace, to the bar. There he said something to the others, and they all looked my way and shook their heads – again, sadly, as if I were in a very bad way indeed. . . .

* Although these various 'put-on's' are directed against an individual, he will often serve in part as a symbol of a wider group – the adult world, police authority, white people, etc.

We watched them for a moment. Every glance and gesture was carefully aggressive. They stuck out their legs so that Andrew carrying a tray of drinks had to circle round to save tripping – and watched him silently as he did so. One leaned over and took a tray of chips off someone else's table – unsmiling, pointedly unapologetic. Another at the bar began flipping olive stones at the bottles. Belle told him to stop. He apologized with an exaggerated bow and flipped another stone straight away.

"For God's sake *play* something," said Belle.

I got up. It had been a mistake to talk about them so openly. They knew they were being discussed, and now, as I went to the piano, saw that their orders had been obeyed. You could almost feel them spreading themselves. So I began to play the dimity notes of *Humoresque* to put them back a little.

Of course, it did not work. The common quality of all these young men is their watchfulness. They sit and watch everything with dull dislike. This gives them that famous "pinched" look. As my tinkling established itself, one of them sauntered across, hands in pockets, chin down, and stood above me. He simply stated, as an order, the name of a disc-hit. Apart from this plain rudeness, a pianist's biggest bugbear is to be asked for another tune when he is clearly playing – so I gritted my teeth and tried to close my ears. He nudged my right arm off the notes with his elbow and said simply; "mush". And repeated, louder, his request.'*

I am suggesting that minor behaviours can be employed as a serious invitation to a run-in or show-down. One type of truncated act should be mentioned specifically. It is the use of the style of standing or walking as an open invitation to action to all others present. Thus there is a 'delinquency strut' which in effect communicates an authority challenge to adults present, simultaneously conveying not only that the first move has been made but also that it has not been faced up to by those at whom it was and is directed.†
The special swagger of the bullfighter in the ring, *Sandunga*, is the stylization of the same expression.

* W. Sansom, *The Cautious Heart* (London: Hogarth, 1956), pp. 100–102.

† Sometimes called 'walking pimp'. On this and other collapsed moves employed by delinquents, see the useful study by C. Werthman, *Delinquency and Authority*, M.A. Thesis, Dept. of Sociology, University of California, Berkeley, 1964, p. 115, and throughout Ch. LV, 'Gang Members and the Police'.

Since communications or expressions, not substantive matters, are involved in these games, there is little to keep the symbol from becoming increasingly attenuated in duration and visibility until it has practically disappeared. In consequence, a sequence of moves can be exchanged between two players and a winner established with hardly any visible activity at all, as implied, of course, in G. H. Mead's analysis of communication.

Earlier it was suggested that an individual can become reputed among his peers as an action seeker – always on the make for any desirable girl he happens upon, or ready to 'make something' of the slightest affront, or to see everywhere something that can be bet on. Similarly, an individual may acquire the reputation for always being available *to others* for a particular type of interpersonal action, ready at all times to provide a definitive test of anyone seeking definition. The Western 'gunfighter' is often portrayed as the archetypical example. Well-known pool players find themselves cast in this role. Bet-a-Million Gates apparently attracted bettors in the same way.* Today the police, being committed (as already suggested) to obtaining immediate deference from all civilians they contact, and to enforce this demand with an immediate willingness to invoke physical sanctions, sometimes find themselves forced into the tester's role. Male movie stars who are type-cast into tough hero roles may be utilized as testers by those who chance to meet them in public places. Highly regarded jazz musicians who allow the practice of 'cutting' provide another example, at least for those who write about them.

Whether an individual constantly seeks out character contests or is constantly sought out for them, we can anticipate that he won't last long; anyone so inclined will eventually be removed from competition by the workings of probability. So long as each play involves an appreciable gamble, the persistent chance-taker ought not to plan on a long future. The action role is itself long-lived, but its performers can last only briefly, except on television.

Just as there is specialization of persons, so there is specialization of signs. Particular affronts can be defined as those an honourable individual ought not to tolerate. There are critical points understood by all those involved as the ones past which things will have gone too far; once they are reached, the offended

* See Lucius Beebe, *The Big Spenders* (New York: Doubleday, 1966), p. 85.

person must disallow excuses, feel things seriously, and take steps to re-establish the normative order if he is to preserve his honour. Among the many words an honourable cowboy can hear, he must, however peaceful his intent, recognize the few that everyone knows are 'fighting' ones. Once such specialized function is given to acts, they can be employed by aggressors as an unavoidable call to action. Performed in a measured and pointed way, these acts test the recipient's honour, that is, his readiness regardless of price to uphold the codes by which he lives. The actual offence is understood by all parties to be incidental, a mere convenience; the chief significance of the act is to serve as a frontal test of the individual's tacit claim to honour.* Thus a conventionalized statement, 'You lie in your throat', was the traditional *mentita* – the act by which an offended party forced the offender to challenge the speaker to a duel.† Spitting in the other's face is a less gentlemanly and more common example. In current American race relations, the white person's use of the word 'nigger' is equally provocative. Other acts serve as tests in more circumscribed groups. A teacher in an urban slum school who affirms the school rule against lateness exposes himself to a pupil's strolling in late and coolly looking him in the eye to underline the challenge.‡ These testing acts are favourite moves in contest contests.

Just as a test can be fashioned out of an offensive act performed by one individual against another, so it can be generated by demanding under threat that an individual act in a way he thinks improper. To establish an individual in a subordinate status, an aggressor may coerce him into openly performing an undignified obeisance or service on the assumption that once he allows himself to give-in he can (and he knows he can) be relied upon henceforth to accede to any demand made of him.§ As with the jockey,

---

* These acts of insolence and pointed insubordination are to be contrasted to bodily acts of deference, acts which are specialized too, but which serve to attest to the actor's current willingness to accept the *status quo*.

† Bryson, *op. cit.*, Ch. IV. As suggested, the offended party could not challenge the offender because this would give the offender the choice of weapons. Offenders were thus tacitly assumed to be honourable enough to allow themselves to be manoeuvred into the challenger role.

‡ An incident of this kind is described in Werthman, *op. cit.*, pp. 68–9.

§ See the treatment of 'obedience tests' in Goffman, *Asylums, op. cit.*, pp. 17–18.

'nerve' is then thought to be lost, but this time in regard to inter-personal activity and its ceremonial order. And, of course, as long as both parties share these beliefs, the social game will be played accordingly.

In considering action I said that, although there is a relation between action and character, some forms of character arise in opposition to the spirit of action. The same qualification must be made in regard to interpersonal action and character contests. There are situations in which approval is given to an individual's refusal to be drawn into a fray of honour, and 'immaturity' is imputed to challengers. It is always possible for the individual to decline to accept the whole ritual frame of reference and, more-over, put a bold face on it, especially when his peers support this style of response:

> But it must be emphasized that, despite prevalent stereotypes, juvenile gangs are not all conflict oriented, and value systems may vary among them as among other human groupings. A 'retreatest' gang, which built its value system around the effect of dope, provides a dramatic contrast.
>
> Although criticized and ridiculed repeatedly by other gangs for their cowardice and lack of manhood, the retreatests seldom responded to taunts, and always retreated from combat. They did not worry about their reputations as fighters – they had none – and did not think them important – in fact, they thought the conflict oriented gangs to be 'square'. Directly challenged to join other white gangs in repelling Negro 'wade-in' demonstrators on a beach in Chicago, they got 'high' on pills and unconcernedly played cards during the entire incident.*

* Short and Strodtbeck, 'Why Gangs Fight', *op. cit.*, pp. 27–8. See also their 'The Response of Gang Leaders to Status Threats', *American Journal of Sociology*, LXVIII (1963), 576–7. A literary example is provided in Louis Auchincloss's novel, *Sybil* (New York: Signet, 1953), pp. 122–3. A man (Philip) at his club with his mistress draws an acquaintance (Nicholas Cum-mings) aside and asks if he would like to meet her. Nicholas declines, and the following dialogue occurs:

'You'd better watch your step, Cummings,' he said ominously. 'You're talking about the young lady whom I intend to marry.'

But Nicholas simply continued to fix him with his chilly stare.

'It's hard for people to know that, isn't it,' he inquired, 'when you're still married to my cousin?'

There was a weighty pause.

'Well, anyway,' Philip said heavily, not knowing what honour might require

Something similar occurs in middle-class bars, where an offended person may feel it beneath him to 'seek satisfaction', at least with the particular opponent of the moment – thus democratizing the chivalric notion that only one's social equals are worth challenging. The victim will be content to lecture his adversary briefly on how 'sick' he must be. In social worlds where honour *is* highly valued and men must be prepared to put up their lives to save their faces, fashions of morality may quickly change, and the act of proving such attributes as one's 'masculinity' may decline in significance.* There has even developed the literary ideal of

---

in so awkward a situation, 'you'd better cut those cracks about Julia. Unless you want your block knocked off.'

Nicholas, however, was remorseless.

'Do you regard the term "mistress" as a "crack"?' he demanded. 'I'm sorry. I had thought it accurate. You're not going to deny that she *is* your mistress, are you? Because I should tell you that as your wife's lawyer, although in no way at her instigation, I have made it my business to find out exactly what your relationship with Miss Anderson is. The word "mistress" appears to cover it exactly. Can you suggest a better? At any rate I must insist on my right so to describe her whenever I have occasion to discuss your affairs with those who may be concerned. If you object, you are at liberty to seek redress, either legally in a slander suit or illegally, as you threaten, in an assault upon my person.'

Philip's breath was now coming in pants. There was no rule for handling a person who so boldly defied the most elementary precepts of good fellowship.

'Would you like to step outside,' he demanded, 'and settle this thing like a gentleman?'

'I most certainly would not,' Nicholas replied. 'I have not come to my club to give you an opportunity to start a brawl in the street.'

Philip stood there for a moment, looking at him uncertainly.

'Oh, go to hell,' he retorted. 'God damn lawyers,' he answered as he moved away. 'Shysters. All of them.'

* Brown, *op. cit.*, pp. 211, 253–6, 261, provides a nice description of ways in which Harlem youth in the 1930s and 40s were taught the necessity to defend their money and their women with lethal fighting, and how, in the 50s in conjunction with the rising significance of drugs, the coercive power of the code declined markedly. This is but a small version of larger histories. The duel of honour, for example, while very popular in France, very rarely occurred in the Northern States, being muchly disapproved by the citizenry. In England, in 1844, the article of the Mutiny Act which obliged officers to uphold their honour by duelling was repealed and replaced by ones that forbade it. The third of the new articles nicely outlines the modern anti-umbrage perspective:

the 'anti-hero' who confidently declines all opportunity to display costly virtues, shows subterranean pride in fleeing from his moral obligations, and takes no chances. Of course, when an individual declines a challenge with coolness or fails to become incensed at an offence he is demonstrating self-command under difficult circumstances, and therefore establishes character of a kind, although not the heroic kind.

In sum, although character contests that can be fought without relevance to physical force are not uncommon, the classic punchout and slap-leather varieties belong mainly to cinematic palaces. None the less, the logic of fights and duels is an important feature of our daily social life. The possibility, however slight, that matters might degenerate in that direction provides mutually present persons with a background reason to hedge expressions of hostility; they have here a constant guide to what is not going to be allowed to happen. (In fact, joking reference to 'stepping outside' can be used as a strategic move to cut back into unseriousness a threatening development in social discourse.) Through a multitude of joint accommodations, the voice of our reason prevails at the cost of hardly any dishonour.

'Approbation is expressed of the conduct of those who, having had the misfortune to give offence to, or injure or insult others, shall frankly explain, apologize, or offer redress for the same, or who, having received offence, shall cordially accept frank explanations or apologies for the same; or, if such apologies are refused to be made or accepted, shall submit the matter to the commanding officer; and, lastly, all officers and soldiers are acquitted of disgrace or disadvantage who, being willing to make or accept such redress, refuse to accept challenges, as they will only have acted as is suitable to the character of honourable men, and have done their duty as good soldiers who subject themselves to discipline' (cited in Baldick, *op. cit.*, p. 114). Baldick comments thus:

'With surprising suddenness, the articles, which were recognized as constituting a British "Code of Honour", combined with the obvious determination of judges and juries to convict duellists of murder, the sarcasm of the Press, and the sheer pressure of public opinion, succeeded in suppressing duelling in Britain . . . the duel as a thriving, honoured and respected institution to all intents and purposes ceased to exist in Britain in the middle of the nineteenth century.' (*Ibid.*)

CONCLUSIONS

The traditional sociological view of man is optimistic. Once you get the beast to desire socially delineated goals under the auspices of 'self-interest', you need only convince him to regulate his pursuits in accordance with an elaborate array of ground rules. (Important among these rules, I want to add, are 'situational proprieties', that is, standards of conduct through whose maintenance he exhibits regard for the current situation.) Accordingly, the main trouble the individual can cause is to fail to acquire appropriate wants, or wilfully to fail to abide by the rules in going about satisfying such wants as he has acquired. But obviously other difficulties must be considered. This essay has dealt with one of them.

Whether an individual is concerned with achieving a personal goal or sustaining a regulative norm, he must be in physical command of himself to do so. And there are times when his aliveness to the contingencies in the situation disrupt his dealings with the matters at hand: his capacity to perform ordinary mental and physical tasks is unsettled, and his customary adherence to standard moral principles undermined. The very intelligence that allows him to exert foresight and calculation in the pursuit of his ends, the very qualities that make him something more complex than a simple machine, assure that at times what he intelligently brings to mind will disrupt his capacity to perform and disarray his usual morality.

The ability to maintain self-command under trying circumstances is important, as is therefore the coolness and moral resoluteness needed if this is to be done. If society is to make use of the individual, he must be intelligent enough to appreciate the serious chances he is taking and yet not become disorganized or demoralized by this appreciation. Only then will he bring to moments of society's activity the stability and continuity they require if social organization is to be maintained. Society supports this capacity by moral payments, imputing strong character to those who show self-command and weak character to those who are easily diverted or overwhelmed. Hence we can understand the paradox that when an immoral deed is accomplished by a well-executed plan that excludes impulsive temptation, the culprit may be half-admired;

he can be thought a very *bad* character even while it is appreciated that he is not a *weak* one.*

A central opportunity to show strong character is found in fateful situations, and such situations necessarily jeopardize the risk-taker and his resources. (An already-decided fate that is now being settled is useful too, but still more costly.) The actor is therefore likely to avoid this chance-taking and squirm out of occasions he has not avoided. In our society, after all, moments are to be lived through, not lived. Further, fateful activity is often itself disruptive of social routines and cannot be tolerated by organizations in large amounts. (Thus, in Europe, duelling throve under monarchies, but monarchs and their leading generals led in trying to curb the institution, partly because of the duelling toll on key personnel.) In domestic and occupational life, most of these hazards seem to have been safely eliminated.

However, there is some ambivalence about safe and momentless living. Some aspects of character can be easily affirmed, but other aspects can be neither expressed nor earned safely. Careful, prudent persons must therefore forgo the opportunity to demonstrate certain prized attributes; after all, devices that render the individual's moments free from fatefulness also render them free from new information concerning him – free, in short, from significant expression. As a result, the prudent lose connexion with some of the values of society, some of the very values that portray the person as he should be.

So some practical gambles may be sought out, or, if not sought out, at least made into something when they occur in the ordinary course of affairs. And enterprises are undertaken that are perceived to be outside the normal round, avoidable if one chose, and full of dramatic risk and opportunity. This is action. The greater the fatefulness, the more serious the action.

Fatefulness brings the individual into a very special relationship to time, and serious action brings him there voluntarily. He must arrange to be in a position to let go, and then do so. The circumstances into which he thus thrusts himself must involve matters that are problematic and consequential. And – in the purest case –

---

* A good recent example is provided by the heroes of timing who brought off the Great Train Robbery. On the regard held for them, see J. Gosling and D. Craig, *The Great Train Robbery* (London: W. Allen, 1964), pp. 173–5.

his dealings with these circumstances must be resolved or paid off during the current span of what is for him a subjectively continuous experience.* He must expose himself to time, to seconds and minutes ticking off outside his control; he must give himself up to the certain rapid resolution of an uncertain outcome. And he must give himself up to fate in this way when he could avoid it at reasonable cost. He must have 'gamble'.

Serious action is a serious ride, and rides of this kind are all but arranged out of everyday life. As suggested, every individual engages in consequential acts, but most of these are not problematic, and when they are (as when career decisions are made that affect one's life) the determination and settlement of these bets will often come after decades, and by then will be obscured by payoffs from many of his other gambles. Action, on the other hand, brings chance-taking and resolution into the same heated moment of experience; the events of action inundate the momentary now with their implications for the life that follows.

Serious action is a means of obtaining some of the moral benefits of heroic conduct without taking quite all of the chance of loss that opportunity for heroism would ordinarily involve. But serious action itself involves an appreciable price. This the individual can minimize by engaging in commercialized action, wherein the appearance of fatefulness is generated in a controlled fashion in an area of life calculated to insulate its consequenecs from the rest of living. The cost of this action may be only a small fee and the necessity of leaving one's chair, or one's room, or one's house.

It is here that society provides still another solution for those who would keep their character up but their costs down: the

---

* Persons differ according to how long they hold their breath for a continuous experience. Zealots and true believers seem to be inclined to stretch things out a bit, sustaining a span of experience and enthusiasm where others would exhale and mark life off into different plays. Of course poets and the religious are wont to argue that if the individual compares the very considerable time he is slated to spend dead with the relatively brief time allowed him to strut and fret in this world, he might well find reason for viewing all of his life as a very fateful play of very short span, every second of which should fill him with anxiety about what is being used up. And in truth, our rather brief time *is* ticking away, but we seem only to hold our breath for seconds and minutes of it.

manufacture and distribution of vicarious experience through the mass media.

When we examine the content of commercialized *vicarious* experience we find a startling uniformity. Practical gambles, character contests and serious action are depicted. These may entail make-belief, biography, or a view of someone else's currently ongoing fateful activity. But always the same dead catalogue of lively displays seems to be presented.* Everywhere opportunity is provided us to identify with real or fictive persons engaging in fatefulness of various kinds, and to participate vicariously in these situations.

Why is fatefulness in all its varieties so popular as an ingredient of living once-removed? As suggested, it provides excitement without cost, if the consumer can identify with the protagonist.† This process of identification seems facilitated by two factors. First, fateful acts, by definition, involve the actor in use of facilities whose full and effective agent is the actor himself. The single individual is decision-maker and executor, the relevant unit of organization. Presumably an individual, real or fictional, is easier to identify with, at least in bourgeois culture, than is a group, a

* James Bond is given a fateful undertaking. He checks with his seniors at an exclusive club whose services he handles very firmly. James Bond takes a room at a plush hotel at a plush resort in a plush part of the world. James Bond makes the acquaintance of an unattainable girl and then rapidly makes the girl, after which he shows how cooly he can rise above her bedside murder. James Bond contests an opponent with cars, cards, 'copters, pistols, swords, spear-guns, ingenuity, discrimination of wines, judo, and verbal wit. James Bond snubs the man about to apply a hot iron. Etc.

† There are, of course, great differences through time and across cultures regarding what persons will allow themselves to enjoy vicariously. I don't think execution-watching is now considered much of a privilege, but there is no doubt that it was once a neat example of thrills through vicarious participation. Thus in eighteenth-century England:

'The curiosity of men about death led intellectuals and people of fashion to be fascinated by the scaffold. Pepys was a frequent spectator and Boswell, Johnson's biographer, is said to have used his great gift for making friends with the famous to the Keeper of Newgate for no other purpose than to get good seats at hangings. On one occasion when he was able to ride to Tyburn with the condemned man he considered himself as fortunate as a modern sports fan with a couple of tickets for a world heavyweight fight. His pleasure was shared by Sir Joshua Reynolds riding in the coach beside him.' (Tholl, *op. cit.*, p. 53.)

city, a social movement, or a tractor factory. Second, fatefulness involves a play of events that can be initiated and realized in a space and time small enough to be fully witnessed. Unlike such phenomena as the rise of capitalism or the Second World War, fatefulness is something that can be watched and portrayed *in toto*, from beginning to end at one sitting; unlike these other events, it is inherently suited to watching and to portraiture.

Consider the following story told by a Negro journalist, driving across the country in order to write a story about what such a trip would be like for a person like him:

I didn't linger long in Indianapolis, nor in Chicago, which was now held fast in the grip of a bitter lakeside winter. Then I was cutting across Ohio, driving dully, the seat belt tight against my waist. In mid-afternoon I saw a patrol car coming up behind me. I checked my speedometer and it read seventy, the limit. I held steady at this speed, expecting the trooper to pass me, but when I glanced around I found him keeping pace with me. Then he signaled me to pull over.

After Kentucky, I had been followed by police or troopers in Georgia, Tennessee, Mississippi; I had been pulled over in Illinois and California. Followed, pulled over and made to know that I was a lone black man in a big car, and vulnerable as hell. I had had enough. I snatched off the seat belt and rolled down the window. It didn't give me room enough, so I practically kicked the door open.

'What's the matter?' I shouted at the trooper. He didn't answer as he walked to the car. And then I decided to commit it all – my body, too, if he wanted it – for I would not take any more harassment.

'Let's see your license.'

'I asked you what the trouble was.' That was not what he wanted. The ritual said that I should hand my license over to him without a word.

'I want to see your license.'

I gave it to him, smelling the odor of a man about to exercise the insolence of office. It was the old game: 'You black, me white, and I'm cop besides.'

He fingered the license and then, leaning casually in the window, said, 'John, what's your occupation?'

I laughed. What does occupation have to do with an alleged traffic violation? Was the nature of my work supposed to tell him that I had money enough to pay him off? Was it to let him know that I was the 'right kind' of Negro, one with political connections that could make it hot for him? Was I supposed to be jobless and transporting drugs, a corpse, or young girls across the state line? Police and troopers of America, comes a slow day, you can always find a Negro or two wandering through your state. Brighten up that day by making like exactly what you are.

'My name,' I shouted, 'is Mr Williams.' I'm sure that cops and troopers use the familiar address with many people who are white, but this one I smelled out. 'John' was synonymous with 'boy'. He snatched his arm from the window. I flung my authorization for the trip at him. I watched him as he read it, and thought, not only am I not the 'right kind' of Negro, not only will I not pay you off, but I am about five seconds away from total commitment – which means five seconds from beating your head.

He glanced over the top of the sheet. 'Mr Williams, you were doing eighty coming down the road. When I caught up with you, you were doing eighty-two.'

'You're a liar. I was doing seventy. Eighty? Take me in and prove it.'

'Mr Williams–'

'Tired of taking all this crap from you guys.'

'Mr Williams–'

'You're going to run this nonsense and yourselves into the ground.'

Cars were slowing as they passed us. The trooper's face took on an anxious look. Yes, I was rambling in my anger, but I was ready to go. What is more, for the insults I delivered, he would have taken me in *had he been right*. Instead, he returned to his car and I drove on – at seventy miles an hour.*

Mr Williams really has this experience and then makes himself and it available in a popular magazine. A dramatic reporting nicely covers the relevant events, as would a cinematic or stage version. We readers become vicariously involved, safely removed from what we live by. What is for him a character contest, a moment of truth, is for us a means to massage our morality.

Whatever the reasons why we consume vicarious fatefulness, the social function of doing so is clear. Honourable men in their scenes of fatefulness are made safely available to all of us to identify with whenever we turn from our real worlds. Through this identification the code of conduct affirmed in fateful activities

* J. Williams, 'This Is My Country Too', Part II, *Holiday*, September 1964, p. 80.

– a code too costly or too difficult to maintain in full in daily life – can be clarified and reasserted. A frame of reference is secured for judging daily acts, without having to pay its penalties.

The same figure-for-identification very often engages in all three kinds of fateful activity: dangerous tasks, character contests, and serious action. Therefore we can easily come to believe in an intrinsic connexion among them, such that he whom character leads to one type of fateful activity will be the sort of person in the sort of life who finds it necessary and desirable to engage in the other two as well. It is easy to fail to see that the natural affinity of the hero for all types of fatefulness probably does not belong to him but to those of us who vicariously participate in his destiny. We shape and stuff these romantic figures to satisfy our need, and our need is for economy – a need to come into vicarious contact with as many bases of character as possible for the same admission price. A living individual misguided enough to seek out all types of fatefulness is merely adding flesh and blood to what originated as consumer packaging.

This suggests that rules of social organization can be given support by and give support to our vicarious world of exemplary fatefulness. The hero of character is not likely therefore to be the man on the street:

Consider the strain on our moral vocabulary if it were asked to produce heroic myths of accountants, computer programmers, and personal executives. We prefer cowboys, detectives, bull fighters, and sports-car racers, because these types embody the virtues which our moral vocabulary is equipped to celebrate: individual achievement, exploits, and prowess.*

Because the portrait is needed, a place must be found for the portrayer. And so, on the edges of society, are puddles of people who apparently find it reasonable to engage directly in the chancy deeds of an honourable life. In removing themselves further and further from the substance of our society, they seem to grasp more and more certain aspects of its spirit. Their alienation from our

* B. Berger, 'The Sociology of Leisure: Some Suggestions', *Industrial Relations*, 1, 2 (1962), p. 41. Yablonsky, *op. cit.*, pp. 226–7, makes a similar point in a discussion of what he calls the 'sociopathic hero'.

reality frees them to be subtly induced into realizing our moral fantasies. As suggested of delinquents, they somehow co-operate by staging a scene in which we project our dynamics of character:

The delinquent is the rogue male. His conduct may be viewed not only negatively, as a device for attacking and derogating the respectable culture; positively it may be viewed as the exploitation of modes of behavior which are traditionally symbolic of untrammeled masculinity, which are renounced by middle-class culture because incompatible with its ends, but which are not without a certain aura of glamour and romance. For that matter, they find their way into the respectable culture as well but only in disciplined and attenuated forms as in organized sports, in fantasy and in make-believe games, or vicariously as in movies, television, and comic books. They are not allowed to interfere with the serious business of life. The delinquent, on the other hand, having renounced his serious business, as defined by the middle class, is freer to divert these subterranean currents of our cultural tradition to his own use. The important point for our purpose is that the delinquent response, 'wrong' though it may be and 'disreputable', is well within the range of responses that do not threaten his identification of himself as a male.*

Although fateful enterprises are often respectable, there are many character contests and scenes of serious action that are not. Yet these are the occasions and places that show respect for moral character. Not only in mountain ranges that invite the climber, but also in casinos, pool halls, and racetracks do we find places of worship; it may be in churches, where the guarantee is high that nothing fateful will occur, that moral sensibility is weak.

Looking for where the action is, one arrives at a romantic division of the world. On one side are the safe and silent places, the home, the well-regulated role in business, industry, and the

---

* A. Cohen, *Delinquent Boys* (London: Collier-Macmillan, 1955), p. 140. Here it would hardly be possible to find a better example than the writer, Norman Mailer. His novels present scenes of fateful duties, character contests, and serious action; his essays expound and extol chance-taking, and apparently in his personal life he has exhibited a certain tendency to define everything from his marriages to his social encounters in terms of the language and structure of the fight game. Whatever the reward and costs of life-orientation to gambles, he appears to have reaped them. In this fantasization of one's own life, Hemingway of course was the previous champ.

professions; on the other are all those activities that generate expression, requiring the individual to lay himself on the line and place himself in jeopardy during a passing moment. It is from this contrast that we fashion nearly all our commercial fantasies. It is from this contrast that delinquents, criminals, hustlers, and sportsmen draw their self-respect. Perhaps this is payment in exchange for the use we make of the ritual of their performance.

A final point: Vicarious experience re-establishes our connexion to values concerning character. So does action. Action and vicarious experience, then, so different on the surface, seem to be closely allied. Evidence might be cited.

Take clothing. Female dress is designed to be 'attractive', which must mean in some sense or other that the interest of unspecified males is to be aroused. And with this arousal the basis is laid for one type of action. But the actual probability of this action occurring is very often very low. Fantasies are thus invigorated, but reality is not. A clearer version of the same vicarious tease is the wide current sale to horseless cowboys of Stetson hats, high-heeled boots, Levi's, and tattoos.* Delinquents who carry knives and own 'a piece' similarly exhibit a heightened orientation to action, but here perhaps appearances have a better chance of intruding on reality.

Lotteries, the 'numbers', and casino keno are commercialized expressions of long-shot gambles offered at a very small price. The expected value of the play is, of course, much smaller even than the price, but an opportunity is provided for lively fantasies of big winnings. Here action is at once vicarious and real.

When persons go to where the action is, they often go to a place where there is an increase, not in the chances taken, but in the chances that they will be obliged to take chances. Should action actually occur it is likely to involve someone *like* themselves but someone *else*. Where they have got to, then, is a place where another's involvement can be closely watched and vicariously enjoyed.

Commercialization, of course, brings the final mingling of fantasy and action. And it has an ecology. On the arcade strips of urban settlements and summer resorts, scenes are available for

* See, for example, J. Popplestone, 'The Horseless Cowboys', *Trans-Actions*, May–June 1966.

hire where the customer can be the star performer in gambles enlivened by being very slightly consequential. Here a person currently without social connexions can insert coins in skill machines to demonstrate to the other machines that he has socially approved qualities of character. These naked little spasms of the self occur at the end of the world, but there at the end is action and character.